MW00579514

Genesis 12:3

MY DIARY
SECRETS

Jean Stromer

by Mrs. Gordon Lindsay

Published by
Christ For The Nations Inc.
P.O. Box 769000
Dallas, TX 75376-9000
(214) 376-1711
Web Site: http://www.cfni.org
E-Mail: info@cfni.org

First printing — 1976
Second printing — 1977
Third printing — 1979
Fourth printing — 1982
Fifth printing — 1984
Sixth printing — 1989
Seventh printing (rev.) — 1998

All Scripture NKJV unless otherwise noted.

Dedication

To my three children: Carole (Shira), Gilbert and Dennis, from whom I've learned so much.

Acknowledgments

With special appreciation to those who helped me so much in preparing this book: Ruth Maier, former assistant editor of *Christ For The Nations* and personal secretary to Gordon and me for many years; Ruthanne Garlock, former editor of *Christ For The Nations*; and Karen Singleterry, one of my former secretaries.

For all inspiration and encouragement received by those who read this book, the glory belongs to God and His Son Jesus, Who is revealed to us by His Holy Spirit.

Table of Contents

Chapter One

An entry in Gordon's log, dated October 16, 1932, reads: "Young lady by the name of Freda saved." It was a strange series of circumstances that had brought me to this pivotal point in my life.

Born in Canada on a large wheat farm that my parents had homesteaded near Burstall, Saskatchewan, I was one of 12 children born to Kaity and Gottfred Schimpf. My father, who was of German origin and who grew up in a German community in White Russia, met my mother, and they were married after they had come to America. While living in Kansas, they heard of the great opportunities in Canada in wheat ranching. The government was offering free land to any who would come up there and homestead. As they were both pioneers at heart, Kaity and Gottfred set out for Canada, looking forward to adventure and an opportunity to support their family on the wheat plains to the north.

When they arrived in Burstall, there was no place to stay. As they needed a roof over their heads immediately and there wasn't time to build a proper house, they hurriedly put up a makeshift sod house of matted turf. It was in this sod house that my older brother, Ted, and I were born. By the time the next child arrived, my father had built a large, beautiful 10-room house.

During World War I, the wheat market was very favorable, and our wheat ranch prospered. However, my mother did not like the harsh winters, where the temperature would dip to 60 degrees below zero, so she prevailed upon Dad to move to a warmer climate.

He set out to seek a new home for our family, and in Oregon City, Oregon, he bought a large apple orchard. When he returned to Burstall, we held an auction and sold all of our household effects and our cattle, then boarded a train for Oregon City. It was 1919 when we began our new life in Oregon.

The apple orchard which my father had bought turned out to be a financial disaster. The post-war years saw the country's economy sadly slumping, and Dad could find no market for the apples he grew. He ended up feeding most of them to the hogs. In addition to this, our cattle, farm and equipment in Canada had been sold on credit. And being so far away, we were unable to collect the money that was owed to us. We were by now virtually penniless.

In spite of the many hardships that were to

come to our family, God in His providence, had undoubtedly ordained this move to Oregon. With my father's loss of his life's savings by the purchase of this farm on which he could not make the payments, he turned in despair to God.

In Canada, our family had attended a Lutheran church; but in Oregon City, we were exposed to the Full Gospel for the first time. As my father cried out to the Lord, the longing of his soul was fulfilled as he was baptized in the Holy Spirit, along with my brothers and sisters. This blessed experience was to elude my mother for 35 years, however, for she never felt she was quite good enough to attain such spiritual heights. It was not until she heard an evangelist explain that the baptism in the Holy Spirit is to be received as a gift from God — it is not something one can earn by his own works of righteousness — that she fully grasped this truth. And she was filled with the Holy Spirit that same day.

The pastor of our church in Oregon City was exceedingly dynamic, brilliant and talented. He was also a compassionate man, for when he saw the financial difficulties our family faced, he offered to adopt one of the children. As it turned out, I was the one he wanted to adopt. I think this was because he liked to hear me sing. For although I was only 6 at the time, he would often call me to the platform to sing a verse or a chorus before the congregation.

At the mention of adoption, my tiny 5-foot-2-inch mother stood erect, squared back her shoulders and said proudly, "If I have to eat bread and water for the rest of my life, not one single child will leave this roof." Later in life, I learned what that love really meant to me. My mother and I were very close until the time of her death at the age of 87.

But the pastor had another side to him — he was a very stern disciplinarian, almost to the point of complete dictatorship in the home. As a result, he alienated his four children. His son, Andrew, who was called "Bub" by his family, and I felt drawn to each other as children, and our friendship developed through the years. Unfortunately, his life was later to end in deep tragedy.

A year after moving to Oregon City from Canada, we had to leave the farm, and from then on, life was filled with many more hardships.

Although my father spoke Russian, German, Polish and Spanish fluently, he never quite mastered the English language. For this reason, the best employment he could get was in a lumber mill where he worked for $3.10 a day. This was not sufficient to feed as many mouths as we had; so every summer while other children were tak-

ing vacations, our family was out picking straw-
berries, raspberries, boysenberries, blackberries,
string beans, prunes or hops. There was little
time to play.

I recall that at the age of 9, I was out in the
field from 6 a.m. until 6 p.m. or later, working
alongside my mother. Sometimes I would wonder why the harvesting of one fruit would follow
so closely on the heels of another. And why the
Lord did not somehow leave a little space
between so we could have a week or so off in the
summer. But that was not to be, for it seemed
when we finished picking one kind of berry,
there was another type ready for harvest.

But if we expected to eat the next winter, we
had to do this sort of work. Generally by the time
school was out the first of June, we had accumu-
lated a big grocery bill that the store owner had
carried for us from the time we had entered
school the previous September. So in order to be
able to get groceries the following year, we had
to work in the fields all summer to pay for the
last year's food bills.

One morning, when I was about 13, my father
returned unexpectedly from his work. His face
was grim. During the night, the sawmill had
caught fire and burned to the ground. He was out
of work! Jobs were exceedingly scarce for one
who couldn't speak the language well. So our

family's small financial security was swept away, and we lived, as it seemed, from hand to mouth; yet I never recall going hungry.

A few months later, my father found a seasonal job in Washington state hoeing sugar beets, so my mother and some of the older children went with him. I remained in Oregon with my two younger sisters and an older brother who had a job there. I cooked, ironed, washed and had practically full care of my two sisters. A month before I was to graduate from the eighth grade, my two sisters and I traveled the 300 miles by train to join my parents in the sugar beet fields of Washington.

I did not know whether my teacher would pass me because I left school a month early. All summer, I worried that I might not be able to start high school with the rest of my classmates. To my delight, when I returned to our home in Portland at the end of the summer, I found my report card in the mail — I had passed!

It was during that summer that I had contracted lockjaw. Since my parents had never heard of it, they didn't know what it was, and really weren't too troubled about it. For about a week, I could open my mouth barely wide enough to get down some liquids and a little food. In spite of this, I didn't miss a single day's work. As I look back now, I often wonder how a skinny girl of 13 lived through that ordeal, with wet feet from the dew in the early morning hours, and a disease which is often fatal. But God was merciful.

My childhood was not unusual in that I probably had the average number of brushes with death. One such occasion was when I was about 10 years old. Our house had an old-fashioned wood lift in the kitchen. This huge, heavy box held a great deal of wood for the kitchen stove; it would be lowered by a pulley to the basement where our supply of wood was stored.

As children, we had been warned not to stick our head in the lift for fear of what might happen. But like a lot of inquisitive children, on one occasion I either disobeyed or forgot the rule.

My grandfather, who although hard of hearing, was a burly, robust man for his age. He had decided to go to the basement to get more wood for the kitchen stove. When he started to operate the pulley to lower the lift to the basement, I heard him and decided to watch the lift as it was lowered. I opened the lift door which was in the kitchen, thinking that I would see the lift already below me going toward the basement. To my horror, I suddenly realized I had put my head into the wood lift! As the lift began to descend, my neck was being slowly closed in upon as in a hangman's noose. I was too terrified to scream.

Just then, my aunt walked into the room, and seeing what was happening, let out a bloodcurdling scream. My nearly deaf grandfather heard her cry — a miracle no one (except God) could explain — and stopped the pulley. My aunt ran to the basement and explained what had happened, and Grandfather hurriedly raised the wood lift. Like a bolt of lightning, I pulled my head from the box and was saved. Never again did I have to be warned not to stick my head into the wood lift.

I well remember my father — a very handsome man with black wavy hair, blue eyes and broad shoulders; how erectly he sat on his horse as he rode. But being from the old school, he didn't believe women needed an education. Therefore, he was strongly opposed to his daughter going to more than the required grammar school.

In my heart, however, was a keen desire for knowledge, so I prevailed upon mother to help me. Father felt he could not afford to let me go to high school, which was true. With 12 children, he did have his hands full. Nonetheless, mother made a secret agreement with me that if I could find a job, she would talk to Dad and persuade him to let me attend high school.

Immediately, I began to look for employment, although I was only 13 at the time. I didn't have far to look, for it so happened that a neighbor a block away had three children and needed help. Both the husband and wife were working, which left the three girls pretty much on their own. Therefore, I was hired to clean house each night, as well as do the washing, ironing and cooking. How well I remember the huge pots of chili beans I had to cook weekly. (And to this day, I can still turn out a pretty good pot of chili beans!)

When I found this job, which netted me $3 a week, mother kept her agreement — she talked to father, and I was permitted to go to high school. Many times I had to walk the entire distance to school, which was four miles round trip, because I didn't have the 4 cents it took to ride the streetcar.

The following year I secured a better position with a lovely Jewish family where I received room, board, clothing and $15 a month. I worked for this family for several years. During my senior year, I worked three weeks at a department store during Christmas time in order to be able to buy my class ring, my graduation announcements, school pictures and a graduation dress.

At midterm, I graduated from Jefferson High School, one of the largest in the city of Portland with over 2,000 students. That semester, only two scholarships were to be given — one to a young man and one to a young woman. Imagine my surprise to learn that the faculty had selected me to be the recipient of one of these scholarships!

This scholarship, given to me for being "the most deserving girl," provided partial payment to attend the college of my choice. I dreamed all that spring and summer of attending college in the fall, yet knowing all along that there wasn't the remotest possibility that I could go. I could depend on no financial help whatsoever from my parents, as they had a hard time even providing food and clothing for my other brothers and sisters.

As fall came, and I watched some of my classmates go off to college while I worked as a domestic in a home for $30 a month, I felt completely frustrated. Life didn't seem worth living. And I was plagued with serious and dark thoughts that robbed me of my peace. It was now the fall of 1932.

The Still, Small Voice

It was then that I visited my sister who told me about a revival meeting in progress. The evangelist was a young man by the name of Gordon Lindsay. My only recollection of Gordon at that time (he was eight years older than I) was a mental picture I had of him from some years earlier. I had watched him and several other young men forcefully preaching on a street corner opposite the downtown mission that both his family and mine attended.

For want of something better to do, I decided to attend the revival that night. When the invitation to accept Christ was given, although under conviction of the Holy Spirit, I was too proud to go forward, knowing that the people in the church were aware that I came from a Christian family. I deluded myself into thinking they believed I was Christian. I am sure most of them knew that during my years of working away from home, I had left the path of following the Lord.

After the dismissal prayer, I nonetheless made my way to the altar at the front of the church. There the devil told me I would live a dull and drab life if I were to become a Christian (yet now as I read over my diaries, they sound like storybooks), that I would never have any friends, and on and on. Nevertheless, with the Holy Spirit tugging at my soul, I surrendered my life to the Lord that night and was gloriously converted.

While I was kneeling at the altar, the Lord spoke to me in a still, small voice and told me that if I would be faithful to Him, I would one day marry Gordon. I was as sure of that as I have been at any time in my life when God has revealed something to me. But I did not tell a soul about it for the next few years.

By now Bub, our first Full Gospel pastor's son, was an outstanding saxophonist and musician. No longer serving the Lord, he was employed at a Portland radio station, and played in dance bands at night. We had dated on occasion and always enjoyed each other's company. But after I accepted Christ as my Savior, Bub came to see me only once. When I told him about my conversion, he teased a little, then disappeared from my life forever.

Several years later, he married. But his life had degenerated into one of drinking and dissipation. After making one suicide attempt and failing, he succeeded the second time when he attached a hose to the exhaust pipe of his car, rolled the windows up and asphyxiated himself. When his father found him, his body was still warm, but his spirit had already exited. What a tragedy for a handsome young man who, with his abilities, could have gone so far for God.

Although I had opportunities to date other young men, I could never seem to become interested in anyone, knowing what the Lord had revealed to me about His plans for my life. During the next few years following my conversion, I saw Gordon only about once a year when he would return to Portland to visit his family. He seemed rather disinterested in girls, and when, on rare occasions, I would visit his sister in their home, Gordon was generally reading, surrounded by stacks of books.

A number of times Satan would say to me, "Wouldn't you be surprised if you heard that Gordon was engaged? Or if he came home married?" To each of these harassments, I would affirm my faith in what the Lord had told me, and leave it there. I had learned earlier that if Satan can get a Christian into the arena of debate, he has won the battle. I decided to encourage myself on the other hand by faith in God's promises.

In the meantime, I felt a need to prepare myself for the role of a minister's wife so I could assist Gordon in any way he might need me. I enrolled in the Foursquare Bible school's night classes, as by now I was working as a cashier in a large department store. This Bible training no doubt changed the entire course of my life. And I was to learn throughout my life that some doors of opportunity seemed small, but before I even realized they were doors, I was through them. And had I not gone through the first one, the others would never have opened.

The Bible school classes were from 7-10 p.m. And since I made only $1.40 a day during those depression years, I sometimes did not have the carfare to ride to school. I had to walk the two miles to school from the store where I worked.

Of course, the 25 cents it took to buy a meal was entirely out of the question. So generally, I had to wait and eat my evening meal after I arrived home about 11 p.m.

Two years after I was saved, my father died suddenly of a heart attack. This left an even greater financial strain on my older brother and me to support the family. (The night my father died was the only night I missed classes during the three-year Bible school I attended.)

Besides working in the department store and attending Bible school, I was very active in church. I sang in the choir; assisted in the young people's meetings; spoke at the rescue mission on Saturday, at the downtown street meeting and in the jail services; and served on the communion board.

One night four years after my conversion, as I was singing in the choir, I saw Gordon unexpectedly walk into the auditorium. With him were his two sisters, who were about my age, and within minutes he was surrounded by a number of girls (which was customary on his visits home). I decided right then and there, "Here is one girl who isn't going to run after him."

That evening when the service was concluded, though I had not seen Gordon in some months, instead of going back to greet him, I decided to slip out through the basement door. I caught the streetcar, transferred to the bus and went home.

As I lay awake that night the devil harassed me again saying, "Aren't you the smart one! You expect to marry Gordon, and you didn't even go to say 'hello' to him." I reminded the devil that if my marriage was to be the work of the Lord, then God didn't really need my assistance anyhow.

So in one way I was surprised, yet in another I wasn't, when two days later, I looked up from my work at the sound of my name. There stood Gordon! When I asked how he had found me in that large store, he said he had called the office. I knew then that this was not just an "accidental" meeting. Instantly, I felt that this was to be the beginning of our courtship.

That evening he took me out to dinner, and later, we walked along the shores of the Columbia River. It was a beautiful night, and one for which I had been waiting four years. A few days later, Gordon left for the South again. (The back seat of his old car was stacked nearly to the ceiling with *Reader's Digests* which dated back for years. Besides this, he had built wooden bookcases which he carried on the left running board of the car. I wondered where he would put a wife, if he had one!)

"Dear Freda ..."

Before leaving, Gordon asked me if I would answer his letters if he wrote me. I told him I would. Thus began a casual friendship which led to our marriage a year later. The following letters are a few among the many he wrote me during this time.

Nearly four years after my conversion came this first letter:

Jackson, Mississippi
August 17, 1936

Dear Freda,

... In Dallas stopped to see the Centennial Exposition. The greatest thrill was to talk over a television system, both hearing and seeing another party at the same time. What part will television play in the diabolical grip the Antichrist will have over the world? Time will tell — but future events cast their shadows before! ...

... You spoke of a certain young couple's not quarreling. What a monstrous idiocy and colossal folly for mature people to quarrel. They invite bitterness and crush forever the beauty of living. They have sold their happiness for a mess of pottage. The firebug who burns his house over his head is a wise man in comparison. Only people with a streak of childishness will quarrel.

True, problems ever arise, but they must be dealt

with sympathetically, diplomatically and unselfishly. Seventy-five percent of marriages are comparative failures! Why? First, they rush into it rashly. Second, they are blindly drawn by physical attraction and never question the fact of spirit compatibility. Third, they talk twice and think once; with sharp words, they build up resentment and bitterness that can never be undone. Fourth, they cannot learn to compromise nonessentials. Fifth, they quit showing love at the time of their marriage. Anything else in life they study with care and caution, but the art of living is butchered and mangled — and they succumb to the inevitable law of reaping what they sow.

But does the average unfortunate individual realize his mistake? Rarely. With incriminations and recriminations, he blames everything and everybody but himself. This morbid delusion both comforts and confirms him in the fatal course of his own choosing. ...

> Your friend,
> Gordon Lindsay

* * * * * *

> Noxapater, Mississippi
> September 5, 1936

(Written to me in my appointment to position of president of the 200 young people of the Portland Foursquare Church.)

Dear Freda,

(1) Always seek to work in the closest harmony with the pastor. (2) Always show a spirit of optimism and faith before the young people. (3) Try to keep them looking forward to something. Young people are restless and energetic. They must have something to dissipate their energies. ...

The glaring mistake of young people seems to be that they rely on physical attraction alone. But this soon plays out. Man is nine-tenths spirit. Thus if there is no spiritual harmony, it becomes a dragged-out affair, waxing worse and worse, going from bitterness to hatred, and finally crashing on the shoals of the divorce court. Marriage is absolutely a 50-50 proposition. I have often noticed that one will expect of the other what he refuses to give himself. The most expensive thing in married life is the first unkind word that is spoken. Well, that's enough soliloquizing.

>   Your friend,
>   Gordon

✳ ✳ ✳ ✳ ✳ ✳

>   Noxapater, Mississippi
>   September 7, 1936

Dear Freda,

... The other night I was listening to the radio. Something happened to me that was quite striking. A voice boomed over the radio: "This is the

U.S. senator for Louisiana, Huey P. Long, speaking." This was 1935. It wasn't a ghost nor had time turned backward. Long's voice had been preserved by electrical transcription. The message he gave that night was 100 percent realistic.

The works of the dead live after them. No doubt our lives are recorded faithfully on the annals of heaven. And when they are reproduced at the judgment seat of Christ, I hope I won't be ashamed of mine. ...

Always your friend,
Gordon

✳ ✳ ✳ ✳ ✳ ✳

Noxapater, Mississippi
September 10, 1936

Dear Freda,

... Of course, the only thing worthwhile is to be in the will of God. All else is dross. But God has the best for those who will put Him first. ...

I am glad you want only to be yourself. Too many want to be themselves, plus. An artificial front is hard to maintain. Too much flash is hard to maintain. I have been acquainted with preachers who have a most impressive appearance in the pulpit, but who are a total failure at home — capricious, fickle, magnificent exhibitions of dual nature. At the best, they are crude imitations.

Have you noticed that the tendency of humanity

from the highest brackets down to the lowest and humblest stratum of society runs to the dual nature? It is interesting to watch the poor swain put on his little show. Bedecked in a lavender suit and flashy tie (if he possesses that much "wherewith"), he purchases a watch, notable in size, and fastens it to his vest with massive links. If he owns a car, it is apt to be a ponderous hulk of "ancient vintage," but towering seven feet into the sky. And the stagey puts on her little show with gaudy beads from the 10-cent store, a bracelet of iron, rings set with paste and earrings that flatten the lobe of the ear.

And so the whole world puts on its show — although in the higher circles, the artificialities become exceedingly more refined and subtle with an understanding heart, a cultivated mind and a sparkling spirit. ...

... Am glad you believed my "explanation." Although nowadays people are so loose with the truth that one oft gets his confidence shaken in some of those to whom he looked for better things. But a lie is about the most detestable thing under creation. It is sad that many will trade their character for the temporary relief it affords. They are like the little boy quoting, or rather misquoting, Scripture, who said, "A lie is an abomination to the Lord, and a very present help in trouble."

Yours as ever,
Gordon

✳ ✳ ✳ ✳ ✳ ✳

Biloxi, Mississippi
October 6, 1936

Dear Freda,

... It surely is a joy at the close of a revival to have folk come up with tears in their eyes and thank you because you have been instrumental in the providence of God in their salvation. Evangelistic work to one not called soon loses its glamor. And though sometimes I become quite weary, yet the glory of soulwinning never fades to me, and its charm is one of the lasting things of life. ...

You say that October marks your fourth birthday. My "log" of October 16, 1932, says, "Young lady by the name of Freda saved." You see, I have a record book — not exactly a diary — just a line for each day — runs back 10 years. Each line proves a key to events of that day, and when referred to, brings back a flood of memories that would have otherwise retreated forever into the chambers of the subconscious mind. ...

Always your friend,
Gordon

✳ ✳ ✳ ✳ ✳ ✳

Coalinga, California
November 12, 1936

Dear Freda,

... Our last week at Biloxi was a success. A

good number of souls were at the altar, and on one night, the auditorium was filled to capacity and over, although it is of considerable size. A young woman was to go to the hospital to be operated on for appendicitis. She and her mother called at the house for prayer, and I felt that God had really touched her. Her mother had her go to the hospital anyway, but before they could operate on her, she was shouting with victory. She left the hospital, and the doctor, seeing what had taken place, said, "Pray for me."

> Yours as ever,
> Gordon

* * * * * *

> Coalinga, California
> November 28, 1936

Dear Freda,

Greetings from sunny California!

... I'd rather be in the will of God than have all the wealth of earth at command. ...

> As ever,
> Gordon

Marriage Plans

Gordon returned to Portland in time for the holidays, and shortly after Christmas, we announced our engagement.

I remember a Sunday that very winter when

it had begun to snow in the early morning hours. I made it to Sunday school and the 11 a.m. service. But in the afternoon, the radio continued to give warnings that a heavy snow was anticipated, and no one should be on the street except for emergencies.

I then had a decision to make: I was president of the young people's group of 200, and each Sunday from 5-6 p.m., we had a prayer meeting at the church. Then we had a young people's service until 7:30 p.m., at which time the main evening service started. With radio warnings coming every few minutes, I wondered whether I should go.

After prayer, I felt definitely led to make the effort. My brother, sisters and mother decided if I was going, they would come for the evening service, and we could drive home together.

There was hardly a baker's dozen there that evening in the huge church building, but nonetheless, we felt the Spirit of the Lord present. At the conclusion of the sermon by Mrs. Harold Jefferies, she gave an altar call for those to accept Christ who had not done so.

I had volunteered sometime earlier to be a personal worker. I saw a young woman raise her hand and immediately felt drawn to her, as she was about my age. So I went forward with her and began talking and praying with her. She accepted the Lord as her Savior that evening, as did also her husband who drove a beer truck for Blitz-Weinhard Company. As far as I recall, I had no further contact with her.

Many years later when we were in Texas, I received a letter which said:

Dear Mrs. Lindsay,

Could you by any chance be the Freda Schimpf who prayed with me on the night of Portland's worst snowstorm? There was a young girl who was really a tremendous help to me, and she seemed to be led of the Lord to speak about the very things that were troubling me. As a result, I was able for the first time to understand; and I received Christ as my Savior that night. If you are that person, then I would like to tell you what happened to me in the intervening years.

After leaving Portland, my husband and I attended LIFE Bible College. We later pastored several churches. After earnestly seeking the Lord, we both felt led to enter the mission field. We are now in Colombia, South America, where we have established a strong church for God. Over a thousand have received the baptism in the Holy Spirit since we have been here, and we give God all the glory. I thought if you were Freda Schimpf, you would be interested to know this.

Sincerely,
Virginia Knapp

How delighted I was to receive this letter and to realize that God did indeed lead me to go to church during that blizzard. Well did I remember that night after the service when we left the church in the blinding snowstorm. Scarcely a car was on the streets except ours, and we crept along at a snail's pace the five miles to our home. But when we were about five blocks from the house, the car stalled in the deep snow. My brother, Dave, tried everything he could to keep the car moving, but it finally balked completely.

So Dave, my younger sisters, my tiny mother and I trudged slowly through the deep snow with the wind howling about us unmercifully. In several places, it looked as if we wouldn't make it in spite of the fact that we had only five blocks to go. Finally we made it to the house, and I remember crawling in between my two sisters in their bed to keep warm — I normally slept on a cot in the same room.

All traffic was halted for several days, but after things began to open up a bit, I looked out the window one afternoon and noticed Gordon approaching the house, stomping through the white, flaky snow.

When I answered the door and invited him in, he had a big smile on his face and said, "I have something for you." He opened the little box and pulled out a diamond engagement ring and put it

on my finger! (Sometime later, he told me he had
paid $75 for the set of two rings, but to me, it was
the most beautiful diamond ring in the world. I
proudly wore it in anticipation of our wedding
day.)

I was in Los Angeles attending a convention
when the following letter arrived, after which
Gordon resumed his evangelistic meetings:

> Portland, Oregon
> January 3, 1937

My Dearest Freda,

... You have come to mean more to me than
anything else in the world. May it ever be thus.
It gives me a thrill to be able to write, not Dear
Freda, but Dearest Freda. ...

> From your sweetheart,
> Gordon

* * * * * *

> Silverton, Oregon
> January 18, 1937

My Dearest Freda,

... On my journey south, I had gotten some
little distance past Salem when I was peculiarly
checked in the Spirit. Something seemed to say
that I had passed by the very place where the
Lord wanted me. So after vainly arguing with
myself, I turned north. Leaving Salem by another

way, I was forced onto a detour, which led for a short distance to the Silverton road. This was the first time I had even thought of Silverton. So I went by the city as it was not much out of the way. I called on the pastor. He insisted that I stay over Sunday, and if possible hold a meeting, as the people had been praying that God would send an evangelist their way. I stayed. ...

But you know, I confidently expected to see you later. And then by the vagaries of fate, to be deprived the privilege by somehow missing you, makes me feel most acutely how much I love you and how much I miss you when you are absent. You will ever be the center of my affections and love.

> Your sweetheart,
> Gordon

✳ ✳ ✳ ✳ ✳ ✳

> Silverton, Oregon
> January 27, 1937

My Dearest and Only Sweetheart,

... Drove down after dinner and went through the town of my childhood, Scotts Mills. It was there that I first went to school. Strange indeed are the impressions I received. It seemed as if for the moment, time had crazily turned backward. The town has not changed in over 20 years. And it seemed as if the lapse of time was only a dream, and I was a little boy again, running about the

town. Once in awhile I grow poetical. It is a bad
verse, but the old town gave me a little inspiration. I'll write it as it comes to me:

Today I stood on a green swarthed hill,
Below me rolled the wheel of the mill,
Turning forever by winding stream,
Turning back time as I watched in my dream.

A score of years swiftly rolled away
Back into the land of yesterday.
And I saw myself a child once more,
Running breathlessly from open door,
To gateway of a bridge across the way,
Now battered by time, neglect and decay.

How oft did I stand by the old mill stream,
To wonder and ponder in childish dream,
On what the future held in store,
When I should be a child no more.

But as the old wheel rose and fell,
What it seemed to say I cannot tell;
But today I said, "The story's told,
I've found that *one* with heart of gold,
That which I yearned for in my dream,
As I sat by the banks of the old mill stream."

... Well, sweetheart, you and I can together
become coheirs of the inheritance of grace,
knowing that God shall be with us in all that lies

ahead. Each time I leave you it becomes a wee bit harder to say goodbye. So darling, let me say, I love you, I love you, I love you.

> Always your sweetheart,
> Gordon

✻ ✻ ✻ ✻ ✻ ✻

> Salem, Oregon
> February 9, 1937

My Dearest Sweetheart,

... Surely it will pay us to live close to the Lord these days. When the dam of world hatred breaks, this old Earth will be drenched in blood. ... The present lull is merely the awful hush before the battle. ...

> Your sweetheart,
> Gordon

✻ ✻ ✻ ✻ ✻ ✻

> Silverton, Oregon
> February 25, 1937

My Dearest Sweetheart,

... My darling, you write that you hope you won't be a burden to me. Now I know that you are joking. For you could be none else than a joy and a blessing. Be assured of this forever! My only qualm of conscience is (and may the Lord forgive me for a purely human wish) that I won't

be able to lavish upon you the material blessings
that I am sure I could if I were in secular work.
But we are working for a better world than this,
are we not? ...

> Your sweetheart forever,
> Gordon

✴ ✴ ✴ ✴ ✴ ✴

> Silverton, Oregon
> March 3, 1937

My Dearest Sweetheart,

> ... For what is the setting without the stone?
> What purpose a ring without a gem?
> Or throne, without the diadem?
> Ah, as I saw you in that evening's gleaming,
> I knew you were the jewel — O my darling!

> > Always and forever yours
> > and yours only,
> > Gordon

Gordon's Pioneer Work

Gordon now felt led to take over a new work
in San Fernando that had floundered and then
shut down. With no permanent building, only a
few remaining interested families, and an accu-
mulation of past-due bills, the picture that
greeted him was not an exciting one.

San Fernando, California
May 5, 1937

Dearest Freda,

... As for the bills that were due here when I
took over this work, they never bothered me very
much. They are a small matter beside the weight-
ier considerations involved in establishing a
good work. In fact, God answered prayer completely in that respect; in one day, He sent in over
$40 (in less than 24 hours). (Forty dollars is not
much, but it is a lot when there is no natural
source.) In the morning, we agreed before the
Lord in prayer that God would answer that day
in the settlement of bills. About noon, I felt led
to drive and see a lady in the country who was
involved in a meter dispute. She never belonged
to this church, and I was anxious to show her that
we were settling up the bill that had not been paid
since January. She gave me a *warm reception*
when she saw me. I let her cool off, and then
showed her that I had already paid one bill and
had come out to give her the receipt.

Say, you should have seen the change. She at
once became a friend and to prove it, she insisted
on the privilege of coming in and paying every
unpaid bill. (Of course, I wouldn't stand in her
way.) So the Lord answers prayer. ... I'll be happy

indeed when the time comes that you can take part with me in "our" work. ...

> Your sweetheart,
> Gordon

✳ ✳ ✳ ✳ ✳ ✳

> San Fernando, California
> May 19, 1937

Dearest Freda,

... I am glad that you have a taste for reading. Certainly an appreciation of books greatly broadens one, and gives him an understanding of human problems that he would never get in any other way. ...

God has given us encouragement in many ways, and considering the extremely discouraging situation when I first came, I must truly say, God has been with us.

There is a piece of property I am eyeing. It is in the very center of town, has room for a tabernacle, as well as two houses on it. I believe we could get it for $3,500 with $500 down. It would be wonderful if we could secure it upon which to set our tabernacle. One house would make a good parsonage, and the other could be rented to liquidate the debt and later sold. It may be premature to consider purchasing property this soon, especially when there is positively no human source upon which to look. However, if it is the will of God, He can make it possible in a short time. Pray that God's will shall be done. ...

> Your sweetheart,
> Gordon

✳ ✳ ✳ ✳ ✳ ✳

> San Fernando, California
> May 28, 1937

Dearest Sweetheart,

... I truly know that our union is in the will of God, and certainly the perfect will of God is the only place I desire to be in this troubled world.

> Always your sweetheart,
> Gordon

✳ ✳ ✳ ✳ ✳ ✳

> San Fernando, California
> June 8, 1937

Dearest Freda,

San Fernando is only a few minutes drive from Hollywood, California. Today Hollywood is in mourning: Jean Harlow lies a corpse in a mortuary. She sowed to the flesh and of the flesh reaped corruption. She made her debut in that notorious picture, "Hell's Angels." Today she is witnessing a realistic version of it. It is a well-known fact down here that she died from the effect of alcoholism. ...

We are continuing to advance for the Lord

here in San Fernando. I just checked over the books a few minutes ago to see how our finances were totaling. God has been good to us. A year ago, the books showed about $50 per month income for the struggling little church. This tapered off to the vanishing point, until finally there was nothing. Not a single hope in Israel when I came about the first of May. *But God is not dead.* We paid off $35 worth of bills the first day by miraculous answer to prayer. ... We took up our first missionary offering, and it was over $15. About $68 came in altogether during the week, making a total of $240 in the past month and a half.

Yours forever,
Gordon

* * * * * *

San Fernando, California
June 18, 1937

Dearest Freda,

... Getting work like this in motion requires untiring efforts. My only avenue of escape is the dividing of responsibility with others as fast as competent workers are available. One of the secrets of leadership is the ability to get others to do what one alone cannot do. ...

Last Sunday I prayed that if it be the Lord's will, we would receive the complete $100 in our offering for the property. As I believe I have already explained, I have been praying for some-time for some very valuable property in the very midst of town. It has two houses, a garage and plumbing shop on it. The area is one-third of an acre. The property, as property is now selling, might well be worth $5,000 or $6,000 with just a little retouching of the houses. The people asked $4,500, and I believe it is worth it without a question, but felt I would not want to enter into a debt of over $3,500. But would the people accept such an offer? And $500 was needed for the down payment. How could we get control of the property?

After much prayer, I felt led to attempt to get an option on the property. Then we could tear down the plumbing shop, use the lumber for the tabernacle, and during the life of the option, get the balance of the down payment. In the natural, we could expect no such results. But prayer and faith prevailed. Last Sunday without anyone being asked for a dime, the $100 came in. By faith, I made out the option, drove to Ventura, and asked the lady if she would sign it. She did! Now, we can set up our tabernacle, with all materials for it assured. So we're looking for-ward to a citywide campaign July 27. (By faith, I arranged for the evangelist beforehand.)

Surely this is God. The location could hardly

be better. It is in the exact center of town, one block from the high school. Across from it are beautiful dwellings and buildings. Sweetheart, if the balance of the money ($500) comes in by October, I would like our marriage to be at that time. So, you pray that God will indicate His will in the matter. I will surely need your presence and help at that time. By faith, God can send in the $400.

> Always yours,
> Gordon

＊ ＊ ＊ ＊ ＊ ＊

> San Fernando, California
> June 28, 1937

Dearest Sweetheart in the World,

... All in all, it is doubtful if very many churches have made the progress that this church has made in two months, when it is realized that on the first of May, it was from every standpoint, utterly defunct. The past history of the place elicited from our brethren only discouragement. However, they are beginning to see that God is able to do things wherever there are those who will lean on Him. ...

Brother "C" has been assisting me for the past week. He and his wife get along wonderfully together. Only this I noticed: They seem to be in bondage one to the other. She can hardly stand to have him out of her sight. And if occasion demands that he be away for one night, she regards it as a major tragedy and cannot sleep.

Darling, I can truthfully say that you found a place in my heart that neither time nor space can affect except to make that feeling even more acute. Pray that "the days may be shortened" till the time we will meet again, to part no more. ...

Your sweetheart,
Gordon

✳ ✳ ✳ ✳ ✳ ✳

San Fernando, California
July 3, 1937

My Darling Sweetheart,

... You speak of it as being six months since we became engaged. To me, they have been six months of joy to know that the Lord, in His providence, has been so kind as to bestow on my lot such a wonderful girl. I shall be happy when our engagement shall terminate — being superseded by that "more excellent way" (I Cor. 12:31 KJV). Now abideth hope, faith and love, but the greatest of these is love. ...

All, from least to greatest, must bend to the standard of what they preach, and by falling below it, they become automatically disqualified. ...

New items of the week: Brother "C" has been assisting me some in the past week. He is the young man about whom I wrote before, whom I helped get out in the ministry. He is a fine young man in many ways. We got a fairly good offering for him Sunday night, but I had prayed that he might get something extra, especially as he was helping us in laying a foundation.

The other afternoon, he was working with a pick and said, rather jokingly, that he didn't mind a pick and shovel as he might dig up a treasure. During the afternoon, his pick hit a small object. He picked it up and examined it incredulously, hardly knowing what it was. I took one look at it and perceived it was a $10 gold piece. If things happened like this once in awhile, we might call it luck, but God is answering prayer day after day in strange ways. We hope to have the tabernacle up and dedicated by July 29. ...

Eternally yours,
Gordon

* * * * * *

San Fernando, California
July 8, 1937

Dearest Sweetheart,

Isn't it sad about Amelia Earhart Putnam (the woman pilot)? A daring girl she was. But it appears that it would have been better if her energies had been directed in less hazardous channels. Toying with life for the empty baubles of earthly acclaim is rather poor policy. The example of touring the world with someone else's husband does not seem good ethics or a good example. The timeworn proverb might appear in this form also, "O science, what crimes are committed in thy name." Hope has not all gone, but it is dwindling fast, and it seems the ceaseless roaring of the waves of the Great Pacific are singing this time, a death song.

> Yours forever,
> Gordon Lindsay
> (I signed my whole name
> by force of habit.)

✳ ✳ ✳ ✳ ✳ ✳

> San Fernando, California
> July 17, 1937

Dearest Freda,

"Whatsoever ye do in word or deed, *do* all in the name of the Lord" (Col. 3:17 KJV). For a number of years, I have been occupied in the establishing of churches in new fields. For this, I have been duly criticized by some of my best friends, from the standpoint that I could be much further ahead financially. It is true about the financial part. In fact, I could be driving a new car had I discontinued new field work last year. However, it is a brittle thread indeed that connects us to earthly possessions, and after all, as I look back through the years, the only thing one can retain are the treasures laid up in heaven. Then too, there is the exquisite pleasure of being conscious of the hand of God over one's life — coming to San Fernando less than three months ago, entering into a desperately hard field where all others had failed, starting from absolutely nothing — less than nothing. God's hand has been with us all the way, and now we have a beautiful piece of property with two houses and a tabernacle nearing completion. Then too, with the rush over, I want to make a down payment on a car.

I wish our wedding could take place this fall. In fact, I need you here to assist in building up the work. Only this stands in the way: Putting on a program as I have here has made it impossible to be in a financial position in which I could finance a honeymoon such as we described.

> Your sweetheart,
> Gordon

* * * * * *

> San Fernando, California
> July 26, 1937

My Darling Sweetheart,

In your letter you make the following remark, "Nevertheless, if you think it would be working too much of a hardship on you and the church, perhaps we had better wait a year or so."

In the first place, dismiss from your mind forever the idea that your coming to San Fernando in any sense of the word could possibly work a hardship. The idea is preposterous and unreasonable! Why darling, your presence will prove a great blessing, not only to me, but to the church. The question is just the other way around. We would be the gainers. The problem is resolved in the fact that it is my natural desire to arrange such conditions as should be necessary to your comfort.

In your particular case, you will be leaving a lucrative job, also leaving a church that has grown to large proportions with great opportunities, to enter a field that in many respects is still new, and the church still in its infancy. Although up to the present time, the blessing of the Lord has been upon it. I have a vision for the future. ...

Darling, I feel that this fall would be the time for the great event, as far as I am concerned. But I must leave the decision with you. It is only honest and right in a life's partnership to be frank and above board in everything. So it is necessary that I tell you just how everything is. I, therefore, await your decision, sweetheart. Only remember: Another year is a long time to wait.

Your lover,
Gordon

✳ ✳ ✳ ✳ ✳ ✳

San Fernando, California
August 5, 1937

Dearest Girl in the World,

You would keep me in suspense, wouldn't you? Ha! However, I honor you because you are taking time to wait on the Lord. That is the only way to go through life. Some people butt their way through life; others take the more profitable way of the Scripture, "The steps of a *good* man are ordered by the LORD" (Psa. 37:23 KJV).

Dear, I had a rather unpleasant experience the other morning. Some enemy of the work hired a prostitute to come to the house at 7:30 in the morning. Fortunately, our evangelist and his wife had just arrived the night before. I called Brother Dobbins. Now, under ordinary conditions, I try to treat women with the respect due them. But, so brazen was this woman's audacity, that to say we threw a scare into her is putting it mildly. She escaped the toils of the law by hairbreadth, and she knew it. We'll never see her again. The very thought of succumbing to temptation to the wiles of such a vile creature gives me a feeling of repulsion. Nevertheless, such experiences are unpleasant, and are one the handicaps of a single man.

Your sweetheart,
Gordon

Gordon wrote the following letter to Dr. Harold Jefferies, pastor of the large Foursquare Gospel Church that I attended.

San Fernando, California
August 12, 1937

Dear Brother Jefferies,

... In your letter you write, "We feel that Freda is our own." I am glad that you (as her pastor) are able to feel that way. I know your kindness to her has been a great blessing in her life. She is not the type to push herself forward and, therefore, her promotion (as president of the young people) was due to merits alone, and your ability to judge human nature. I trust your mutual friendship may ever be sustained. May we ever be able to sing that beautiful song, appreciating the richness of its meaning, "Blest be the Tie That Binds."

I fully understand and appreciate the tie that binds her to such good friends. Moreover, I realize the opportunity that lies before her in your movement. ... It would bring poignant regret if I were ever to learn that she felt her future career were in any way hampered by myself. Regarding that one point, I admit that I am easily vulnerable. It is my earnest desire that Freda may get the very best out of life, and that she may be able to realize opportunities that come her way. No other wish could be compatible to the love that a husband should give his companion. ... As for Freda, you of course understand that *she was saved and received the baptism under the ministry of your correspondent.*

> Yours in His service,
> Gordon Lindsay

✳ ✳ ✳ ✳ ✳ ✳

> San Fernando, California
> August 18, 1937

Dearest Freda,

As to the arrangements for the wedding, I am sure I can safely rely on your judgments in all matters pertaining to it. I will be there a few days beforehand so I can get my visiting over and be ready to leave immediately after the ceremonies. I couldn't stand the suspense; therefore, I phoned you Sunday evening.

As I explained in my letter to your pastor, my only qualm of conscience is that I hope you will never have to feel your opportunities were sacrificed by your marriage to me. ...

> Ever your sweetheart,
> Gordon

✳ ✳ ✳ ✳ ✳ ✳

> San Fernando, California
> August 27, 1937

Dearest Freda,

It is indeed refreshing in these days of fast living

and marital indiscrepancies (even among professed Christians) to find a couple as your pastor (and his wife) so closely bound by the cords of love. Of course, the secret of a happy married life is to become absolutely one, not in tastes altogether, for variety is the spice of life, but one in spirit.

> Your sweetheart forever,
> Gordon

＊ ＊ ＊ ＊ ＊ ＊

> San Fernando, California
> September 3, 1937

Dearest Freda,

It is said of Jacob that the seven years he waited for Rachel were only as days, but you know that these two months seem as years. However, every time I think of how close the time really is, I feel like praising the Lord, for He has surely given me the one girl out of the many thousands I have seen, that I can really love. Dr. Jeffries may tie the knot, but you are already knitted to my heart inseparably.

> Your darling sweetheart,
> Gordon

＊ ＊ ＊ ＊ ＊ ＊

> San Fernando, California
> September 8, 1937

My Darling Sweetheart,

... You ask if I mind the church wedding. Sweetheart, I hope that nothing I have written would give you the impression that I was displeased, for I am not. True, if there were no one to consider but myself, I should prefer a more quiet arrangement. But we are to consider others beside ourselves. As you say, our folks would appreciate a more spectacular affair. It is always my policy to give in on nonessentials. It is only on essentials, where I feel that the will of God is at stake, that I am adamant. ...

It is true as you say, a life lived alone is, to a great extent, empty. One needs another to balance his judgment and to be a complement in his life. Life was meant to be shared. I have seen many things in my brief span, but the real pleasure of all experiences is in being able to share them with someone else.

Did I tell you that in renting the tent, I did not know where the money was coming from? But on the morning I needed it, an old friend dropped in and advanced the money of his own volition. God surely answers prayer. If I let up on definite prayer one day, what a difference in the way things work out.

Ever and forever yours,
Gordon
* * * * * *
Ajo, Arizona
September 20, 1937

Dearest Sweetheart,

... Honey, please don't worry about your coming up to expectations. You are beyond my expectations. Maybe it should be the other way around — maybe I won't come up to yours. But anyway, no one could love you more than I.

> Always your love,
> Gordon

＊ ＊ ＊ ＊ ＊ ＊

> San Fernando, California
> October 13, 1937

My Darling Sweetheart,

... If only the devil, in a final fit of rage, does not try to effect some evil scheme to secure further postponement of our marriage. ...

It is my deepest conviction of the equality of men and women, intellectually, spiritually and otherwise. ...

> Your eternal sweetheart,
> Gordon

＊ ＊ ＊ ＊ ＊ ＊

> San Fernando, California
> October 22, 1937

Dearest Sweetheart,

... Love is a most delicate thing, and I treasure it above all. Its beauty is easily marred and fragrance lost, unless carefully guarded. ...

Women are and should be equal to men. Man does not want either a superior or an inferior helpmate. Men and women are not competitors but should be an inspiration one to another in the battle of life. Of course in my case, that is not true. For you are the best of all girls, and I am not the best of all men. ...

Forever yours,
Gordon

Chapter Two

O ur wedding day finally arrived — November 14, 1937. It was to be a big wedding since Gordon and I had both grown up in Portland and had many friends and relatives there.

The Lord seemed to show His love toward us in so many small ways. With my father dead, and my mother without funds to help me, it was remarkable how the Lord came to my rescue. My older sister made my satin wedding dress. Gordon, of course, bought the flowers. A younger sister paid for the big wedding cake. But where were we to have the reception? Any place to my liking would have cost considerably more than I could afford.

After prayer, I felt impressed to call the manager of a beautiful clubhouse on Laurelhurst Lake. He informed me that they never rented out the clubhouse on a Sunday night due to a noise problem in that exclusive residential district. I then told him that I was president of the young people's group at the local Foursquare Church and was marrying a young evangelist.

God must have moved on his heart, for suddenly he said, "We will make an exception, and you can rent it for $15." My joy knew no bounds, and I lifted my heart to the Lord in gratitude. For this is a place where a rich girl would have held her wedding reception, and now the Lord was making it possible for me, a poor girl, to have it for *my* reception.

I was also concerned about what kind of platform decorations we would have, because I really couldn't afford anything. To my complete amazement, a commercial window decorator and artist friend, Ben Larsen, donated his time and skill to turn the platform into what looked like a little bit of heaven, with risers of variegated brilliant fall colors. Baskets dripping with autumn flowers hung from the ceiling and were joined by colorful ribbon streamers to two large baskets standing on the floor at the outer edges of the platform. Another basket, tilted slightly, appeared to be pouring out its bouquet of flowers on the bride and groom.

Some 1,600 people attended the wedding. In fact, the church was so crowded that some members of my family who came in late had to stand along the back wall with many others who were not able to find a seat.

I never shall forget, as I stood concealed at the back of the church, hearing the wave of audible "oohs" and "ahs" when the curtains were drawn, and the guests beheld what many said was the most beautiful wedding scene in the history of the church. And all this for a poor little girl and an equally poor traveling evangelist.

I have always felt a wedding should be a very spiritual occasion. Ours was just that with Dr. Harold Jefferies officiating. (Thirty-five years later, my oldest son, Gilbert, said of our marriage, "If ever a marriage was made in heaven, I'd say yours and Daddy's was.")

Following the reception in the beautiful clubhouse, we left that same night in the secondhand car on which Gordon had made a down payment. It was loaded to the hilt with wedding gifts. We drove as far as Salem, Oregon, a distance of 50 miles, and found about two o'clock in the morning, a very average-looking, small hotel. It sounded strange to hear Gordon register us as Rev. and Mrs. Gordon Lindsay. When we went to our room, immediately Gordon asked that we kneel and have prayer as he wanted our life together to start with prayer.

This great emphasis on prayer was no doubt the most outstanding characteristic of his life — as I was to learn in the 35 years I lived with him. His habit of daily prayer took a man, who might otherwise never have been heard of, and placed his name before millions the world over. Only eternity will reveal the many souls who found

Christ because of him.

Becoming a Pastor's Wife

The next day we left for California, stopping en route to visit some friends who were pastoring in Modesto. From there, we went on to spend a couple of days with Gordon's sister and brother-in-law, Gladys and Leon Hall, who were pastors in Coalinga.

By Sunday, we were in the pulpit of the new church Gordon was starting in San Fernando. Actually, it was a crude tabernacle with a canvas top. However, the location was ideal, and the work was growing. Some time later after we resigned from that church, the pastor and congregation sold the property to the city. On that very spot now stand the police department with the city library next to it. The church Gordon established was then moved to another location and is still existing today with a sizable congregation.

Adjusting to the role of pastor's wife from that of a young businesswoman, had its joys as well as its difficulties. I found myself doing a lot of things for which I really was not qualified. But in a new work, one doesn't fill out an application and examine one's qualifications and limitations. He just gets in there and does what needs to be done. So as Gordon's assistant, I found myself leading the singing, singing solos, speak-

ing, preaching, teaching the young people, coun-
seling, directing the choir, helping clean the
church, etc. Visitation was something I always
enjoyed, as I loved people.

After being there only two months, I felt led
to complete my Bible school training which I had
begun in Portland. One semester was all I needed
to finish the four-year course (which I actually
completed in three-and-a-half years).

So Gordon decided to return to evangelistic
work while I moved on campus at LIFE Bible
College in Los Angeles. By securing the position
of secretary to one of the faculty members, I was
able to earn my tuition and help toward my
support. Every few weeks, Gordon would come
and spend a day with me. We loved to sit beside
Echo Park Lake and dream together of what God
had in store for our lives.

Some of my family and friends were
extremely critical that, after being married such
a short time, "we would each go our separate
ways," as some stated. (I wouldn't advise this for
many couples, but for us it seemed the right thing
to do.) I had always been a stickler for finishing
whatever I started. And today as I look back over
the years, I feel I made the right decision. The
beautiful part about it was that I had Gordon's
full approval, without which I would not have
gone.

After graduation, we pastored the Foursquare church in Tacoma, Washington. There again, we saw the value of house-to-house visitation. We took a church that had missed its golden opportunity by moving from an ideal location to one on the outskirts of the city in a declining area. We, nevertheless, saw God move as we reached the hearts of the people by making ourselves available to them.

As Gordon and I went from door to door offering our services to anyone in need, it made an impact on the community. Instances of salvation and healing took place in the lives of some whom we met for the first time.

Finances were scarce. I recall on several occasions, Gordon and I would walk the four-mile round-trip into town to treat ourselves to 7-cent lamb chops.

It was in this city that a friendship was born that perhaps made as great an impression upon Gordon and me as any we made in the years to come. The friendship I am referring to was a very close one with our beautiful young people's leader, Helen. But I shall reserve that story for a little later.

Pioneer Ministry in Montana

After eight months in Tacoma, we were asked by our denomination to start a new church in

Billings, Montana. The Lord helped us to secure a pastor to take our place in Tacoma, and the church is still serving the community today.

On our way to Billings, we felt led after prayer to hold a revival in Butte, Montana. As we drove along, we were deeply grateful to the Lord for helping us make our $30 car payment. It seemed to take all the faith we could muster to believe God for that *huge* sum of $30 each month. And how grateful we were, too, for the car heater in that cold climate — that was a real luxury in those days.

We began the meeting in Butte on Sunday, and were conscious of new faces curiously watching every move we made. But Gordon had an unassuming way about him that gave him ready acceptance wherever he went. At the same time, his positive, faith-building sermons always brought results. Everywhere he went, souls were saved, healed and baptized in the Holy Spirit.

My diary records that our love offering was $2.89 that night. A heavy snow fell during the night, so on Monday, Gordon and I shoveled snow to clear the sidewalks around the church. Afterward we gathered to pray. The pastor asked us to pray for one of the men in the church who, although prominent in the community, was defiant and was disrupting the work of the Lord. He was in fact all but tearing it apart. Hearing the

details, Gordon read aloud I Corinthians 5:4,5:
"In the name of our Lord Jesus Christ, when ye
are gathered together, and my spirit, with the
power of our Lord Jesus Christ, to deliver such
an one unto Satan for the destruction of the flesh,
that the spirit may be saved in the day of the Lord
Jesus" (KJV).

Few ministers and far fewer believers grasp
the full import of this verse, and rarely is it ever
put to use. When a crisis in the church occurs,
most resort to a human way of dealing with it,
although God has already made provision in His
Word for handling the problem.

As the four of us knelt, we delivered this
troublemaker over to Satan for the destruction of
his flesh, but asked that his spirit be saved for
eternity. Before the week was over, this man was
seriously injured in a mine accident. God spared
his life, but only after he called the pastor to the
hospital and repented with many tears. By the
time the revival drew to a close, he was back in
the church making restitution, a humbled man,
but now the cooperative leader God intended
him to be.

From Butte, we went to Billings to start a new
church. (This city was to become a battleground
to test our faith.) Gordon and I helped finish the
tabernacle that was under construction. I remember the back-breaking job of evenly spreading

the sawdust which was to serve as our floor. When finally the last shovelful was in place and the crude benches dusted, we both breathed a sigh of relief and went home to clean up.

"Home" was a two-room, upstairs apartment in an old frame house — terribly hot in the summer (air conditioning was unheard of), and not too warm in the winter. The roof was slanted, so we could stand upright only in the center of one room.

We were going to hold a revival campaign to get the new church off to a good start, and our first service was to be held on Easter Sunday. The ladies and I made some curtains for the platform and fixed a paper cross for the background. I typed copies of the words to the hymn, "Christ Arose," and several other Easter songs, as there was no money to buy songbooks. Several of us distributed handbills to the homes advertising the services. Everything was in readiness down to the last detail. Now we expectantly waited. Though the building was quite cold, some 25 came for the first service. God met us in a glorious way, and we felt the day was a success.

My diary records that the offering was 92 cents which Gordon felt led to give to the evangelist, as we were to be partially supported by the home missions department at $50 a month. But six days later, we received a letter from the home missions secretary telling us that due to a drop in income, our promised support was withdrawn. My diary for that day reads: "Have faith in God."

Each month we received a $10 offering from Gordon's parents, which to us was a windfall. It greatly encouraged our hearts and helped us with those $30-a-month car payments, which always seemed to come around too soon.

On the second day of the revival, snow began to fall. Gordon and I spent part of the day painting a large oilcloth sign which announced the services. The rest of the day was spent in prayer. Only two people came to the meeting that night.

Some mischievous neighborhood boys threw rocks at the church and broke some of the new windows. The wind came howling through. Later in the week, some boys interrupted the evangelist's sermon by continually throwing rocks on the roof. Gordon and one of the men went outside to curb the disturbances. The boys took off running with the men close at their heels. Finally, they caught one of the boys. After giving him a sound scolding, the men returned to the tabernacle.

When I saw Gordon sit down in the rear of the church, I wondered what had happened. His face was all bloody! After the service, he told me that he had run into the neighbor's clothesline while chasing the boys and had cut his face quite severely. Anyhow, that was the last night the gang of boys threw rocks on the roof.

Billings was a long way from nowhere; therefore, we were continually called upon to share what little we had. We made it a policy never to turn anyone away. My diary records: "An old woman and her (demented) son to whom we gave food and 50 cents." And again: "Fed stranded evangelist."

Gordon and I felt the only way to reach the community was to go door to door, and visit the people and minister to their needs. Then we invited them to the services. As we did this, our attendance grew.

After the snow melted, the spring rains set in. Leaks developed in the roof. It seemed as if Gordon and I were continually on the roof making needed repairs. The rain was also seeping into the tabernacle from the ground. So belatedly, we dug trenches around the tabernacle, but not before the sawdust was soaked. With little heat in the building and continuing rain, it was impossible to dry out the sawdust floor.

By now the revival had come to a close, and the evangelist had left. Gordon was preaching every night and playing the piano. I was the janitor, Sunday school superintendent, young people's leader and song director for those first two months. As soon as qualified persons joined our efforts, I gladly relinquished one position after another. The hardest one to fill seemed to be that of a song leader. So each night after I finished leading the singing, I would leave the platform and sit on the front row, with my feet on the wet sawdust.

Weary already from making continuous house calls, and perhaps a little overheated from the exertion of leading singing, I developed a heavy cold. Several weeks went by. Instead of getting better, the coughing increased. So Gordon decided I needed rest.

A minister and his wife wanted to go to Oregon. They offered to pay for the gas and oil if Gordon would drive them. Here was our chance. Gordon decided I should go to my mother's in Portland for that rest. We drove the 1,000 miles back to Portland. It was a wearisome trip for me, with roads none too good, and with very little sleep at night, due to my persistent coughing. My weight had dropped to 94 pounds.

We arrived at mother's around seven o'clock one evening. She hurriedly kissed Gordon and me. It was prayer meeting night, and by 7:15 p.m. she must leave for church. So rapidly, she pulled all sorts of food out of the icebox, set it on the table, told us to enjoy it, and off she went.

Feeling a little hurt at my mother's leaving after not having seen me for some time, I mentioned it to Gordon. His answer was, "I wish I had a church full of members just like her."

Tuberculosis!

Gordon stayed a couple of days, then headed back to Billings, leaving me to rest at mother's. But instead of getting better, I seemed to be losing ground. Every other day it seemed, I took a fresh cold — cold upon cold.

One morning while my next older sister, Emma, was visiting me, I attempted to pick up a small footstool. The weight of it was too much for me, and I fell on top of it. I decided to go back to bed. A few minutes later, Emma came into my room. Weeping, she said, "Freda, we hate to tell you this, but we all think you have TB."

Tuberculosis — how that word pierced my heart! Over and over again, the possibility of it had been haunting me. Now my sister said I had it! Could it be that I, a young woman married only one-and-a-half years, was doomed by this oft deadly disease? Together we wept.

An appointment was made for me to be X-rayed. When the X-rays were developed, the doctor brought them to the house. (In those days doctors made house calls.) Never shall I forget his words to me: "Young lady, I have bad news for you. You have TB in both lungs. See (and he pointed as he held the X-ray up to the window for light), this is your best lung. It is completely spotted. The other lung is so full of water it shows up as a blur. The only thing in your favor is your youth. *I want you to spend one year in bed.* Don't even put your feet on the floor to go to the bathroom. If your family isn't able to give you that kind of care, then I'll make plans to get you into a sanitarium." And with that he left.

Back in my room, my heart was breaking. "No, no," I cried. "It can't be." One year in a sanitarium! And what after that year? Maybe two, three, five, 10 years? Who could tell! Maybe a slow, lingering, hemorrhaging death after that? Could that be the will of God for me? Never! I refused to accept it.

Gordon's parents had been married in Zion, Illinois, and he was born there. Zion was the headquarters for Dr. John Alexander Dowie, who brought back divine healing to the Church at the turn of the century. Thousands of miracles took place there. Thus, the Lindsays were strong in faith. Immediately upon hearing about my diagnosis, Dad Lindsay called Gordon telling him the news, and admonishing him to return at once to Portland to be at my side.

Bundled up and lying on a cot in the backyard of mother's home, I was deep in thought about the future. I did not see how Gordon could possibly come to be with me. The church was so

new, he couldn't leave it. Besides, with the $30-
a-month car payment, plus $10-a-month rent for
the apartment, I knew he just couldn't afford it.
Nevertheless, Gordon did decide to return to
Portland. I later learned, he succeeded in getting
a minister friend to fill in for him at the church.
And somehow he scraped up enough money to
buy gas for the return trip, but not enough to sleep
in motels (though the cost was only $2 or so a
night).

So he drove until he was tired, pulled alongside the highway and slept for a few hours, then
proceeded again westward. The old car could
barely average more than 30 miles an hour, so a
1,000-mile trip, with roads not too good, was
really an undertaking. Thus, not expecting him
in the least, I gave a cry of joy when I saw his
frame round the corner of the house. "Gordon,
what are you doing here?"

He embraced me as I raised up on my elbow
on the cot. Looking at me very seriously, he said,
"I hear the news of your condition is not good.
But this is not the will of God for *us*. The devil
is trying to destroy my ministry and to take your
life."

Oh, how good it was to have him near — to
encourage me when I needed him most. He
talked on about it being the will of God to heal
me, quoting Scripture after Scripture. And you

know the Bible says, "Beloved, if our heart does
not condemn us, we have confidence toward
God" (I Jn. 3:21). So with that he left me to
myself.

Back in my room, I began to call on the Lord.
I asked Him to forgive me of every sin — of
omission or commission — of which I was
guilty. After communing with the Lord for several hours, I felt completely clean within. It was
as though I had had an internal bath; nothing
between me and my Lord and Savior. I knew I
was ready to be healed!

Later that evening after visiting his parents,
Gordon returned. I told him I was ready — ready
to be healed! So together we prayed, Gordon
leading out in a strong, clear voice, cursing the
devil, and asking the Lord to heal me in Jesus'
Name. I was agreeing with him. "If two of you
agree on earth concerning anything that they ask,
it will be done for them by My Father in heaven"
(Matt. 18:19).

So with that as the declaration of my faith, I
arose from bed, declaring I was healed. I did not
consult my feelings, for had I done that, I would
have stayed in bed. No feelings came at first. But
back and forth I walked, praising God and thanking Him for healing me, while Gordon shouted
with me. After a few minutes, I *did* feel stronger.
Praise God! For some 15 or 20 minutes this went

on. Then feeling a little weary, I climbed back
into bed, only to arise a few minutes later and
proceed again to thank God for my healing.

That night, I slept almost unbrokenly — the
first time in several months. The next morning
when mother came to ask what she could bring
me for breakfast, I told her that I was joining her
and Gordon at the table. After breakfast, she
urged me to "crawl back in bed and not overdo."
I informed her that I would dry the dishes for her,
which I did.

Less than two weeks later, on July 16, 1938,
I helped Gordon pack, and we were on our way
to Billings, stopping en route at Yellowstone for
a day or two. On August 3, I was back in church,
helping in the services, healed by the power of
God! (Later, my sisters told me that when they
and mother waved goodbye to me that morning
in Portland, they thought the next time they saw
me, I would be in my coffin.)

Some have asked if I had a relapse or a recur-
rence. To this I must say, that for a few months,
I would occasionally have "symptoms." But
Gordon, being the strong and thorough faith
teacher he was, had cautioned me that "lying
symptoms" would return. And when they did, I
was to immediately recognize that they came
from the devil, and I was to resist them with all
that was within me. "Resist the devil and he will

flee from you" (Jas. 4:7). To emphasize it, Gordon would gleefully point out, "You notice, he won't just walk away. He'll put his tail between his legs and run for all he's worth." And so it worked! Praise God!

And though it had seemed at that period of my life I would never reach age 30, I have indeed lived a full life — working 12, 14 or 16 hours a day for 35 years by the side of my husband who prayed the prayer of faith for me — and I am still going strong today.

Chapter Three

After Gordon felt his ministry in Billings was completed, we left for the evangelistic field. It still thrills me to recall some of the ones who came to Christ in those revival meetings.

One such four-day engagement was in Elma, Washington, one month before our first child was born. In those days, evangelists couldn't afford to stay in motels. At least the ones we knew couldn't. During this particular meeting, we stayed in the country with a quaint family. The mother had died, leaving only the father and daughter.

I noticed there were no knobs on the doors. When I asked about this, the old man told me, "Door knobs only invite thieves."

"But how do you keep the doors closed?" I asked.

"Oh, just use some old newspaper and give the door a slam. It'll hold."

The meals, too, were something long to be remembered. It was exceedingly hot in the house, and there were flies by the multitudes. After dinner we left the table, and a moment later,

looking in from the adjoining room, I saw a
dozen or more cats of every color and size on the
kitchen table. They had come through a big hole
in the screen. When I called attention to the cats,
the girl went to the table, and waving her arm
said, "Shoo!" The cats scrambled off the table
and disappeared out the hole in the back door
screen. The old man explained, "Oh, they do that
every time we finish a meal."

The daughter then removed the food to the
warming oven of the old wood stove. And the
next day, we finished what the cats had left the
night before. Needless to say, with the birth of
our child only a month away, for some reason,
my appetite was not up to par.

But if I thought the meals left something to be
desired, I was even more dismayed to learn of
the sleeping arrangements. When the old man
showed us to our room, he instructed us to be
sure to put our clothes, shoes and socks under the
covers. At first, Gordon and I both smiled, thinking he was joking. But curious, I asked, "Why?"

His answer was anything but amusing, "Well,
you see," he replied, "when you turn out the
lights, the pack rats in the attic will carry your
things away if you let them." I was horrified, but
followed his instructions.

Surely enough, as soon as we turned out the
single, dim light hanging from a long cord in the

ceiling, the "graveyard shift" went into full swing, dragging *something* over the rafters *all night.* Every so often, I would sit up in bed, trying to feel if our clothes were entirely covered, getting very little sleep for wondering if our personal belongings would be there the next morning.

But whenever we would stay in an "unusual" home, Gordon with his ever-present humor, would always encourage me with something like, "Well, we're not buying this place. I've learned I can live anywhere as long as I know it's not permanent." Or, "We'll soon be moving on."

Our "love offering" in Elma was $4.50 that week. But as we left that community, we knew we had reached souls who, because of our coming, would spend eternity with Jesus. That compensated for any inconvenience.

A few days before our firstborn was due, we headed back to Portland. The day before the baby's scheduled arrival, my labor pains began. Checking in at the hospital, after examination I was told that a serious problem had developed in the position of the child.

When Gordon had brought me to the hospital, he carried with him his usual satchel of books. To the surprise of the doctor, he asked for a desk where he could study. She offered him her own, which he accepted. But when he learned of my difficulty, he earnestly began to intercede for me, claiming the Scripture, "She will be saved in childbearing" (I Tim. 2:15). God did intervene, and though it was a breech birth, Carole Ann was born a half hour later, weighing nine pounds — a healthy, beautiful child. Five weeks after Carole was born, I became a naturalized U.S. citizen, having been born a Canadian.

That same year, we received news of the sudden death of Earnest Lindholm, a missionary in the Congo. He was our first missionary in that he came from San Fernando, and our church there was helping in his support. Shortly before his death, Ernest's wife had given birth to their only child.

Earnest had gone hunting to secure some meat and being unfamiliar with the ways of the forest, he was attacked by a water buffalo and was instantly killed. (His young wife and son stayed on for years in Africa continuing missionary work.)

His homegoing had a very sobering effect upon both Gordon and me, for here was a young man totally dedicated to the Lord whose life was so suddenly cut short. We could not explain to the parents why he was taken. We shall have to wait for the answers to some things in life until we get to heaven.

Back on the Evangelistic Trail

Shortly after Carole's birth, we returned to evangelistic work. I recall one four-week revival we held in Grants Pass, Oregon, at the church of Leon Hall, Gordon's brother-in-law. This was a strong church in many ways, yet it had an air of complacency. So we initiated a plan to visit as many in the city as possible. We divided the church, and sent the workers out two-by-two.

After everyone had selected a partner, one rather uncouth and awkward-looking man remained unchosen. So it fell Gordon's lot to take him. He noticed that the man said very little as they went door to door, but nonetheless, seemed to be very observant — noting everything Gordon was saying.

After a few days, this man said to Gordon, "I believe I could do that myself." Gordon encouraged him with, "Why, sure you can!" So he chose someone to go with him, and away they went.

To make a long story short, this "least-likely-man-to-succeed" brought by far more new people into the church during that revival than anyone else. In fact, it so stirred his soul that he became what the pastor said was the most successful soulwinner in the whole church. In addition, he was later voted upon by the people to serve on the church board. He remained active in the church until his death some years later.

At the conclusion of that revival, my diary notes: "Starting south, not knowing where."

After several overnight stops, we arrived in Ajo, Arizona, where Gordon preached, and a number found Christ as Savior that night. The following day, we visited the "well" — Ajo's source of water. This 650-foot well (the only one in the world bored through solid rock) has arms reaching out for three miles.

To this city, Gordon, as a very young preacher with but a few cents in his pocket, had come alone in the early '30s. With seemingly no response to his ministry, and without even sufficient money for gas to leave the city had he wanted to, he became desperate with God. Going alone into the desert for a period of prayer, he mightily called on the Lord. God heard his prayers, and that night four men were saved. Revival broke out, and he stayed on for a number of weeks. Night after night, men received Christ as Savior.

On a Monday night during that revival (this was supposed to have been his "rest" night), Gordon was invited to visit the "well," seven miles from the city. There he spoke and told of God's plan of salvation. Of the seven families who maintained the well, three of them accepted Christ as Savior that night and became pillars in the church.

Now several years later, Gordon, I and little Carole were guests of one of the families at the "well" who had been saved in that meeting. We had been warned by a number of people that it was folly to take Carole into the Arizona desert at that time since she was less than a year old. In fact when we arrived in Arizona, some of the ministers told us the same thing. Nevertheless, there we were, and both of us felt God had led us.

Scarcely had we settled down to take the Ajo pastor's place during his vacation than Carole became ill. She had a severe case of diarrhea, was unable to eat, ran a very high temperature, and was passing blood. It seemed that, from the natural, those who had warned us were right.

We now had a grave decision to make. What would we do? We decided to trust God, and that we did. We had special prayer for her and committed her to the Lord, then went about our work, thanking the Lord for her healing. Almost immediately, we could see the change. The bleeding stopped, and the fever broke. Within a few days, she was completely well. And her picture, taken six weeks later when she was 1, shows her to be an exceedingly healthy child.

I never shall forget one certain Sunday morning while we were at Ajo. The service had just ended, when suddenly someone came into the church, saying that five young men from Ajo had turned over in a convertible. According to the report, all of them were injured. One was a member of a very devout family. The parents of a second boy had belonged to the church but had somehow gotten their eyes on people and off the Lord, and had left. As a result, this particular boy was not serving the Lord and had not been in church in some years.

We left immediately for the hospital. Upon arrival, just as the parents, who had come directly from church were coming into the waiting room, we asked to see the boys. The nurse escorted us, along with the parents, into the room of a boy who was in the throes of death. His face was completely covered with blood. He was unconscious, groaning and rolling from side to side in his bed. The mother took one look at him and began to cry out. The nurse, Gordon and I led her back into the waiting room.

Some 15 minutes later, while we were endeavoring to console the mother, suddenly the nurse came back in and said to this mother, "We have made a mistake. That was not your son. Your son is in another room, and is scarcely injured."

The parents seemed to be in a state of shock. They could not comprehend what had just been told them. We asked the nurse where their son was. We led the mother down the hall into the room. There, seated on the bed with but minor scratches, was the mother's son. Incredulous at first, then overcome with joy, the mother threw her arms around her son, and laughed and cried all at the same time.

The boy that we had just seen in such agony, was the one whose family had dropped out of church, and had gotten away from the Lord. He died shortly after we saw him, and we conducted his sorrowful funeral several days later.

A third boy was seriously injured. His family had been somewhat careless, but now they rededicated their lives to the Lord, and the boy completely recovered. The two other boys had escaped injury.

Later, we talked to the parents who had been mistakenly led to the wrong boy, then to their son. We asked them how it felt when they walked into the room and saw their son alive and well. They answered, "It was as though he had been raised from the dead!"

And that is really the message of salvation for every one of us. Actually we deserve death, and the judgment of death is upon each one. But Christ has taken the judgment for us and has paid for our salvation, which brings with it eternal life. If we accept Him as Lord and Master of our lives, it is as if we were raised from the dead.

A Soul Won Through Obedience to God

World War II was in progress and gas rationing became a necessity. However, we were able to drive on from Ajo to the little town of Wickenburg, Arizona. There God gave us 25 beautiful converts.

In these meetings, Gordon would play violin solos and preach, and I would generally sing a solo and lead the singing. Together, we prayed with those who came forward with a need, whether it was for salvation, healing or the baptism in the Holy Spirit.

I recall one meeting in Tillamook, Oregon, one of the cheese centers of the world. This scenic little town on the coast had some wonderful people in it. Many of them were farmers and dairymen. One 19-year-old, Paul Zerker, belonged to a Swiss family. His father had died a year or so before, and the operation of their large dairy farm was thrust upon him, the eldest son.

Paul's mother and sister shared their great burden with us that he had never accepted Christ as his Savior. During the course of the revival, I had a tremendous burden for this young man. Each night, he would come into the service — often a little late due to many chores. He would seemingly be very moved, but when the service came to a close, he failed to come forward to accept the Lord.

Finally, the last night of the revival arrived. I sang a solo, "My Mothers Prayers Have Followed Me." Again I could see a visible conviction on this handsome, clean-cut young man's face. I felt sure this must be the night. But when Gordon gave the invitation, the boy again failed to act upon it.

After the close of the service, I went to the back door to shake hands with the friends we had made, but I was still greatly troubled in my spirit about Paul. As I saw him coming toward me, the Holy Spirit spoke to me to ask him to accept Christ. I began to reason with the Lord, saying, "Well, the service is already over, and it would be hard now to convince him to go forward, especially since the meeting has already broken up."

But the closer he came in the line to shake hands, the more my heart pounded. I knew if I didn't act, I would be disobeying God, and a soul might be lost forever. So when he finally stood before me, I put my arm around him and said, "Paul, this is your night."

Immediately he began to weep, and without any hesitation turned and walked to the altar. A marvelous conversion resulted, and years later, I heard that Paul married a lovely Christian girl. He became a very real strength in the church and

was one of its elders. I have often thought back
and wondered what might have happened had I
not obeyed the Spirit's leading that night.

In that particular city, I notice in my diary on
one day my schedule was as follows: I helped
canvass — that is, give personal invitations from
house to house — helped paint signs for the
revival, attended the street meeting, helped on
the radio broadcast, and led the song service.
This, of course, in addition to caring for Carole.

Cloudburst in Clovis

From the west coast we went south again, and
as we arrived in Clovis, New Mexico, we found
ourselves in the midst of a cloudburst. Our motor
stopped, and I well remember the strange feeling
I had as suddenly our car began to float for
several blocks right down Main Street. Gordon
had absolutely no control over the car. The streets
were deserted, and we had the road to ourselves.
But where it would take us we really could not
tell as we were in unfamiliar territory. (Yet the
paradox was that we were gliding along so
peacefully.)

Both of us began to call mightily on the Name
of the Lord. After we had drifted through town,
the car finally came to rest on a little rise. Greatly
relieved, we just sat there and rejoiced. Suddenly
from nowhere, a man appeared in a truck and

asked if we wanted him to pull us to a higher area on the highway. We told him we did (though secretly we were concerned because our money was almost at the zero point). To our relief, when he finished, he charged us only $2.

The Conversion of Bill Sutter

From Clovis, we went to Tucson, Arizona, to hold a revival. Years before, when we were in Billings, Montana, we ministered to a family by the name of Sutter. They had two sons, one of whom was named Bill. He was like a lot of teenage boys — wanting to do his own thing, and not especially interested in serving the Lord.

Shortly after we began to deal with him about the Lord, Bill became very, very ill with rheumatic fever. He was so sick, he was not even able to walk except with intense pain. We prayed with him, and God marvelously healed him. But still he would not serve the Lord.

After we left Billings, we lost track of the Sutter family. Now we were down in Tucson. We placed an ad in the paper announcing the revival, and Bill Sutter read it. He was in the army, stationed at a nearby base. With little else to do in the evening, he decided to visit the revival, and see if by any chance, we could be the Lindsays who had prayed for his healing in Billings.

That very first evening, Bill came forward to

accept the Lord as his Savior, and was gloriously saved. The following nights, he brought soldier after soldier to the meeting. They, in turn, found Christ as their Savior and Baptizer.

One soldier in particular, I recall, testified that he received the baptism in the Holy Spirit on his way home from the service. He was so happy and excited that he ran around a school building several times, unable to control the overwhelming joy and love that was welling up within his soul. The other soldiers just stood on the sidelines and rejoiced with him.

Bill later married a fine Christian young woman and settled in Chicago. There for years, he held a top-level job in the cattle-buying industry while active in the Stone Church. When I heard from him not long ago, he was still a solid Christian engaged in similar work with his family back in Billings.

"Let the Little Children Come to Me" (Mk. 10:14).

One interesting note in my diary says, "Carole had a prayer burden." We were in the city of Turner, Oregon, and had a day of fasting and prayer. The unusual thing about this notation was that Carole was only a little over 2 years old. I recall how she laid her little frame over the altar and travailed in prayer as an adult would.

In our generation, the sad thing is that so many parents exclude their young children from worship services and prayer meetings because they believe "children are just too young to understand." I am sure most parents would be surprised if they realized how much children *do* understand. And how often those parents miss opportunities to affect their child's life by failing to let him attend and participate in their spiritual activities.

During the years we raised our three children, "babysitting" and nurseries were unknown. All three of our children were raised in church. When they were tired and sleepy, there was always a little pillow or blanket by their side where they would relax, and many times they would fall asleep.

In many churches today, there are good, spiritual children's programs. This is fine, but should never become just a place of entertainment "to keep the children occupied." I'm a firm believer that once a child begins public school (and perhaps a couple of years earlier), he should share in at least some of the adult worship services — preferably seated beside his parents.

Our second child, Gilbert, was born three years after Carole. A month after his birth, we were on the evangelistic road again.

When Gilbert was 6 weeks old, we were

holding a revival meeting in Oakland, California. It was Sunday morning. I was up early to get the two children bathed and ready for Sunday school and church. Because it seemed chilly in the house we were staying in behind the church, I lit the gas oven (or thought I did), and pushed the bassinet with Gil in it, close to the oven.

I then joined Gordon in the opposite end of the house, and was giving a final check to the notes on the Sunday school lesson I was to teach. Gordon was working on his morning message. Suddenly he said to me, "Is the baby all right? I keep hearing a little gurgling sound coming from the kitchen."

I dashed toward the kitchen, and suddenly heard the escaping gas! Looking in the bassinet, I saw that Gilbert's eyes were rolled back in his head, and he was scarcely breathing.

I cried for help, and Gordon came racing into the room. He rushed Gilbert to the opposite end of the house, and placed him near an open window. Immediately after I had turned off the gas and opened the back door, we prayed desperately that God would spare our son's life. He did, and within an hour, the color had returned to his face. And we took him to service that morning.

Slam the Door on Fear!

During one revival we held in California, we

stayed (as was the custom) in the home of the pastor and his wife. They were a lovely couple; but the wife, who was about my age, was becoming crippled with arthritis. She had been from doctor to doctor, city to city, treatment to treatment, and nothing seemed to avail. That her arthritis was getting progressively worse was apparent. There seemed to be a fatalistic attitude in the home about her condition, and no amount of praying made much difference.

After the conclusion of our campaign, I recall a sort of depression or shall I say fear, settled upon me. This pastor's wife had told me all of the symptoms she had had when the disease began. As I thought sympathetically upon her condition day after day, and having lived with her those weeks, I suddenly realized that I was having the same symptoms. My bones began to ache, and my joints were in real pain. After some weeks, I shared my great concern with Gordon, and fortunately he had the answer.

He said to me, "Fear is the door that will give the devil a wide entrance into your body, and unless you overcome it now, you will find yourself in the same condition as the pastor's wife with whom we just stayed." He scolded me, reproved me, and then loved me and warned me that fear was a luxury I just could not afford. And unless I really became outraged at the devil's attempt to put his diabolical, crippling disease upon me, I would certainly be the loser.

He gave me a number of Scriptures, including Job 3:25, "For the thing I greatly feared has come upon me, and what I dreaded has happened to me."

Realizing what the devil was doing to me, I earnestly sought the Lord and resisted the devil with all my might. Deliverance came shortly after this as I told the devil that that was one disease I refused to have, and for him to take his trick and leave. He did! Praise the Lord! And that disease has never troubled me since. Years later I saw this dear pastor's wife at a camp meeting. She was almost immobile — relying on her family for her care. How my heart went out to her, for she was yet a comparatively young woman and was so physically bound. I was grateful then that I had a husband who did not make the mistake of nurturing my fears and pampering them, but challenged me to claim healing and health which was purchased for me at Calvary.

Sometimes in our married life, I would almost envy the wives whose husbands were so patient and kind during long, protracted illness. For it seemed that Gordon had no tolerance for sickness, and any time I was not feeling well, he showed absolutely no sympathy. In fact in the natural, he seemed brusque and even harsh at times. Realizing that I would get no comfort or assistance whatsoever from him in that regard, I decided it didn't pay to be sick. I might just as well be well.

Since he believed so strongly that sickness was the work of Satan, he would ask me, "How can we pamper the work of the devil? That would be totally unscriptural." So that was his attitude, and his actions were consistent with his convictions.

Often years later, I would meet the women whose husbands had been so long-suffering and tolerant. I reflected that these same women would have been a million times better off, had their husbands been like Gordon, and not had such tolerance and forbearance for the work of the devil.

Child Miraculously Healed of Severe Burns

In one campaign in Grass Valley, California, a young lad whose last name was Huff, attended. When he was a small child, he was playing with several older boys in a garage. They discovered a gasoline can and decided "to make some sparks." So they poured gasoline in a jar and set it down, throwing a match on it.

This Huff boy was the youngest, and stood closest to the jar. When the gas ignited, it sprayed

fire on the child's clothing, burning him badly.
He was hospitalized for a long time, and except
for scars, came out of the episode fairly well,
with one exception: The burn under one arm
never healed. Time and time again, the skin from
under his arm would attach itself to the body, and
operation after operation resulted. The flesh was
never dry, and it seemed like there was nothing
medical science could do for him.

His mother brought him to our meeting. Gordon and I prayed for him and told the mother to
go believing. The following night, the mother
and child came to the service, excited beyond
comparison. The boy's arm had been completely
healed. All of the drainage had stopped, and he
was now able to raise over his head the arm that
had been more or less impotent. In fact, he swung
it as though he were getting ready to throw a fast
curve on a baseball field, much to the delight of
everyone present. He came night after night, and
the miracle was complete.

Pastor's Daughter Accepts Christ

In Reno, Nevada, the pastor and his wife had
a great concern for their wayward daughter who
was in her late teens. Each night as Gordon
would plead with souls to accept Christ as their
Savior, this particular girl would sit unmoved in
the rear of the church with her friends. In fact,

judging from the company she kept, some wondered if God had a chance in her life.

On the last night of the meeting, to our heart's joy, this girl came forward and took a stand for the Lord. We left Reno the following day. Time and time again, as we continued praying for the girl, the devil would inject the thought in my mind, "Well, that was the last night. She just came forward because a lot of the young people did. She will never stand. After the excitement of the revival is over, she'll go right back to her sinful companions." Again and again, however, the Lord brought her to my mind. I would pray for her that she would become a strong and stable Christian.

It was my pleasure to see her mother later and to find that this young girl had indeed stood true to the Lord. She had broken ties with some of her unsaved companions, and was at that time, enrolled in Bible school preparing to work for the Lord. To God be all the glory!

Chapter Four

A fter several years on the evangelistic field, we received a call in July 1944 to pastor the Assembly of God church in Ashland, Oregon. Here was a congregation of about 40 wonderful people. The great Dr. Charles S. Price had held an area-wide revival in this community 20 years earlier, and had made a lasting impression on many lives.

A nucleus of about 40 in that one community had founded this church, but due to lack of leadership, the church had not grown. We were told that for 20 years they had been praying that the Lord would give them 100 in Sunday school. Yet the attendance remained around 40.

One of the first things Gordon and I did after assuming the pastorate, was to start visiting every family in the community as time would allow. Immediately, new faces started appearing in church, and this indeed excited the "old regulars."

As Sunday school increased, there were no rooms available. So with volunteer help, we started digging out the basement. Since there was no way to get a piece of earth-moving equipment under the church, the dirt had to be handled a shovelful at a time. Gordon and the men spent several weeks laboriously removing every square foot of earth to make room. We then built our first Sunday school room, and as time went on, we dug an entire basement under that church, to provide extra classrooms.

One day an evangelist stopped in to see us. After eating and praying together with him, we felt he should be our first evangelist. He had a nice appearance, though we realized he was uneducated, and his grammar was rather poor. Later, when he wrote us a postcard, to our horror, we saw that he had misspelled practically every word on it. This made us realize that he had even less education than we had thought.

There were about a half dozen teachers in our small congregation since it was a college town, and we were musing over the thought, "What will be the response of these teachers to this evangelist?" In the natural, we almost recoiled from having to face the issue.

However after prayer, Gordon still felt that this was the evangelist God wanted at that church at that time — perhaps to shock our staid, sophisticated people into activity, seeing how God could use a man of even his meager background. So Gordon wisely "warned" our people that we had an evangelist coming who would no doubt

"murder the king's English," but who nevertheless had the anointing of God on his life. If we
could be charitable in overlooking his grammati-
cal mistakes, he knew God would give us the
revival for which we had been praying.

Needless to say, this was exactly what was
necessary. And when the evangelist came,
instead of the congregation rejecting him, they
stood behind him. As a result, there was nothing
like it since the days of the Chautauqua orator,
Dr. Charles S. Price. Some 23 were filled with
the Holy Spirit — a record for that community.
Many others found Christ as Savior.

Feeling that music has a vital part in church
worship, we started praying for an orchestra and
choir leader. To the surprise of many people
there, God sent us a Dutchman who was an
accomplished violinist, and had actually played
before the queen of Holland. Within a short time,
we had a terrific choir and an orchestra, which
was admired by every church in the southern part
of the state.

Attendance climbed steadily until we were
averaging 300 in Sunday school (in this community of only 7,000 people). In fact, at times our
Sunday school was running higher than any of
the other Assembly of God churches in that state.

One splendid family, the Karl Oesers, began
attending our church. Shortly after our arrival,

the wife, Geraldine, really prayed through and touched God. But her husband of staid German background, held back. However, after much prayer for him, Karl accepted Christ as His Savior. They and their families have been pillars in that church ever since.

Carole Falls From Moving Car

Once when Carole was 5 years old, we were riding home from church. A young assistant of ours was seated in the back seat of the car with her. As we turned a corner, suddenly the car door swung open. Carole decided to get up and close it. With Gilbert in my lap, I was unable to reach her. And I saw her as she lost her balance and rolled out onto the pavement.

Gordon immediately stopped the car and ran to where she was. He picked her up and found that the side of her face where she had hit the pavement, was bruised and bleeding, and she was groaning.

We rushed her home, and she began to spit blood. As Gordon enclosed her in his arms, it appeared she was going into convulsions. He walked the floor with her, calling on the Name of the Lord, as we felt that was our only recourse. Slowly she became calm, and we took her to bed with us.

After a couple of hours, she fell asleep. And

by morning, she was greatly improved, although her bruised face looked like hamburger. Nevertheless, several days later, we attended a convention in Grants Pass, Oregon, and God had so completely healed her, that it was impossible to see even a scar.

In a pastor's home the word "deacon" is often used. We had an excellent group of deacons in our Ashland church, so that was a common household term in our family.

It had been my conviction that we should start teaching the Bible to our children at an early age. I always made sure that Carole knew her memory verse for the Sunday school lesson. When she was 6 years old, one of her lessons was about the creation. The memory verse for the week was, "In the beginning God created the heaven and the earth. And the earth was without form, and void; and darkness *was* upon the face of the deep" (Gen. 1:1,2 KJV).

When she repeated her memory verse to her daddy on Saturday night, she said, "In the beginning God created the heaven and the earth. And the earth was without form and void; and darkness was on the face of the deacons."

An Answer for Weight Watchers

Gordon's dry sense of humor often made him a popular figure among young people. He always had a Bible answer to any question, and would give it in such a way that it would both strike home and yet at times could be very funny. One time, a beautiful young girl in our Ashland church came to him with a problem. She said that she planned to be married in a few months but was quite a bit overweight and would not look nice in a wedding dress. She asked him to pray for her.

Gordon looked at her very solemnly and then said, "My dear sister, 'this kind goeth not out but by prayer and fasting'" (Matt. 17:21 KJV).

A Dream Concerning Charismatic Catholics

The people of Ashland treated us like kings. In my diary I note: "God has been wonderfully good to us — better than we deserve." The annual church election was held, and we received 100 percent of the votes. The people then voted that they would not have another election as long as we chose to remain pastors.

While in that city, the Lord gave me a perplexing dream about three o'clock one morning. I dreamed of the end-time persecutions. In this dream, I saw my friends and myself being called out of a dungeon to stand trial and to be persecuted for our testimony of Jesus. As I ascended the stairs, I was surprised to discover a Catholic priest in our company. He was there because of his love for Jesus! This was back when we did not personally know of any truly born-again priests.

When I awoke I was puzzled. Little did I then realize the significance of the dream. It was foretelling this very day when Catholic priests and bishops, nuns and the laity, are going out, filled with the Holy Spirit, and boldly proclaiming that Jesus Christ is the same yesterday, today and forever.

Twenty-seven years later, I remembered that dream as I sat one cold, rainy day in June 1974 in the Notre Dame stadium watching 30,000 born-again Charismatic Catholics testifying of their love for Jesus. Truly this was a fulfillment of Joel 2:28.

The Ashland Parsonage

In Ashland, I had my eye on a beautiful colonial style house right behind the church which I felt would make an ideal parsonage. After sharing my idea with Gordon, we began to pray about it. We heard the owner was not interested in selling, but a few months later, the owner did indeed want to sell. Upon getting a unanimous vote of the board, we purchased the parsonage, and after some minor remodeling moved in.

A few days later on August 29, 1946, our third child, Dennis Gordon, was born — a healthy youngster whom the hospital staff called "the football player" because of his size.

Shortly after this I lay in bed one night, exceedingly grateful to the Lord for my beautiful family, for the spacious parsonage, and for a congregation that loved us so dearly. I began to help the Lord plan my future. I reminded Him that now I had everything I really wanted, and that with Ashland being a college town, I would be perfectly satisfied to remain there. My three children could attend college up the street about a mile, and I felt Ashland would be a good place for the Lord to look for our family when The Rapture took place.

Opportunity after opportunity for service arose in southern Oregon. We were on the radio, and involved in a lot of spiritual ministries outside the church. Carole was now $5\frac{1}{2}$ years old, and was singing on the radio as well as taking piano lessons.

God's continued blessing was upon our ministry in Ashland, and notes from my diary state: "Brother Clark, one of the board members, received the baptism after 17 years." "Ben Peterson, another board member, received the Holy Spirit after 22 years." And on and on goes the amazing story of what God did in that city.

A Ministry to Those Seeking the Holy Spirit

Gordon's ministry was always strong in the areas of salvation, prophecy and healing. We had

had two evangelists, Rev. John Stovall and Rev.
J. E. Stiles, who were strong in ministering to
those who wanted to receive the baptism in the
Holy Spirit. (In J.E. Stiles' meeting alone, 52
people were filled with the Holy Spirit.) But
Gordon didn't seem to have much success in that
area of ministry.

One night after speaking on the baptism in the
Holy Spirit, when he came home from the service, I mentioned to Gordon several areas where
he should have been more clear. I felt that he
could have been more effective had he included
some simple instructions at the close, and I suggested what he should have said.

Gordon turned to me saying, "I believe the
Lord wants you to teach the new people how to
receive the baptism in the Holy Spirit."

"Oh, no," I replied. "I could never do that!"

"Yes, that is exactly what the Lord wants. He
wants you to instruct people, and I am going to
announce on Sunday that you will be speaking
next week on how to receive the baptism in the
Holy Spirit."

"No, no, never!" I protested.

Again he remonstrated, "Yes, I am going to
announce the service."

For the next few days I earnestly sought the
Lord, for I felt I was on the spot. To my surprise
when I did speak and instruct the people, a new

faith sprang up in my own heart. I was able to
minister to those who needed the baptism in the
Holy Spirit in a way which surprised me most of
all, and several were filled that night. (In years
to come, I noticed that God had given Gordon a
spirit of discernment. He seemed to sense what
a person's ministry was to be and would encourage him to step out in faith in it.)

From then on, Gordon would almost never
pray with an individual to receive the baptism in
the Holy Spirit, but would refer them to me. We
worked as a team. He would make up for my
deficiencies, and I would try to help where he
lacked. There was never a spirit of rivalry, never
a spirit of jealousy. We felt God had brought us
together and that each was to complement the
other. In fact, if anything, Gordon always
"pushed" me harder than I really wanted to go.
It seemed he was always thinking up more
opportunities than I could possibly fulfill.

When sometimes I would see a vying for position and an undermining of one another in the
homes of some ministers, my heart would bleed.
Actually, if only ministers could realize it, a wife is
probably the most loyal, the most unselfish, the
most economical, the most dedicated worker he and
the church will ever have — if the relationship in
the home is what it should be.

With regard to the faith the Lord gave me to

instruct those who desired to receive the Holy Spirit, I recall one convention I attended in the East in those early years. The morning classes were divided, and it so happened that one of the speakers failed to show up for his class. Gordon saw me in the lobby and asked me to "fill in." With not a minute's time for preparation, I grabbed my Bible and went hurriedly to the waiting class.

What should I speak on? Why, the baptism in the Holy Spirit of course. So after my time of instruction, I asked those to come forward who were candidates. Everyone who came was filled!

The noted evangelist and Bible teacher Dick Mills later told me he attended that service. He said to himself, "If God can use a little woman like that, then He can use me." From there, he took his first trip to the Caribbean Islands and, he said, "got with it." Since then, God has mightily used him.

I remember when in later years, we conducted a tent meeting in Topeka, Kansas. Gordon preached the main evening service, and I gave the morning instruction. Present in one of those day sessions was an elderly man who came to receive the baptism in the Holy Spirit. When I asked him how long he had been seeking, he said, "Since Azusa Street," which was in 1906.

I have always felt it is good to be positive

rather than negative in trying to help people. So to keep from discouraging him further I suggested, "Well, you should be ready to receive by now then, shouldn't you?" He agreed. After a few simple instructions, he receive without further delay along with others who were present.

The Torn Stocking

It was in Ashland that an incident occurred which showed God's mercy and love for our family. Our parsonage was located beside a huge gas station. Gilbert was now 4 years old and loved to ride his tricycle up and down the sidewalk. We had warned him to stay away from the gas station. Both the church and the station were on Main Street, which was actually the highway from Sacramento to Portland and on north. A lot of trucks stopped at this station.

On this day, Gilbert was kneeling on the ground near the gas station tying a rope to his tricycle when suddenly a huge truck began backing toward him. The station owner told me later that when he saw the truck backing up, all of a sudden, he saw Gilbert seemingly right under its wheels. He let out a cry to the high heavens and waved his arms for the trucker to stop, but apparently the trucker did not hear him. So he shut his eyes as he was certain Gilbert would be crushed to death.

A moment later, the truck eased forward and went on its way. The station owner rushed over to Gilbert who stood there crying because, "That mean ol' truck tore my stocking off."

How grateful I was to God when I examined him and saw that although the truck had indeed torn his stocking off, his foot was unscratched. Had the truck gone an inch farther, his leg would have been crushed, and he could well have lost his life.

Through this event, the Lord dealt very strongly with me that it is most important to be continually in close fellowship with the Lord and to be in His *perfect* will.

Chapter Five

J ack Moore, a friend of Gordon's from
  Shreveport, Louisiana, arrived one day on
our front steps in Ashland, inviting us to go with
him to Sacramento to attend the meeting of a
Baptist man by the name of William Branham.
We decided to go with him on this trip — one
which was to completely change our lives.

It was while we were at the Sacramento service that the Lord impressed upon both Gordon's
and William Branham's hearts that Gordon,
because of his wide contacts in Full Gospel
circles, would be the logical one to manage
Branham's meetings. Now we had a Herculean
decision to make. What would we do? Leave the
church where I had just told the Lord I would be
when The Rapture took place? The thought was
out of the question!

However after much prayer, Gordon and I
both felt he should go with Brother Branham. So
he asked for a year's leave of absence from the
church. I was to remain behind with our three
children and oversee the church. Gordon would
secure evangelists from time to time to come and

help me. It was a difficult decision, but both of us knew it was of God.

Following are a few of the letters Gordon wrote me while traveling with Brother Branham:

Shreveport, Louisiana
January 13, 1948

Dearest Freda, Carole, Gilbert and Denny,

How is my family? ... I certainly miss you all. If it were not because there are matters that appear to be tremendously important, I would certainly not be separated from you. However, God will make up to us many times any sacrifice. ...

Brother Branham is a very simple brother in many respects, and is utterly incapable of coping with the cunning and shrewdness that he meets on every side. He has definitely turned over the management of the campaigns to Brother Jack Moore and myself. ... There will be breaks between the meetings, so we will have opportunities to visit home. ...

It appears now that we shall have to start a magazine. ...

I have been holding a few services here in Shreveport. There have been a number that have come forward for salvation. There is a large number who have not received the Holy Ghost. I surely wish you were here as I know you have a ministry in that work.

How are Carole, Gilbert and Denny? I am expecting a good report from them. Lots of love and
kisses to you all. I miss you very, very, very much.

Gordon

* * * * * *

Shreveport, Louisiana
February 1948

Dearest Freda, Carole, Gilbert and Denny,

... Well, I miss you all so much, but know that
the time is short, and what sacrifices we make for
God will be repaid manyfold. Soon the last phase
of Armageddon will come, and the treasures of
this world will turn to ashes. ...

Freda, don't worry. Take care of your
strength. Carole, help Mama with all you can.
Gilbert, be a good boy and do what Mama says.
Denny, don't get into things. Say hello to all the
church.

... We are preparing to put out a magazine, and
all this requires much work. Our plans for the
printing are not yet complete, and there are many
things to consider.

Scores of invitations that have come to
Brother Branham have been forwarded to us
here. ...

... We shall return to Florida in a few days. F.F.
Bosworth is there, and he is mightily stirred over
the ministry of Branham. He used to have great

healing meetings himself. ... He used to work with Dad in Zion City. ...

... I have been very busy — almost have the manuscript for the book on divine healing completed, but will want Brother Branham to check it before it goes to press. I miss having you around, especially when checking manuscripts is necessary.

Lots of love,
Daddy

✻ ✻ ✻ ✻ ✻ ✻

Shreveport, Louisiana
February 13, 1948

Dearest Freda and All,

... Glad to hear the Sunday school is holding up well. Honey, please be careful and don't overdo. You must learn not to worry so much, but to rest in the Lord. Remember the proverb that says, "A living dog is better than a dead lion" (Eccl. 9:4 KJV). So a live lady is better than a dead one. Ha! ...

Love,
Daddy

✻ ✻ ✻ ✻ ✻ ✻

Miami, Florida
February 18, 1948

Dear Freda and Family,

... We drove to Mobile and picked up Brother

Branham. I read Brother Branham the manuscript of the book on divine healing which I had
prepared, and he was quite enthusiastic to get it
on the press at once. Have much to do in getting
the magazine ready for the press. ... There are a
thousand details to work out in these Branham
meetings, but God is helping us.

                              Lots of love,
                              Daddy

                    ✳ ✳ ✳ ✳ ✳ ✳

                         Tampa, Florida
                         February 23, 1948

My Dearest Freda and Family,

    We have had some great services the last few
days — many remarkable healings have taken
place, and the crowds have grown and filled the
tent, which is remarkable, considering the fact
that the tent is several miles out of town, and the
fact that every church has a revival meeting
going on, since we did not make advance prepa-
rations here.

    The Martz evangelistic party, which begins at
the Evangel Assembly of God, is staying at the
same tourist home. They have a little girl who is
only 7 years old, and she is the most prominent
girl evangelist in the world, having attracted
huge throngs all over the world — has been
publicized in *Look* and other magazines. She

seems quite remarkable for a child. Since the party does not begin until today, they have been attending our meetings. The little girl was quite impressed and said, "Daddy, I'm going to pray for the sick because it's in the Bible. ..."

I will have to get busy on the magazine, which will be called *The Voice of Healing.*

> Lots of love and kisses to
> my family,
> Your Daddy

✳ ✳ ✳ ✳ ✳ ✳

> Shreveport, Louisiana
> February 1948

Dearest Freda, Carole, Gilbert and Denny,

... We had a good meeting in Miami, even though it had practically no organization. Several hundred came forward for salvation Sunday afternoon, and most of them were weeping as Brother Branham told his life story. Three hundred souls — and most of them seemed to mean business — are more than a good evangelist sees saved in a year. We took up subscriptions for our magazine, *The Voice of Healing,* and got around 500. There were many outstanding miracles of healing. ...

... We now have a Webster wire recorder, and it is wonderful. I want to get one for you so we can use them for communication. I can read

Bible stories and talk to the children. I think it will be a great pleasure to us.

Jack Moore's oldest girl, Anna Jeanne, will be circulation manager of the magazine. I believe she is quite well qualified for the job. ...

Lots of love and xxxx,
Daddy

✳ ✳ ✳ ✳ ✳ ✳

Pensacola, Florida
April 3, 1948

Dearest Freda, Carole, Gilbert and Denny,

Arrived in Pensacola yesterday afternoon. The party met me at the bus depot. They told me a bad storm had blown down the tent. So we went to the armory. It was packed — 2,000 at 6:30 p.m., and the rest turned away. It was a most excellent service, and some fine healings. The tent is going up today.

Wish you all were here,
Daddy

✳ ✳ ✳ ✳ ✳ ✳

Shreveport, Louisiana
April 6, 1948

Dearest Freda, Carole, Gilbert and Denny,

... I'd get lonely, too, if it weren't for the fact that I'm so busy, I hardly get time to sleep. I surely miss my little family. It is hard to be away, but I know God is really in this great work. I want to say that the smile on the face of a little girl who wore braces and now was able to walk, was beautiful to behold. Pensacola was shaken in an amazing way, and multitudes gave their hearts to Christ.

... Am back in Shreveport — and up to my ears in work — another issue of the magazine to get out, and letters without number to write. Thursday evening we'll leave on the night train for Kansas City.

Lots of love and xxxx,
Daddy

* * * * * *

Shreveport, Louisiana
April 8, 1948

Dearest Mama, Carole, Gilbert and Denny,

To our folks in Ashland, greetings! The city of Pensacola was shaken for God. Many thousands attended. Great and notable healings took place. A lunatic that ran mad was delivered, and at last report, is now in his right mind. Fifteen hundred or so responded to a salvation altar call, but we had no place to put them. Our magazine is coming along fine — received 800 subscriptions in Pensacola. Will run out 15,000 next issue.

Love to all,
Gordon

✳ ✳ ✳ ✳ ✳ ✳

Kansas City, Kansas
April 10, 1948

Dearest Sweetheart, Carole, Gilbert and Denny,

Here in Kansas City, I had opportunity to meet many ministers. One young man, Oral Roberts, is having an outstanding ministry of healing also, in which many signs and wonders are taking place, though not on the scale of Branham's meetings. He attended our meetings, and you will see him, the tall fellow, in one of the pictures. ...

... We are in the midst of a great meeting in Kansas City. Last night was one of the most powerful services I was ever in. ... This work gives me opportunity to get acquainted with outstanding men of God everywhere, which of course is interesting.

I preached yesterday afternoon to a large crowd, including perhaps 40 ministers. I can preach as often as I desire, but many other problems take up my time. Also got acquainted with Oral Roberts, who also has an outstanding healing ministry. He is staying through this meeting. He has crowds that run into the thousands, too.

Lots of love and xxxx,
Gordon

* * * * * *

Elgin, Illinois
April 23, 1948

Dearest Freda, Carole, Gilbert and Denny,

I stopped Sunday night and Monday with Oral Roberts. God has greatly blessed him in a healing ministry. Had fine conversation with him. Will have article about him in our magazine which is just coming off the press. ...

Was surely happy to learn Carole had received the baptism. That's really fine. Must say bye-bye — and lots of love,

Daddy

* * * * * *

Shreveport, Louisiana
April 22, 1948

Dearest Honeybunch and My Little Ones,

... Maybe I'll have to have you and family come down here to Shreveport later. I could be with you more often, and in your spare time, you could help with the magazine. Everything depends on Brother Branham's strength. If that keeps up, we see great possibilities.

Lots of love and xxxx,
Daddy

* * * * * *

Shreveport, Louisiana
April 24, 1948

Dearest Mama, Carole, Gilbert and Denny,

... I do feel in the will of God in this work. If Brother Branham's health keeps up, I suppose this will be permanent. Would you consider in the future coming to Shreveport? I would rent you a house, and you could assist with the magazine. This is all theory yet. ...

Lots of love and xxxx,
Daddy

The Man, William Branham

Gordon highly treasured the time he spent with Branham. William Branham was a man of Baptist background. He had come from an exceedingly poor family. His father was a heavy drinker; therefore, Branham's earthly advantages were few. An angel had visited him and given him the gifts of healing. Scarcely anybody who attended his meetings doubted that this was actually the case.

Perhaps no minister in our generation had as great an effect upon the lives of so many other preachers regarding the supernatural, as did William Branham. He came to the fore at a time when the ministry of divine healing was at a low ebb. But when men saw what God was doing again in the world through this simple man, they too were inspired to believe God for a greater outpouring. And as a result, many other preachers sought God for and received a supernatural ministry.

But William Branham was not an easy man with whom to work. At the very beginning, Gordon had to act as a liaison between the sponsoring pastors, for it seemed that Branham had some erratic ideas. In fact, at first, some of his opinions, because of his lack of sound teaching and background, bordered on the occult.

Brother Branham was a man easily influenced. Therefore, when Gordon was with him, he did succeed in helping straighten out some of Branham's doctrines. However we noticed almost from the start, a trait of which most people were never aware — that Brother Branham was exceedingly vulnerable to flattery. When men would get around him in public, he appeared to shun them; but in his private conversations, it was apparent that he thrived on their flattery.

In later years, some of those who made the deepest inroads into Branham's life and held the greatest influence over him, were those who would put their arms around him and publicly present him as the greatest preacher on earth.

Gordon loved Brother Branham and was most

charitable in all his dealings with him. But with Gordon having been born in Zion, Illinois under the ministry of Alexander Dowie, he knew what flattery could do. In Dowie's case, it took a man who had a great miracle ministry and brought him to disaster.

So it was that Gordon had a great burden and concern for William Branham when he saw that unscrupulous men, in order to gain their own ends, would flatter him. This ultimately led to God removing Branham from the scene, to preserve His own glory and to keep Branham from teaching errors he fell into as a result of his weakness.

In some ways, Branham was actually child-like. Time and time again after a citywide meeting was scheduled and planned for months in advance, the advertising was out and the auditorium was packed, Brother Branham would fail to show up. Branham's reason: "Well, I just didn't know it was that far." He'd eventually arrive a couple of days late.

Gordon worked with Branham for about six months, during which time *The Voice of Healing* magazine was started, in order to carry the message of the revival that had broken out under Brother Branham's ministry.

Crisis!

A meeting had been scheduled in Eugene,

Oregon, and Gordon asked me to be present since it was close to Ashland. How can I ever forget what took place there?

After the closing service, Gordon and Branham met together for a lengthy conversation. Gordon had cautioned him that he was going beyond his strength as he prayed for countless thousands, but Branham failed to heed his advice. Now, Brother Branham advised Gordon that he was leaving the field that night, and "might never return again" because he was exhausted, and felt he was on the verge of physical breakdown. He was returning to Indiana to get back his former job as a game warden.

When Gordon asked him what would happen to *The Voice of Healing,* Branham replied, "That's your baby. That was your idea in the first place."

So after midnight with heavy hearts, Gordon and I headed south toward Ashland. (By now we had already turned in our resignation to the Ashland church, which would be effective as soon as Carole was out of school in May.)

Since it was en route, we decided to drive as far as Grants Pass, where Gordon's sister and brother-in-law, Gladys and Leon Hall, pastored. About 3 a.m., we dropped wearily into bed. The next morning at breakfast, we were introduced to an evangelist whom we had not met before.

Leon introduced him by announcing that he had a ministry similar to Branham's. We were, of course, very interested. After spending several hours together, the evangelist asked Gordon to arrange and direct his campaigns, and Gordon felt led to do so.

A letter from Gordon tells of one of those campaigns:

Salinas, California
June 7, 1948

Dearest Freda, Carole, Gilbert and Denny,

We have had fine meetings here in Salinas. Many miracles are taking place under this man's ministry. In deaf and blind cases, I think his ministry excels that of Branham's. The tent holds only 1,000, and Salinas is not a large community. This minister is not known yet as Branham is. But I believe his crowds will grow, and his ministry will eventually have as great a scope as Branham's. There was a deaf and dumb case healed last night, which really moved the congregation. ...

Lots of love and xxxx,
Daddy

The year away from Gordon was not easy. Over and over again in my diary are notations such as: "Miss Gordon a lot." "Very lonesome." "So happy to see him." "Lonesome for our

Daddy." Shortly after school was out in May, I was more than ready to leave the church and the people I loved to travel full time with Gordon.

We bought a 15-foot trailer and moved everything we could into it from our huge parsonage. The five of us traveled that summer as a family, and we enjoyed every moment of it. When fall came however, I realized it would be best to put Carole in school. When I told her we were sending her to Portland to live with her aunt for the school year, she cried all night. However, once she started for the plane, she dried her tears. But it was very difficult for me to put her on the plane when she was only 7 years old. My diary says of her: "She is a very brave, little soldier."

We traveled with this evangelist for some eight months, during which time, his ministry took on tremendous proportions. Gordon and Leon Hall would teach the people and pray with them in the day services, and God honored His Word with outstanding miracles in every meeting. I note one diary entry of a meeting: "Gordon spoke; five deaf mutes delivered, 17 saved." He seemed to have a real ministry of praying for the deaf. One notation dated January 26, 1947, reads: "Gordon seems to have the gifts of healing, and the deaf and blind are healed." Another entry in my diary: "Every disease healed in Jesus' Name."

Our last meeting with this particular evangelist was held at the Shrine Auditorium in Los Angeles where 7,000 people were packed, and hundreds were on the outside trying to get in. The newspaper clipping I have from that meeting reads, "KING-SIZE TRAFFIC JAM AT SHRINE." Then it went on to say, "Not since the days of Aimee Semple McPherson has there been such a meeting at the Shrine."

But it was at that particular meeting that Gordon and Leon left the team, for it was obvious that the evangelist's wife had an exceedingly jealous spirit. (Later the couple had some serious marital problems. After a separation of some years, however, I understand there was a reconciliation.)

The wife urged her husband not to let Gordon and Leon pray for the people in the day services, as she felt it would detract from her husband's ministry. (Actually, the line of people wanting to be prayed for was so long that in no way, could he have prayed for them all.) Besides this, she insisted that her husband have his own magazine. And, though the minister did ask Gordon to be the editor of his proposed new magazine, Gordon felt that he could not do justice both to his own magazine, and to that of another at the same time, so he resigned.

During these eight months, Gordon had been

instrumental in projecting this man, though previously virtually unknown, into a worldwide ministry.

Chapter Six

It was while we were in Los Angeles that a remarkable experience took place, and one to which I referred earlier. It concerned our young people's president from Tacoma, Washington. Gordon had asked me to write the story earlier, so I'm reprinting it here:

The End of the Trail

She was a beautiful girl — a rather tall, slender blonde. Her grace and charm won her many friends. Her musical talent gave her an open door of service. When she stood before an audience, there was a natural poise about her that was both fascinating and relaxing. But above and beyond all this, there was a genuine consecration to the cause to which she was dedicated — so much so, that she spent many of her Sunday afternoons at the church praying for the young people whose meetings she led at 6 p.m. Her entire family was spiritual and a credit to our church. To sum it all up, she was an outstanding leader, with a bright future if she continued to wholly follow the Lord.

After knowing this girl for several years, our

close contact with her was broken when we left that part of the country for other fields of labor for the Lord. We heard indirectly that she had gone to Los Angeles to attend Bible school.

But while in school, she made the same mistake that many others have made — that of getting her eyes on people instead of keeping them on Jesus. She became lonesome, disillusioned and discouraged — a fertile field for the devil to begin sowing his seeds of doubt and discontent.

Next, she began attending in her hometown, a church whose standards were considerably lower than those she upheld. Then came the report that the pastor was keeping company with this blonde. How could this be? He, a married man with a family? But it was true! And finally came the news that they had run away together!

But the wife had something to say. Soon the police were on their trail, and shortly after, apprehended them. The minister was put in jail and convicted of stealing, as the car he had used for his rendezvous was in his wife's name, and thus was her personal property.

And there in jail was born a most satanic-inspired false religion. The minister, instead of confessing and forsaking his sin, decided to go on a fast. To get an individual to repent is a Herculean task, unless the Spirit of God is given place to work. The guilty would rather do almost anything than to confess and forsake his sin. It has been said that the two hardest words to say in the English language are, "I'm sorry." But God's Word says, "To obey is better than sacrifice" (I Sam. 15:22).

Finally as he continued his fast, a voice spoke and said, "You must start a new religion. All other religions are wrong. The Christian faith is error. Christ is a bastard. You must overthrow them all. You must start this new doctrine now. Call this new religion Yahweh."

Immediately, he sent for his newly acquired wife. As he told her of his "revelation," a strange power came upon her — a strong delusion from hell — and she embraced this cult, utterly forsaking Christ! But this man had to serve out his term in the penitentiary. Who was to carry on in the meantime? Why she, of course!

And so it was that after our party had just completed a large salvation-healing revival in Los Angeles which ended in the Shrine Auditorium, with some 7,000 in a single night's attendance, we picked up the local paper, and there saw an announcement of a Sunday afternoon service by this strange cult. I felt I must attend and see for myself, as the reports were hard to believe about one who had been so close to us.

Making my way to where the meeting was to

be held in a large auditorium at one of the downtown hotels, I slipped into a seat near the rear of
the room, breathing a prayer that I would go
unnoticed. Several hundred people were present.

Soon the service began. Someone led some
songs, all of which were unfamiliar to me. I
looked anxiously for our friend. At last she made
her way to the platform. There she stood, beautifully clothed in a long, shining garment, with a
corsage on her left shoulder. All eyes were upon
her!

What I was to see and hear during the next hour
even yet brings cold chills to me, and will remain
indelibly imprinted on my mind as long as I live.
All at once, a spontaneous praise and worship of
Yahweh broke forth from the people, as they rose
to their feet with hands stretched toward heaven.
This occurred again and again. I felt at times I must
run from the building, so oppressive were the pow-
ers of darkness. But I decided to weather it, sitting
silently with my hat somewhat pulled over my face
to avoid recognition.

And then came the sermon — a bitter attack
against Christianity. The blonde mistress stood
there and cursed and blasphemed Christ again
and again, calling Him "bastard," while the congregation shouted, "Praise Yahweh!" She read
Scriptures from the Bible concerning the Holy
Spirit, the Virgin Birth, the Resurrection. She

would describe the event in a lewd manner, and pervert it into a sex joke, amid a mighty roar of "Praise Yahweh!" from her adherents.

At long last, the service came to a close. Refreshments were served, but I could not partake as they were offered to "strange gods." Then I stepped in line to shake hands with the speaker. When suddenly she recognized me, her face became ashen white, and she began to tremble. Calling me by my first name (which she had never before done), she asked, "Were you in the service?" I replied in the affirmative. I then asked her to accompany us to dinner as Gordon was to join me momentarily. She declined with many varied excuses, but I insisted.

Gordon arrived. Another hour passed, and it was apparent that she was stalling for time, hoping we would leave. She disappeared into a dressing room, outside of which we "stationed" ourselves as the minutes ticked wearily away. Finally at long last, she emerged with several "attendants," who, she informed us, must accompany her. We drove to Clifton's Cafeteria and there persuaded her to leave her "escorts" so we could be alone while eating.

Once inside, there was a coldness in the atmosphere. Nevertheless, we tried to be friendly and encouraged her to talk. Finally, she opened up and told us that not many years hence, she was to give birth to the true Messiah out in the desert, in a haven that was even now being established. As for Christianity, she had forsaken it because it was dying.

Then Gordon asked her if she had heard of the large meeting our party had just closed in the Shrine. No, she hadn't heard. Nor had she heard of other similar campaigns in various cities with many thousands attending. We assured her that the real Christian revival was just getting underway; thousands were getting saved and healed, and God was pouring out His Spirit on all flesh. Her face registered surprise and bewilderment as we continued to show her the error of her decision. Then nervously she quickly arose, shook hands with Gordon, threw her arms around me, hugged and kissed me and walked away to join her "escorts."

Back at our trailer, we prayed that if she had not already committed the unpardonable sin, for God to restore her and halt her in this terrible delusion which she was spreading as a new religion. We stayed in the city an additional two weeks. Each Saturday, we would look for her ad. Each time, it stated, "Due to illness of (the young blonde) — no service will be held." We learned later that week from a relative of hers, that immediately after she left us, she developed throat trouble and was unable to talk. We felt God had at least temporarily closed down the services while we were in the city.

For a long time we had no further news concerning this cult, though occasionally we got a letter in our office from one who had fallen into the devil's trap. "Because they did not receive the love of the truth, that they might be saved. And for this reason God will send them strong delusion, that they should believe the lie, that they all may be condemned who did not believe the truth but had pleasure in unrighteousness" (II Thes. 2:10-12).

Now comes the most startling development: I had been seeking information concerning the status of the movement, and also the sequel to what had happened to this young woman.

I was dictating a letter to a Los Angeles newspaper for possible information, when my secretary, Ruth, who had recently been a resident of Denver, Colorado, suddenly paused and looked up in an excited manner, exclaiming, "Why, I know what happened to that woman!" This of course took me by surprise, that my secretary would have knowledge of the matter. We wrote to the *Rocky Mountain News* in Denver for more information.

We learned from this newspaper that at the time this young woman disappeared from our contact, she entered the entertainment field and in 1950, was known in Houston as the "Blonde Bombshell" in various nightclubs where she sang and played. After several years of nightlife, she decided to turn again to her strange religious delusion. However, by this time, and we quote from Denver's *Rocky Mountain News*, March 4, 1957:

> She separated from her husband — divorce proceedings were under way.

> Miss _____ leased her offices in Denver a week ago, with plans to lecture and write on physic phenomena, stressing the use of extrasensory perception. She planned to establish headquarters here for the Kingdom of Yahweh, a religious cult.

> She told police that she was working late Friday, when she was accosted. ... She said the man raped her, after smashing a pop bottle over her head, and striking her in the mouth and stomach. The assailant then knifed a janitor who came to her aid.

> One day later on Sunday morning, Miss _____ was found by her hostess, with her feet resting on the bed, and her head and shoulders on the floor. It appeared she suffered a convulsion. Death occurred at 6:30 a.m.

The *Rocky Mountain News* carried inch-tall

headlines on the front page of Monday's paper — with a seven-inch photograph — saying, "BLONDE MYSTIC DIES AFTER ASSAULT." So ended the career of one who might have been greatly used of God had she followed in His footsteps.

Gordon added this comment: "This is a terrible story, but it is an entirely true one. The strangest thing about it all was the apparent gullibility of so many people in accepting this obviously blasphemous new religion. We truly believe that we were brought in touch with this new cult of Satan just in time. No amount of reasoning could seem to change those who were caught in its toils as we learned that night. By turning the whole matter over to God (I Cor. 5) at the crucial hour of its inception, its rapid spread was apparently halted.

"As we learned later, this woman ceased her role as high priestess of the cult in Denver to go on stage. When at length, she tried once more to set up headquarters for the cult in Denver, she was murdered within a week. If such delusion can get a grip on people in these days of enlightenment, what will happen when the Antichrist is revealed with his supreme deceptions?"

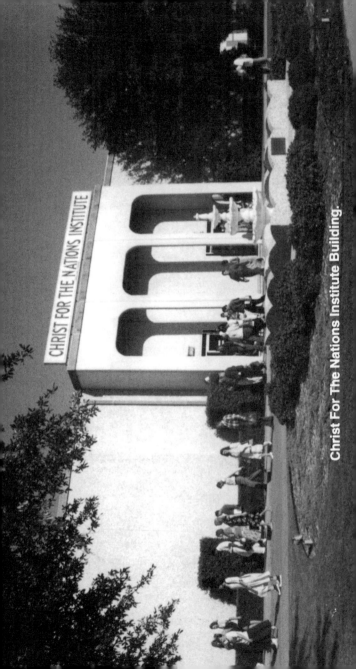

Christ For The Nations Institute Building.

Caribbean Christ For The Nations located in Montego Bay, Jamaica.

CFN's German Bible school — Glaubenszentrum — in one of Hitler's former facilities.

CFN has helped build over 10,000 Native Churches; the first one was completed in 1962.

Gordon Lindsay's books have been translated into 79 languages; over 50 million are in circulation.

Freda's parents, Gottfred and Kaity Schimpf, with her brother Fred and sisters Esther and Emma.

Freda at age 6 with her two younger sisters, Edith and Elma.

Freda at age 23 just prior to her marriage.

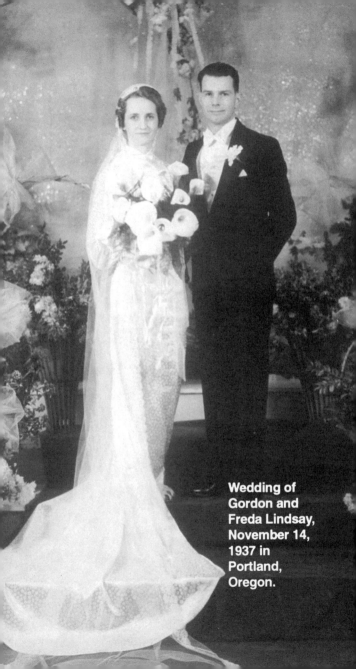

Wedding of Gordon and Freda Lindsay, November 14, 1937 in Portland, Oregon.

Gordon Lindsay, while pastoring the Ashland, Oregon church.

Gordon and Freda on one of their first evangelistic tours.

The Lindsay family of five while pastoring in Ashland, Oregon.

The Lindsay family of five now grown up — in Dallas, Texas, 1970.

The Lindsay Family (back row, left to right): Shira, Ari and Ayal Sorko-Ram; Dennis, Ginger, Missy, Freda, Julia, Shirley and Gilbert Lindsay

Gordon Lindsay Tower (formerly the Sheraton Hotel) now the CFNI men's dorm in Dallas.

Chapter Seven

After we left Los Angeles, both Gordon and I spent a number of days fasting and praying for God's perfect will for our lives. A few days later, Gordon felt we should go to Mexico to see for ourselves what the healing ministry could do in a foreign land.

We went unannounced to a church in Ciudad Victoria. When we told the pastor there that we would like to hold revival meetings, he was quite reluctant. He said the Americans who came there had had some real problems. The people had stoned his car and broken the windows.

To my surprise, Gordon, who had never in our ministry asked for a meeting, insisted. Gordon told him that many sick would be healed during the meeting. When he said this, the pastor's ears perked up, and he quickly agreed.

Before the first service started, our two little boys were in the car with me while Gordon and the pastor were inside the church. As I sat there with the windows rolled down because of the heat, a drunk man came over to the car and began to curse and swear at me. (I assumed this by the tone of his voice, and the pastor later verified it.) With eyes filled with hatred, he began to swing his arms as though he wanted to strike me. Immediately, I remembered what the pastor had said about these people not liking Americans.

I rolled up the windows and locked the car. As I sat there trembling, I called on the Name of the Lord. I didn't know if the man might break the windows. After what seemed like hours but were actually just minutes, the pastor and Gordon appeared around the side of the church — to my great relief.

As the pastor saw the man yelling loudly, he remonstrated with him in Spanish; and finally with the help of a couple of other men, got him away from the side of the car without his injuring anyone.

"Gloria a Dios"

At the first service, there was a medium-sized crowd in the quite large church, and the people seemed only mildly interested. But at the close of the service when Gordon began to pray for the sick and a deaf person was healed, the meeting suddenly came alive. People began to shout "Gloria a Dios!"

My diary records that next night: "Ours was the only car at the church; altar lined with sinners. Had to urge Christians not to come in order to make room for sinners. Lord healed many. Place packed."

The following day, my diary says: "About 50 for salvation. A deaf mute boy delivered." The next day: "About 100 for salvation." The day after that: "About 125 for salvation." The final day: "About 175 for salvation. Prayed for 200 for healing. Great miracles."

In the prayer line on the final night, I was overjoyed to see the man who on that first day had threatened me outside our car. I scarcely recognized him. This time he was not drunk and unkempt, but looked quite neat. When it came to his turn for prayer, his request through the interpreter was: "Pray that the profane devil in me will be cast out." Gordon did pray, and the profane devil left him. How do I know? Because he immediately raised his hands and began to cry and laugh for joy as Christ came into his heart.

From there, we went to Monterrey. My notes read: "About 50 at the altar for salvation. Miracles greater than those I saw in Branham's meetings on a first night." Again Gordon seemed to have outstanding miracles with regard to the deaf. My notes read: "A little boy, stone-deaf for two and a half years, instantly healed."

"The Baby Has Died!"

One incident I recorded concerns a baby who

was very sick. The parents had brought him to the service where he began to get progressively worse. Because of the crowd, the mother was afraid she couldn't get to the platform for prayer, so she decided to take the child home.

On the way to the house, suddenly the child died in her arms. Weeping, she hastened her pace to her home. Along the way, she met a friend who was going to our meeting. When the mother told her friend what had happened, the latter urged her to take the child back to the service to see what God would do. So together they came with the dead child.

By the time they had entered the service, Gordon was praying for the sick. It would have been almost impossible for her to make her way to the front. However, as she told the people that her child had died, they squeezed together to make room for her to push through. Finally, she reached the platform, and our interpreter talked to her. The mother told the interpreter that the baby had died.

In the midst of the shouts of praise for healings already taking place in the service, it was hard for Gordon and me to hear what the interpreter was saying. We thought she said, "The baby is dying," but she actually said, "The baby has died."

We did notice that the child lay perfectly still

and was pale. But he was so well wrapped that only a part of his little face showed; therefore we did not realize he was actually dead. Gordon laid hands upon the child and began to pray. In an instant, the child began to breathe and opened his eyes. When he did, pandemonium broke out in the church! It sounded as if the roof were coming off!

Gordon and I didn't fully realize why this tremendous outburst until the interpreter, seeing our restrained response, explained that this baby had been dead, and God had brought him back to life. It was only then that we understood why there was such jubilation, weeping and joy.

Months later, we received a letter from the parents stating again that the little child had been dead for a half hour or so when the mother brought him, but was very much alive now, and normal in every respect.

More Miracles in Mexico

Another healing that took place there which stands out vividly in my mind, is that of a man who was bent over, almost in half. He was brought by two young men and was bodily lifted to the platform since it would have been impossible for him to climb the stairs. In addition, he was shaking terribly with the palsy.

After prayer, the man sort of shuffled his feet

to the edge of the platform. Then he jerked loose from the hold that the two men had on him. I watched him carefully, and for a moment, I almost held my breath, thinking he might try to walk down the steps. But I needn't have worried. Swinging his arms backward, instead of walking down the steps, he made one flying leap off the side of the platform to the surprise and delight of everybody present.

Like a little boy, he ran up the steps, went to the edge of the platform, and leaped off again, as those seated on the floor beneath him scattered to give him room to land. This performance went on for several minutes, and a more excited, happy crowd I never saw in my life. A thousand persons were present to witness this healing. It was a scene I shall never forget.

My diary continues: "Man stone-deaf for 16 years instantly healed. Little girl blind received her sight. One hundred and fifty at altar for first time." (We had to ask those who had ever come to the front for salvation not to come this time, in order to make room for the new people.)

How quickly children adapt to new situations and environments. What wonderful missionaries they make. I recall one motel in Mexico in which we stayed. Gilbert, who was 4, was out playing, while Dennis, age 1, and I were taking a nap. Later when I went to find Gilbert, he had disappeared. Finally, I saw him with a group of men. I overheard him talking to one of the men in English. I asked him, "How did you know any of the men would speak English?"

"I just asked them if anybody knew about Humpty Dumpty, and one man answered me."

So children on the foreign field have a way of adjusting and of solving their own problems.

Upon the conclusion of these meetings we again returned to the United States, and both Gordon and I felt we were ready to go full time in overseas meetings. But after prayer, the Lord indicated to us that he had another ministry for us at that time.

Runaway Trailer

We hitched up our trailer and headed north from Shreveport, Louisiana, where we were printing *The Voice of Healing* magazine. We had scarcely left the city behind, when all of a sudden, we heard a loud "crunch!" Gordon and I looked back to see if the house trailer was intact. We saw nothing amiss.

Shortly thereafter, I looked out the right side window and to my horror, there was our trailer almost abreast of the car. I let out a cry: "The trailer!" Gordon hit the brakes, and then suddenly realized the trailer had broken loose and was going on its own momentum. There was nothing we could do but pray, and that we did *immediately*.

There had been deep trenches along the road to the right and left. But at that very spot where the trailer broke loose, the land was level. So going about 40 mph, the trailer moved right along. Occasionally, as it hit a rough spot, it jumped, and we would instinctively hold our breath, praying it would not turn over.

Finally, we came to a little incline alongside a railroad track, and when the trailer hit this spot, it came to a standstill. Gordon and I jumped out of the car, lifted our hands and praised the Lord, because all our earthly possessions were in that little trailer.

We were just about two blocks away from a garage that had a tow truck. A man towed the trailer in, fixed the broken hitch (while we witnessed to him of God's wonderful keeping power), charged us about $5, and we were on our way rejoicing in the Lord.

The Ministry of T.L. Osborn

It became clear that Gordon's ministry was to instruct younger preachers who were launching into the healing ministry. One of them was T.L. Osborn. He had gone as a missionary to India, but had lost his health and had come back from the field, broken in spirit and disillusioned.

It was during the Branham campaign in Portland, which Gordon was managing, when Mrs. Daisy Osborn attended. She went home and told her husband what she had seen and heard, and he came to see for himself. Then he started fasting and praying for a similar ministry. He realized that this was the kind of ministry it would take to reach the heathen. Shortly after this, God did begin to use him.

Osborn went to Chicago and rented a building, but he was having a difficult time getting a crowd and making ends meet. It was at this juncture that he invited Gordon to work with him, and Gordon accepted.

Our first joint meeting was in Reading, Pennsylvania, where we erected a secondhand tent. Gordon contacted the ministers in the area, and several of them decided to cooperate in the meeting, though their response was not altogether enthusiastic. In the opening service, only 300 people were present in that large tent.

Gordon noted that when T.L. spoke, he made some rather negative remarks about Full Gospel people. This, no doubt, he did partly because he felt he had been rejected by some of them when his ministry had failed the first time in India, and probably partly because he wanted everyone as a whole to feel welcome — not just Full Gospel people. However, Gordon pointed out to him that if he continued doing this, he would alienate the Full Gospel people. T.L. followed his suggestion and from then on was careful in his remarks.

When it came time to pray for the sick, those at the head of the line were usually the ones who had been prayed for in every campaign, over and over again, without appropriating God's promises for healing. When these failed to receive their healing, the effect was not good. So, because of unbelief not too much happened in the first services.

After seeking God, Gordon felt impressed to have a talk with T.L. and made the following recommendation: "Your wife seems to be an alert, observant, spiritually-sensitive woman. When the people come forward for prayer, why not have her mill through the crowd and talk a few moments individually to the ones to whom the Lord leads her? Then let her select those who she feels have the faith for their healing and put them at the head of the line."

T.L. acted on this suggestion and from then on, the results were electrifying. When the first got healed, it was like an atomic chain reaction: Scores were healed successively.

Our crowds began to increase, and two weeks later, my diary records: "Three thousand at service tonight." A week later: "Four thousand under the tent." The following day: "Two thousand

standing on outside of tent." And on the great
closing day: "Five thousand present."

Gordon taught as well as prayed for the sick
in the day sessions where the attendance would
reach 2,000. On the closing night, there were still
many people needing prayer. They were coming
from hundreds of miles away.

So it was that in that final service, nine prayer
lines were formed, and my notes read: "Blessed
beyond words to see the Lord heal so many
through the prayers of our fellow-ministers.
Amazing things took place in each line." What
we had done was ask each of the cooperating
pastors to take a line and pray for those in it. The
results were beyond anyone's expectations!
After that Reading campaign, a number of men
were moved of God to enter similar ministries.
Among these was a young Mennonite man,
Gerald Derstine, who found Christ as his Savior,
and has become an outstanding teacher and
evangelist.

Faith ran so high in that meeting that curious
things happened. For instance, one lady came to
me at the bookstand and pointed to a large goiter
in her throat. She had planned to go into the
healing line for prayer but was afraid. I asked her
if she believed she could be healed of that goiter.
With a surprised look, she said, "Certainly."

"Well," I questioned, "what's the problem?"

"Well you see, I have a heart condition. And when I am prayed for and that goiter disappears instantly, I'm afraid my heart won't take it!"

Smiling, I instructed her, "My dear lady, the same God Who will make your goiter disappear will also instantly take care of your heart."

"Both at the same time?" she asked.

"Both at the same time," I assured her.

She went rejoicing on her way and was not disappointed when the Lord took care of the conditions "both at the same time!"

A Gift for Carole

It was while we were at Reading that a lady came to the book table and handed me two books to read. I glanced at the covers and noticed they were about child preachers. I knew it would be a total impossibility for me to find time to read them during the 30-day meeting. I was just handing them back to her when all of a sudden, a still, small voice within me said, "Give them to Carole to read." So I did. She was 9 at the time, and she especially liked to read. She showed an immediate interest in them.

The next morning when Carole arose, she said to me, "I didn't sleep all night."

"What was the matter?" I asked. "Were you sick?"

"No," she answered, "I was praying all night.

God came to me, and told me He was giving me a gift."

My first response was a little incredulous, but I did not make any remark. The Lord must have wanted us to do twice as much listening as speaking because He gave us two ears and only one mouth.

A little later, I heard her go to the other end of the trailer and tell her father exactly what she had told me. Gordon asked her, "What gift did He give you?"

Her reply was, "He didn't tell me."

A few days later, Gordon and I were in the trailer bedroom with the door closed. We carried along a little spinet since Carole had been taking lessons and playing since she was barely 5. But on this particular day, we heard music coming from the piano that sounded like an adult playing. Gordon looked surprised and said, "Who is that playing?"

"I cannot imagine. Could it be Carole?"

"No," he answered. "It's an adult."

I opened the door just wide enough to look out, and behold, it was our 9-year-old Carole!

It seemed that overnight God had given her a gift, and from then on, she played the piano for song services, as well as accompanying me on my solos in some of the largest religious conventions and meetings going on in the nation at the time. A concert pianist who was her teacher, later tested her and told me that Carole had absolute pitch — she could identify any chord the teacher played, even though she was in another room.

Sometimes I have seen missionaries' and ministers' children making what some would call great sacrifices because of their parents' divine calling. But as I have observed these children through the years, God seems to make it up to them in other ways. Rarely have I ever seen one who came up shortchanged. For God is debtor to no man, and this includes the children. If anything, these children often have the advantages as their own adulthood will show.

Happy in the Work of the Lord

From Reading we went to Athens, Tennessee. The fact that Athens was a small town in no way hindered the meetings, for within a week my diary records: "Four thousand under the tent."

It was in that tent campaign that I began holding afternoon services for those who wanted to be filled with the Holy Spirit, and it seemed that many times everyone who came forward did receive.

Between meetings, Gordon would fly back and forth to Shreveport. I remember on one occasion, his plane touched down in Dallas just ahead of another one that had made an unsuccessful attempt to land, and 28 people were killed.

We had decided not to send our children to public school so they could be with us. Thus, it fell my lot to teach them. This I did besides attending two meetings a day, leading the singing, singing solos, plus helping Gordon prepare the magazine as we traveled, taking care of our laundry and cooking, and helping in the driving, pulling the house trailer from city to city. There was very little time for "extras," but we were extremely happy to be in the work of the Lord.

Chapter Eight

F or a while we worked with several other
evangelists, helping them in getting their
ministries established. It was at this juncture that
Gordon felt led to have a convention of what
were called healing-deliverance evangelists. The
first such convention took place in Dallas, Texas,
and on the final night, the Music Hall was packed
out. This was to become an annual event for the
next 12 years. We went from city to city filling
the largest auditoriums.

How well I remember those annual Voice of
Healing conventions. The message, though old,
was fresh and alive. The crowds were con-
tagiously enthusiastic and responsive. Tremendous miracles took place. Multitudes came to the
Lord, and there was a sincerity about them that
was unforgettable.

In those first few meetings, the 100 or more
evangelists would meet a few days early to fast
and pray and seek God for His anointing. But as
the years came and went, more and more, Gordon and I were dismayed by the change in some
evangelists whose meetings were carried in *The*

Voice of Healing magazine. The conventions, sad to say, were gradually deteriorating to the point that some used them merely as a vehicle in which to further their own careers, rather than as an opportunity to further the Kingdom of God.

At one particular meeting of the evangelists, on the night before the convention was to open, I remember hearing one of the most vociferous say, "Let's get this thing over with as I want to go up and watch the fight on TV." My heart cried out as in the past the nights preceding the conventions had always been unusual times of blessing as collectively we waited on the Lord. Now however, it seemed the thing some of the speakers were most interested in was how big a "cut" they were going to get out of the convention.

As Gordon and I reflected on the gradual change that became apparent, I recall his summing it up this way: "When ministers become successful and have large crowds, too often, they forget to wait on the Lord daily and study His Word. They depend on their reputation. And instead of being men of God, they become showmen."

For many years, Gordon was president of the association of evangelists, and he was respected by all of the men. One day, I heard one minister say about him to a group of preachers, "The Lord has really used Brother Lindsay." Another preacher spoke up and added, "And He is not the only one who has used him," implying that preachers had "used" him, too.

When problems arose among the evangelists, it was not Gordon's nature to want a confrontation. In fact, he shrank from such when perhaps had he taken a stronger stand, it would have helped. His nature was always loving, tenderhearted, forgiving. As I sometimes said about him, "If the devil had knocked on our door at midnight and said, 'I am in trouble,' I almost felt Gordon would have invited him in with the words, 'Let me see what I can do to help you.'"

So Gordon had a history of helping everybody and anybody. Then sometimes when a preacher had "used" him, as someone said, "he would give Gordon a swift kick and even forget to say, 'It was nice knowing you.'"

But no matter how many times Gordon was taken advantage of, he never became bitter. He would just pick up the pieces, which sometimes included huge indebtedness that had been incurred for radio time and campaigns. In spite of what happened, somehow he would always rise above it again.

I would remind myself that even Jesus had such problems during His earthly ministry. Out of the Twelve He had around Him, one — Judas Iscariot — was a thief and a robber, stealing

money from the treasury (Jn. 12:6). So I suppose
looking back over our ministry, our average was
not much different. Some of the evangelists we
worked with in those early days were sincere and
dedicated men, and have remained so to this day.
Through the years, Gordon and I have counted
them among our dearest friends.

The years have come and gone, but the results
of those conventions still live on. Every so often,
I meet people as I travel the world over who say
to me, "I was saved in such and such convention." "I was called into the ministry." "I was
healed." And I am certain that all of the lasting
results will never be known this side of heaven.
Those conventions served their purpose. They
had their day.

"A Great Big Jesus"

It was while working with T.L. Osborn in a
tent meeting in Corpus Christi, Texas, in October
1949, that Gordon received a call from William
Branham, asking him to go with him to Finland.
After prayer, Gordon decided it was the thing to
do, so he and his good friend, the late Jack Moore
from Shreveport, Louisiana, joined Branham.

In the meantime, I was back in Shreveport
living in the trailer and helping at the office with
the magazine. The subscriptions had grown considerably and mail was often heavy.

While I was in prayer on Easter Sunday afternoon, Dennis, my 4-year-old, was playing around me as I knelt beside the couch. I noticed the church bulletin with a picture of Jesus on the cover lying on the couch and handed it to him. He looked at it disdainfully and said, "Ah, that's a little Jesus. Last night, I saw a great big Jesus."

My first reaction was, "Oh no, you didn't," to which he replied, "I did, too."

So feeling I had said the wrong thing, I quickly added, "What did He look like?"

"Had eyes, had hands, had feet, had mouth," was his reply.

"Did He say anything to you?" I asked.

"Yes."

"What?"

"Coming back!" he said.

Our two older children were present when Dennis related his experience. One of them asked, "Mommy, do you think he means Jesus is coming back?"

"I'm sure He does," I answered them. Then I questioned Dennis, "What was He doing?" Dennis extended his little hands, palms downward in a blessing position. A tremendous heavenly atmosphere suddenly came into the little trailer, and I was certain this child of 4 had actually been visited by the Lord.

I wrote of it to Gordon in Finland, and shortly

thereafter, he printed the account in the magazine. Not long after, I received a beautiful letter in a halting, almost illegible handwriting from an old, old saint of God in the East, who said she asked the Lord not to take her until He had given her a sure sign that His coming was in this generation. "And as I read the account of the Lord's visiting your little son," she wrote, "I was confident this was the verification the Lord sent me."

Gordon remained with Brother Branham in Finland, and the largest auditoriums were continually filled. A boy was raised from the dead in Kuopio, fulfilling a prophecy that had been given some two years earlier when Gordon was with Brother Branham in Florida.

While Gordon was in Scandinavia, the Lord showed me a little token of His love when I received a telephone call informing me that a letter written by Carole (who was 10) titled "Why I Think My Mother is the Most Wonderful," won first place. (This was a Mother's Day letter-writing contest for children up to age 12.) So I was asked to sing on the radio on the Young Americans Club and was presented with my first orchid.

Branham Tent Meeting in Minneapolis

Upon Gordon's return home, Brother Branham asked him to set up a series of meetings. Our first one was to be held in Minneapolis, Minnesota, several months later.

Gordon had a new tent made in the South with funds that came to *The Voice of Healing,* and had it shipped to Minneapolis at considerable expense. He had benches made on location to seat 4,000 or more, and placed advertising in the daily paper as well as in *The Voice of Healing* magazine.

The night before the meeting was to start, Gordon became concerned when he was unable to get through to Branham by telephone. Near midnight, he sent a relative to Brother Branham's house and insisted that he answer his phone. Branham called him back and said that he just felt led not to come to Minneapolis. A little preacher friend of his not too far from where Branham lived wanted a "little meeting," so he just decided to go there and help this dear brother.

Gordon, of course, was rightfully distressed. He reminded Brother Branham that he had asked him to set up this meeting; that Gordon had spent thousands of dollars in having the tent made and in shipping it to Minneapolis, plus getting the seats, the advertising, renting the organ and piano, etc. In addition, Gordon told him that all future meetings would be canceled unless Brother Branham was a man of his word and kept his appointments.

Brother Branham's response was unbelievable — almost childish. He said very meekly, "Now Brother Gordon, if you really think I should come, I will get in the car and drive all night long to get there. I didn't really think it made all that much difference."

To make a long story short, he did drive all that night, and got in just in time to go to the platform to preach, without even having a chance to change his clothes.

Early in that tent meeting, an enormous storm struck with high winds. It looked as though the devil was trying his dead-level best to rip the tent apart and make it impossible for us to hold the meeting.

Leon Hall, his family and I were in the tent. When we saw the storm coming with its mighty, roaring force, we went to prayer. The noise of the wind was so loud that even though we prayed at the top of our voices, we could not hear one another.

The huge center poles seemed to literally jump up and down. Every stake on the outer edges of the mammoth tent was straining and groaning under the tremendous pressure. It seemed all hell had let loose. But when the fierce wind finally subsided, there stood our tent intact! We knew the hand of God had prevailed, and we were in for a great meeting.

And the meeting in Minneapolis was a tremendous success. Thousands poured into the tent and were delivered, either when Branham ministered or when others who were assisting in the meeting prayed.

I remember one woman who brought a small boy into the prayer line the afternoon Gordon was preaching and praying for the sick. (Brother Branham generally spoke only at the evening service.) The boy was clubfooted. Gordon turned to the lady and said, "Are you the mother of this boy?"

The woman answered, "No, I am the grandmother."

"Well, where is the mother?" he asked.

"She isn't here." When Gordon asked if she and her husband were believers, she answered, "No."

"Well, you tell the parents to bring the child back," Gordon said, "and we will pray for him."

At this, the grandmother began to weep as she implored, "Brother Lindsay, I have been fasting and praying for this child. Please pray for him. I believe God will heal him."

Gordon was moved with compassion, and picked the child up in his arms as we prayed for him. He then set him on his feet, and the child began to walk, apparently far, far better than he had been capable of doing before.

With the throngs attending, we did not see this child again until the last night of the meeting, when those who wanted to testify of their healings were asked to come forward. Here in the line stood the mother and family with the boy. He had been made perfectly whole! As he walked on the platform's narrow curtain railing before the eyes of the thousands present, a great round of applause and gratitude to God broke forth.

A man from the state of Washington came to that Minneapolis meeting. He was in the last stages of cancer that was eating out the top of his head. His head was wrapped in bandages, and the putrefying corruption was so intense, that it was continually oozing out through the wrappings.

The front section of the tent had been reserved for the sick. Because of the heat under the tent (the meeting was held in the summer), the odor from this man's cancer was so nauseating, the sick people asked to have him removed as they could not stand the smell. Thus, Leon Hall asked him to sit behind the platform in the makeshift prayer room, telling him that he would try to see that he was prayed for by Branham.

The last night there were so many people present that it was impossible for Brother Branham to pray for them all. So after praying for a number, Branham just told everybody else to look to the Lord, and he left the meeting.

The man with the cancer on his head then came to Leon and me and began to weep. He said, "I had an only cow which I sold so I could have money to come to this meeting in order to get healed. Now my money is gone, the meeting is over. I never did get to Brother Branham, and I am not healed." He sounded so pitiful that I felt like crying with him. But really sympathy was not what he needed.

Leon had a reputation for being brusque. He turned to the man and said, "Man, that kind of talk will put you right in the grave. You don't need to have Brother Branham pray for you. He is just like any other man. Why, I will pray for you, and God will heal you right now." And so with that he laid his hands upon him, and the man and I joined with him. After the prayer, the man disappeared through the crowd.

Some months later, Leon was in a convention on the West Coast. A man came up to him with a big smile on his face and asked, "Brother Hall, do you remember me?"

Leon looked at him intently and said, "I don't know that I do."

"Do you remember the Minneapolis meeting when a person came to you and had sold his cow to get to the Branham meeting and had cancer on his head?" he asked.

"I sure do," Leon replied.

"I am that man!"

Leon looked at him in amazement. There were no bandages. The man appeared to be in perfect health and even had a head of hair. How great is our God!

The Boy Who Sees Through a Glass Eye

One of the most amazing miracles I have ever seen was that of Ronnie Coyne. As a child, he lost the vision in one eye as a result of a playful accident, and so was fitted with a glass eye.

Several years later, he was in a healing meeting and went forward for prayer. When he stood before Osborn's sister, she asked him what his need was, and he said he was blind in one eye. Unaware that the boy actually had a glass eye, she prayed for his healing.

After prayer, she asked him which was the blind eye and he told her. So she held her hand over his good eye and asked him if he could see. "Yes," he answered. He went home and told his mother who was amazed. For the boy could see through the glass eye or through the empty hollow socket, when the glass eye was removed!

Both Gordon and I witnessed this miracle time and time again before thousands of people, as some of our ministers would completely tape his good eye until there was not the remotest possibility of his seeing from it. Then this young boy would read driver's licenses, social security cards, business cards, the Bible — whatever anyone handed him.

The remarkable thing about it was that in the presence of faith, the miracle would operate. But at times, when there was a defiant unbelief also prevalent, the miracle would cease. Then in a day or two, the miracle would be activated again. It was an amazing situation, but one which we could attest to in the highest courts of the land. Like the cruse of oil that never failed the widow in the Bible, so this miracle has continued through the years.

Woman Driver

When our sons, Gilbert and Dennis, were 14 and 11 respectively, we were holding tent meetings with an evangelist and were traveling in a trailer. Sometimes the boys liked to take their sleeping bags and sleep in the tent with the night watchman. In the morning, I would go to check on them and would find Dennis in his sleeping bag under the platform. When he came out, the watchman's little Chihuahua would usually come crawling out of the sleeping bag with him.

One of these meetings was held in a large park in Gary, Indiana, and the tent was pitched in a completely isolated spot. Our family trailer was

parked behind the tent in a wooded area. During
our two-week stay there, we had to go about two
blocks in the park to the public restrooms as at
that time trailers didn't have bathrooms.

One morning after Gordon had left to go back
to Dallas to work on the magazine, I was awakened by a loud knock. I looked out the little
window to see a man who appeared to be drunk,
pounding and wanting to get in. I was quite
troubled because I was there alone with the boys,
so I earnestly began to pray. After pounding for
what seemed a long time, the man finally went
away.

The tent was being taken down that day, and
the driver was leaving at sunset to drive most of
the night to the next destination in Northern
Michigan. Gordon had planned after he finished
the work on the magazine, to return for our next
meeting. But I was worried about staying in the
large park alone with the boys. After talking to
the tent man, I decided to follow him that night.
So the boys and I hooked up the trailer, and when
night came, we hit the road. One rode with me
and the other with the tent man.

I often did much of the cross-country driving
while Gordon was writing or reading in the car.
And I had driven for long stretches before while
pulling the trailer, but never had I attempted
driving such a distance myself, knowing I would

have to drive all night. However, after praying much of the way, we finally arrived at our destination at St. Louis, Michigan, in the early morning hours.

When I called Gordon and told him not to go back to Gary but to come directly to our next stop, he was surprised and a little relieved to know we were safe.

Shreveport, First Home of *"The Voice of Healing"*

During the first years that Gordon managed the evangelistic association, his home base was in Shreveport, Louisiana. His long-time friend, Jack Moore, a building contractor and part-time pastor, had supplied the first office for The Voice of Healing rent free. It was the upstairs of his garage. The sloping ceiling made it impossible to stand erect except in the center of the room. Nonetheless, it was adequate for the time. His lovely daughter Anna Jeanne, the first circulation editor, donated her services.

After the circulation of the magazine grew, Jack Moore provided other facilities, always at his own expense. I have often said, "Gordon never had closer and finer friends in the world than Jack Moore and his family." They have been true-blue for the many years we have known them.

Death on Our Doorstep

Gordon was on the go continually. Sometimes he would ride the bus all night to save money, other times he would take trains. Occasionally, he would fly to meet his schedule.

In 1951, while returning from a trip to Baltimore, he felt a severe swelling at the back of his head. He stopped in Memphis for a medical examination. The doctor informed him that he had a carbuncle at the base of his neck and wanted to hospitalize him immediately. But, Gordon said it was impossible for him to go to the hospital, as he needed to get home. The physician was reluctant to let him go, but Gordon insisted. Only after Gordon promised he would see a doctor the moment he arrived home would the doctor release him. Gordon assured him that he would get in touch with his "Family Doctor."

When he arrived in Shreveport, I somehow missed him at the airport, so he had taken a taxi home. When I walked into the room, he was lying on the davenport. His neck seemed quite swollen, and his face was drawn, as though he were in pain.

The next morning, he was much worse. Several days of continuous pain followed, and it seemed that in spite of much prayer on his behalf, his condition deteriorated.

After the first few days at home, he urged me

to bring a medical dictionary from the office so he could get the information concerning a carbuncle. The next day I read it at the office: "Carbuncle: a very painful and dangerous infection ... often in the nape of the neck ... causing great exhaustion from the poisoning. ... Death often follows." I decided Gordon did not need this kind of "encouragement," so each night, I neglected to bring the medical dictionary home.

Gordon's personal friend, Jack Moore, asked a Christian doctor to come to our apartment to check on him. The doctor was very concerned. He said that not only did Gordon have one carbuncle, but that there were "multiple carbuncles" on his neck. And being at the base of his brain, it could well develop into spinal meningitis. He urged immediate hospitalization, for by now, the neck was a threatening, foreboding deep, red color. But again, Gordon refused the advice, saying that he was trusting the Lord.

The doctor then returned to me and said, "It is up to you. Put hot packs on his neck continually, and see if we can get those carbuncles to burst, or else the poison will go through his entire system, and that will be it."

So having carried the load at the office while he had been in bed, I now became a round-the-clock nursemaid to my patient. After my watching over him, praying with him and encouraging him, finally the carbuncles, one by one, broke. A teacup full of corruption drained from them, and immediately he had relief.

But the devil was not yet finished. That night, he pulled a master stunt. For Gordon's elderly father, who was visiting us and who had been deeply concerned over his son's health, now began to have a blockage of the kidneys and was in excruciating pain. Gordon got out of bed and prayed for his father with all the intensity he could muster.

Returning to his bed, Gordon collapsed from overexertion and by morning, the carbuncles were completely stopped up again, and he seemed to be in a dying condition. His face was turned to the wall, and as visitors came and went, there was no response on his part. He no longer tried to talk with anyone.

I then made several phone calls and sent telegrams to friends of faith to stand with me in prayer in the face of what seemed certain death. Almost instantly, there was again a turn for the better. In several days, he was back in the church, back at work, delivered by the power of the Lord.

A Place to Call Our Own

After living in Shreveport a couple of years, we decided to build a little house. We finally located just the wooded lot we wanted, but when we went to inquire of the owner, we were told that there were four lots together. He said he would not sell one without the others. We knew we could not afford all four, so that lot seemed out of the question.

Yet I had my heart set on that particular lot, and was a little surprised when it was not available to us, since I had claimed the verse, "Ask, and ye shall receive, that your joy may be full" (Jn. 16:24 KJV). I wanted its lovely trees for the children to play under, and it was only a block or so from the office.

So a little disappointed, we looked again and found a less desirable lot a couple of blocks away, one without any trees and with a somewhat sloped bank. The houses on either side were not really all that nice either, but it was not too far from work. We signed the papers, paid the money, and began to make plans with Jack Moore to build a house.

No sooner did we decide on the house plans when a knock came on the door. There stood a building contractor. He said, "Mrs. Lindsay, did you just buy a lot over on such and such a street?" I replied that we had. He said, "You know, I have a contract to build a house for a veteran who is an amputee, and he had applied to the government for a loan on this particular lot. But it took months to get the loan approved, and now finally, here comes the approval in the mail. In order to get approval on any other lot, it would probably take another few months. Really, the man needs desperately to be in his home with his family. Would you possibly consider selling us that lot? Is there any other lot in the area you could select?"

I told him there was one that had been our first choice, but the owner would not sell it to us because he insisted on disposing all four lots at one time. The contractor said, "No problem. I will buy all four of those wooded lots, and you can take your choice. We'll just trade even then."

So that is exactly what we did, and I got the lot for which I originally asked! It made me realize that the Lord is interested in the most minute details of our lives, and how faithful He is.

Jack Moore had been a friend indeed. He built for us the first home we ever owned. It was a nice, small frame house and was far from being paid for, but we did have some equity in it. I was so proud of it. Finally, we had a place we could call our own.

But we had not lived in it one month (in fact, I hadn't even hung the pictures yet) when Gordon decided to move. My first response was, "Oh, you really can't be serious!" But after praying about it myself, I knew it was right, and the move was in the will of God.

Gordon wanted to be in a city that was centrally located where he could have the advantage of fellowship with religious leaders in their world travels. This would also make it easier for him to get back and forth to his office in his cross-country speaking engagements. He also saw the need for a larger labor market. After a considerable amount of time in waiting on the Lord, he felt that Dallas was the place. So on Memorial Day, May 30, 1952, we moved to Dallas.

On to Dallas!

When we moved to Dallas, we sold the home in Shreveport, and with the equity, purchased another house with even more beautiful trees on the lot than the one we had left behind. In fact, this property had close to 100 shade trees.

After living in this house two years, Gordon came to me one day with the news that he wanted to start a printing plant. To say I was shocked is putting it mildly. I asked him what he knew about printing? He replied, "Well, nothing. But we can learn."

Then it occurred to me that it might take some capital. I asked, "How much money do you have to get the place started?"

"Nothing," he replied, "but we could sell our home and use the equity in it."

"And move where?" I asked.

"The basement of our office building" (some two blocks away), was his answer.

I remonstrated by reminding him that the children were small and would be all over the place. All he said was, "Just pray about it." (In any move we made, I never had the feeling I was being pushed into it. Gordon always gave me plenty of time to pray about it.)

When I did begin to pray about it, I assured the Lord that that could not possibly be in His divine plan for our lives. This I did for several days. One morning instead of doing all the talking in my devotions, I became quiet before the Lord and listened. To my surprise, I felt that God did want us to sell our home, did want us to start the print shop, and did want us to move into the basement.

So I placed an ad in the daily paper and sold the house on the first ad. (Not long after, while the new owners were away one evening and we were in church, that house was vandalized and set fire to in several areas with heavy damage resulting.) We moved into the basement apartment, and the next morning, I woke up with joy in my heart, knowing I had been obedient to His voice.

Mumps! Keep Out!

Scarcely a week had gone by when Gilbert, our oldest boy, came in saying he believed he was coming down with the mumps. I asked him if he had been exposed. He replied, "Yes, I have been playing with Butch, and he has the mumps."

So here I could fancy myself living in the basement of *The Voice of Healing* with a quarantine sign above the door saying, "Mumps! Keep Out!" Also, Gordon was away in meetings and could not be there to join his strong faith with me in prayer.

All night long, I battled for dominion in Christ over the situation. By the next morning, the swelling in Gilbert's face had decreased, and he in fact was up, well and playing.

But the devil was now licking his wounds and decided to make a counterattack. Would you believe it, after a few days, I found swelling in my neck? The devil immediately said, "Mumps!" But by now my faith was stronger, and I knew if God had given the victory once, He could do it again. Throwing myself upon the mercy of God, I called upon His Name. Again He brought complete deliverance. The next morning, the swelling was gone, and I was able to go about my work.

God Provides a New Home

With the equity from our home, we built a small printing plant, bought a carload of paper and purchased our first press. By printing our own monthly magazine, we were able to realize considerable savings each month. In addition, Gordon had by now increased his writing output, and it proved to be a substantial blessing to be able to print his books. We opened the print shop on June 12, 1954.

We had lived in the basement about one year when one Saturday morning, a lady who attended the same church we did, knocked on our door. I knew her husband to be an unsaved man, rarely if ever darkening the door of the church. Her words surprised me: "My husband (who was a contractor) was awakened two times last night by an inner voice saying, 'Build a house for the preacher who is living in the basement.'" We were happy to accept this offer.

He went to each of his subcontractors with, "Look, you are not going to make any money on this house. You can do it on future houses. We are building this one for a preacher and his kids. And I want a rock-bottom price from every one of you."

And that is what happened. He built us the most beautiful home we ever lived in for a sub-stantially lower-than-market price. God had compensated for any inconveniences we had experienced that year.

An amusing incident happened on moving day. Always I had tried to a be a helpmeet to Gordon so he could save his energies for the great weight of the work for the Lord that he carried. Rarely did I ask him to give me any assistance with regard to our home or business matters which I could possibly take care of myself. So the day that we were to move, I let him sleep as long as he could. The movers had already loaded the truck with the furniture from all of the rooms except our bedroom. Always being a sound sleeper, he never heard anything (for probably by this time, he was acclimated to the noise from the folding and addressing machines in the office directly over our heads).

Nonetheless, when every room was empty, I ran in, woke him up, and told him to jump out of bed, as the movers were waiting for our bedroom furniture. He did, heading for the shower, and the crew concluded packing all but one nice floor lamp that the office had given us for a Christmas gift.

I was reluctant to let the commercial movers take it, as one of them seemed to have tipped the bottle a little too heavily before breakfast, and I didn't want to trust him with it. So when Gordon finished his shower, I asked him to do me one favor: Carry the beautiful floor lamp across the street to our new home. He readily agreed, and I headed for the new house to instruct the movers where to place the furniture.

Having completely forgotten about the lamp,

I was surprised to look out of the window several hours later, and lo and behold, there it was setting on the street curb! I later learned that just as Gordon was carrying the lamp across the street, some ministers appeared at the office. He began talking to them, set the lamp down, and forgot all about it. I rescued it and took it into the house.

When he came in that evening I asked him where he had placed the lamp. He had at first a rather blank, then guilty look when finally he remembered he left it standing on the sidewalk.

The children used to call him the absent-minded professor. His thoughts seemed always to be on the more important things of eternity instead of on earthly trivialities.

The move was nonetheless consummated, and in my diary at the close of that day I wrote: "How we praise God for our lovely new home."

Chapter Nine

For about a dozen years, Gordon continued his position of leadership in the loosely-knit association of 100 or so evangelists. During that time, he was busy speaking at conventions and often traveling over much of the world. There was a constant stream of ministers to his office, most of whom were looking for some kind of help or favors.

As the years came and went, some of the deliverance evangelists took pastorates, others went into less strenuous types of work, and still others fell by the wayside. When a fellow minister failed, Gordon was always completely broken up about it as if it were his own son, brother or father. He felt it very keenly, and it would cause him to pray all the more and seek God more earnestly.

Finally, a series of circumstances developed that caused Gordon to seriously consider his future. Every time an evangelist associated with The Voice of Healing ended up badly, we would bear the brunt of it. Every time an evangelist failed to pay his bills in whatever city he ministered, we generally got the flack. In fact, at times the creditors would try to collect from Gordon. By now, a number of evangelists had gotten a foothold and had developed their own ministries, often at least partially, the result of the publicity they received in *The Voice of Healing* magazine, which made them nationally or internationally known. Thus, several had gone their own way, and I remember a visit to our home by three of the more prominent of these.

One of these men was very vocal. He told Gordon that he really didn't have a ministry anyway; that he had always just hung on the coattails of other preachers; that, in short, he was just a leech. He concluded that *The Voice of Healing* had served its purpose and that the magazine would be discontinued; that Gordon should go on his way and get himself some little meetings, or take a little pastorate, and maybe publish some sort of little newsletter once a month.

I sat there and listened to the whole thing. Gordon never opened his mouth. I wanted desperately to jump up and show this evangelist the door. Gordon looked very grave. Solemnly, he shook hands with the men and said, "God bless you," and the men went out into the night.

I turned to Gordon and asked, "What are you going to do about it?"

His answer was very, very soft as he said, "Just keep on serving the Lord as I always have."

A Supernatural Visitation

It was about this time that God began to deal with Gordon about not building on another man's foundation (Rom. 15:20). And a very unique thing happened in our lives that again changed the course of our ministry.

We were holding a Voice of Healing convention in Dallas. I recall at times there was confusion as some of the brethren tried to deal with problems that had arisen in the lives of some of the ministers, most of whom were lone mavericks. At times there was also a jockeying for position and leadership.

Several times during that large convention, I had to go to the platform and start the service, as the men would still be tied up in business meetings. I would begin the services by leading the singing, and as the ministers later arrived and preached God's Word, it always brought forth the promised results (Isa. 55:11).

It became very apparent to Gordon that God had something different in store for us. On November 12, 1955, we had come home from the convention exceedingly tired from the weight that was upon us. It was a late hour when we retired. Early in the morning while it was still

dark, I heard the telephone ringing. That is, I
thought it was the telephone, and it sounded like
an overseas ring. (In those days, long-distance
calls had a certain ring.) I started to reach for the
phone. However, when I became wide enough
awake, I realized it was not the telephone by my
bed, but something ringing within my throat. I
could not understand what it was, and as I was
reflecting on it, I thought, "Could this be the
death rattle? Have I overexerted myself, and am
I dying?" I carefully examined my life, in case I
were suddenly to be brought into the presence of
Almighty God.

I lay still and every few minutes, the "phone"
would ring in my throat. Then it shifted from my
throat to my ears. It was as if a phone had been
placed inside my ears. I noticed that Gordon was
aware of it; every time it would ring, he would
pull the covers further over his head. I started to
wake him, but concluded that he was so
exhausted and would have such a full day when
he arose, that I must spare him.

Just then the ringing swiftly shifted to the top
of my head. This went on for some 15 or 20
minutes. I was completely puzzled and had no
explanation for it. Abruptly, the ringing ceased,
and I decided that the first thing in the morning,
I would ask Gordon and see what explanation he
could offer. While I was contemplating these

things, realizing it was not the death rattle and that I had not died, I then fell into a sound sleep.

Shortly thereafter, the alarm clock rang. I jumped up, turned it off, and asked myself, "Now, what was I going to tell Gordon?" But like Nebuchadnezzar's dream, the thing had entirely escaped me. Try as I would, nothing came to my mind. So we went on to the convention, and I thought nothing more of it.

The following day when the convention was over, Anna Schrader, an elderly woman who had a gift of prophecy, was in our home. She had been staying with us for several days. The three of us were in the living room praying and waiting on the Lord.

While we were sharing, suddenly Mrs. Schrader said that one time God had spoken to her through a sort of ringing. As soon as she said the word "ringing," the whole experience of the morning before flashed back into my mind. I began to tell what had occurred, and as I looked over at Gordon, I saw a strange, quizzical look upon his face. He said, "I heard ringing myself. I kept wondering why you did not answer the phone. But I was too exhausted to wake myself sufficiently to ask you."

Then the spirit of prophecy came upon Mrs. Schrader. She said that our ministry was going to be greatly enlarged; the call was a supernatural one. Because it sounded like a long-distance call, God was showing us that our ministry would reach to the nations of the world. Through the ringing in my throat, ears and the top of my head, God was saying that He would speak forth the Word through our voices; many would hear the Gospel through their ears. It would affect their thinking, their minds, and a supernatural experience would result in their lives.

Then she went on to prophesy that the Lord was calling us to build shelters, for these people who were going to be reached with the Gospel would need centers or churches in which to worship. These centers would be built in foreign lands, and God was holding us accountable.

Both Gordon and I were awed by this prophecy; for at the time, we had no immediate plans to go abroad, nor did we have money to build even one church — let alone many churches. However, both of us had felt that God would eventually use us in a worldwide ministry.

The Greenwich Conference

In 1956, Gordon received a telephone call from David du Plessis saying he and Gordon had been invited to Greenwich, Connecticut, to meet with religious leaders. Gordon accepted the invitation, and the two spent all day with these men who were heads of various American denominational churches. It was an unusual opportunity to answer their questions regarding the baptism in the Holy Spirit and divine healing.

At the close of the meeting, some of these men went on record as saying they would not remove from their denominations those who had received the baptism in the Holy Spirit, but would let them remain as members and ministers. And to this day, that commitment has been for the most part carried out.

Tornado!

We were coming from a convention in Greenville, South Carolina, several months later and were on the outskirts of Dallas, when suddenly, I saw a man in the car beside us attempting to tell us something. I said, "Gordon, what is he trying to say?" Gordon looked at him, but couldn't figure out what he meant.

We drove on and came to a stop sign. This man then rolled down his window and said, "I just heard on the radio that there is a tornado over Dallas." We thanked him, and drove on a few blocks to an overpass where we stopped. From this vantage point, we could see a huge tornado traveling northeast over the city. We were still too far away to tell where it was hitting, but we immediately began to earnestly pray. Our three children were at home with their grandmother.

We drove a short distance farther and stopped again, where we could observe the tornado clearly. It was moving with a tremendous force. Black, billowing clouds were churning everything they found in their way. It was horrifying, to say the least.

But as we sat there watching, two more tornados dropped out of the clouds, and I yelled to Gordon, "Look there are two more coming!" We continued praying. Suddenly, the smaller ones that were dropping to Earth went back into the clouds and disappeared. But the big one kept right on coming. We had the radio on and were listening intently.

We heard that the tornado was even then passing through the southernmost part of Oak Cliff, the section of Dallas in which we lived. Oak Cliff was perhaps a world center for Full Gospel churches in those days. Once news of the tornado's touching ground was given, Christians of Oak Cliff began en masse to call on the Name of the Lord for protection.

Later the newspapers and magazines carried this amazing story: This particular tornado, instead of moving north and east as tornados do in that part of the country, moved north and *west;* thus avoiding the Pentecostal belt! The paper said that during the 20 minutes, it was death and terror for some: Ten died, many were injured, and there was $4 million property damage as the funnel passed through 21 miles of the city. But as far as we knew, no Full Gospel person was injured or suffered property loss, which was indeed a miracle!

The Birth of the Native Church Crusade

After giving ourselves to prayer, Gordon and I, along with David du Plessis, Leon Hall and Clair Hutchins, made a missionary trip throughout Central and South America where we saw firsthand the need for native churches.

About that time, we had an unexpected visit from my niece and her husband, Rev. and Mrs. Herman Engelgau, who had served as Assemblies of God missionaries in Upper Volta for many years. Herman said, "You know, Gordon, there are so many towns and villages that need churches. If we had just $250 to help us in these communities, we could build a church."

Instantly Gordon said, "That's the plan!"

So in *The Voice of Healing* (November 1961) magazine, he announced the Native Church program, telling the missionaries that we would give them $250 to assist in building a church. (With inflation, that figure has sometimes doubled, tripled and quadrupled.) We would not pay for the land — the people must purchase it themselves. And we would not pay for the labor —

the people in the church could supply that. The money was to pay for materials only.

Thus, as a result of the announcement that first month, about 30 applications came in from missionaries asking for church assistance. And at the same time, the Lord provided about that number of sponsors. To date, Christ For The Nations (as Voice of Healing was called after a decision by the board of directors in May 1967) has helped build over 10,200 churches in 100 nations of the world. Each year, we build several hundred additional churches, and the work continues to grow. (In August 1997, we completed helping build our 10,000th Native Church. Today, we're well over that number. To God be the glory!)

Chapter Ten

During these years of tremendous opportunity in helping mold the lives of many ministers into sound men of God, our immediate family had its problems. Both Gordon and I saw the need to discipline our children. Living in homes of pastors while we were on the evangelistic field, we had seen much. We knew that if we failed to discipline our children, *we* would be the only ones who could love them.

As Gordon was away much of the time, this burden fell on my shoulders. When he was home, he was snowed under with working on the magazine, meeting people who were coming from everywhere, writing a book each month, and speaking. His own children were constantly neglected.

We would try to conceal from our three children the news of some fellow minister's falling into disrepute. But often our children were close enough to the situation that they learned of these tragedies anyway. That scars were left on their lives cannot be denied. In spite of the fact that Gordon and I would encourage them to keep their eyes on the Lord and not on man, as young as they were, they would sometimes become disillusioned.

I recall when Carole began drifting away from the Lord in her high school years, and when she chose a liberal, secular college of which neither her father nor I approved. She borrowed money on her own and attended. There she had a roommate who was the daughter of one of the wealthiest men in the south — a cattle and oil man. Carole would fly here and there with this family as their guest and would hobnob with the elite of the land, including many political figures.

My heart was broken, and I recall one Christmas when she failed to come home, I was sick in my soul. The devil would harass me by telling me that since our daughter was not serving the Lord, the people would assume Gordon and I were hypocrites. How could we be spiritual leaders when our daughter was behaving as she did? Refusing to come to church, refusing to read the Bible, wanting no part of anything spiritual, and wanting no part of her family.

In addition, the devil called attention to the fact that since Carole was the oldest, she would set the tone for the rest of the family — that her example would cause her two brothers to follow in her footsteps, and that none of our children would serve the Lord. He painted an extremely dark picture.

I recall one Saturday night in particular when I walked the floor all night long praying, not knowing where Carole had gone. I couldn't even think of sleeping. But the next morning, I dried my tears and went to Sunday school where I taught the college class, directing their lives to the Lord. No one in the class knew I had spent a sleepless night, unless my tear-stained eyes betrayed me.

Then Gordon decided to set aside a time of fasting and prayer for Carole. The days stretched into weeks, and finally I became greatly concerned about him — so much so, that I was afraid he would lose his health. When I said to him that I felt he might die from too much fasting, his answer was, "Either Carole will have to die or I will. If she continues in life as she is, she will kill herself and my ministry. So I really don't have a choice."

One day as I had joined him in fasting, I was in my room weeping when Gordon walked in. He said, "What's the matter?"

"Carole," I answered.

"What about her?" he queried.

"Well, every report is that she is getting further from the Lord."

He stood there a moment and finally looked me right in the eyes and said as he raised up my

Bible, "Either this Bible is true or it isn't. If it isn't, let's throw the whole thing out. If it is, let's begin to act like it is. Let's begin to say what the Word says about Carole. Let's refuse to listen to anybody's reports as to what she is doing. Let's just repeat Acts 16:31, 'Believe on the Lord Jesus Christ, and thou shalt be saved, and thy house' (KJV). Let's say it out loud every day — loud enough for the devil to hear — and just see what God will do." Then he went back to his office and left me to myself.

After 30 days of fasting, Gordon felt that God had answered prayer, and that Carole would come back to the Lord, though we did not see any immediate change.

But each day after that, I began to claim what God's Word said about Carole's soul being saved. I did not realize that one day God would keep His Word and do exceedingly, abundantly above what I could think or hope for in her life, though I could and did believe God for her salvation. Nonetheless, I have always felt that Gordon's prolonged fasting projected Carole into the ministry which the Lord finally gave her.

We did not know what method the Lord would use to bring Carole to Himself, but Gordon and I had committed her to the Lord. In the meantime, while Carole was in her senior year in college, she found herself working for a

64-year-old man whose wife was in an asylum. She had noticed on several occasions, he had parked outside her dormitory and would be watching as she came and went to her room.

He seemed to show Carole a lot of favors but her dad reminded her that those favors, she would find before it was over, would have expensive price tags on them. She thought her dad was perhaps a little naive. But one night in the wee, small hours, we received a distress call from her. She had been working late for this man, helping him inventory some clothing in a bankrupt store he had purchased. In the course of his conversation with her, he told her that if she did not break off keeping company with the young man she was dating at the time, he would kill her. She said that by the look in his eyes, she knew he meant it.

She was taken aback by his advances and told him that he was old enough to be her grandfather, and she wanted no part of him. She fled for her life, and as soon as she was able to get back to her room, she called us. She said she was shaking so badly she could hardly hold the phone, because she believed he really meant what he said.

With her dad on one end of the line and myself on an extension, we talked for a while. Then I heard her dad saying to her, "Carole, you have

been running from God long enough. When are
you going to come to your senses? If you are
willing to kneel down by the side of your bed
when I finish praying this prayer, asking God to
spare your life, I will pray for you on the phone,
and God will intervene. Then this man will not
touch you. But if you refuse to make this consecration, then I cannot guarantee you a thing." She
promised she would make the dedication, and as
her dad started praying, she began to weep.

Her dad then told her that when this man with
an evil intent called again, to tell him she had
made a dedication to God, and that she would no
longer work for him. We told her we loved her
and hung up the phone. The man did make an
attempt to see her, but she informed him of her
decision, and he ceased all harassment.

Carole in Spain

After Carole completed college, graduating
with honors, she decided to go to Spain. On the
flight to Barcelona, she was seated beside the
wife of the editor of the largest daily paper in that
city. After Carole arrived in Spain and before the
week was out, that large newspaper carried a
two-column article about her activities for the
Lord, along with several photographs.

This was in 1965 when there was very little
religious liberty in Spain, and some who had

been missionaries in the country for many years had not so much as gotten a line of honorable mention in the paper. Nonetheless, Carole was being pulled apart by two forces. She began modeling for TV commercials, billboards and a line of women's clothes in the largest cities of Spain.

That same year, Gordon and I flew to Belfast, Ireland, for our first meeting there, which was held in the church pastored by Leslie Hale. And though the outpouring of the Spirit was virtually unknown in that country, 10 people received the baptism in the Holy Spirit the very first night. One of these was the pastor's sister.

One night as I finished speaking, a tall, handsome, young man entered the auditorium. His face radiated with expectancy, and he seemed to enter into the spirit of the service in those last few minutes. When I gave the invitation for those who wanted to be filled with the Holy Spirit, this young man was the first at the altar. After a few simple instructions, he received without any difficulty whatsoever along with a number of others.

Later that evening when I talked with him and asked him who he was, he informed me he lived in South Ireland in what is known as Catholic country (about 95 percent Catholic). He said he heard people were being filled with the Spirit in Belfast, and he knew if he could make it to the service, the Lord would fill him. Beaming from ear to ear, he added in his Irish brogue, "And He did! Praise the Lord!"

Some 33 were filled with the Spirit that week, which by American standards was not a great number, but for Belfast it was astonishing!

From there we went to Barcelona, Spain, hoping to see Carole. But because she moved about from city to city, we were unable to locate her. My diary says three days later: "After fervent prayer, we were able to get a call through to Carole and met her in San Sebastian."

After talking to her, both Gordon and I were deeply grieved in spirit, realizing that the life she was living as a model was not conducive to spiritual growth. We prayed earnestly and talked to her about keeping company with a worldly, young, wealthy manufacturer who seemed to be omnipresent. We told her that she was of age and could do as she pleased, but if she married this ungodly young man, she would be unhappy the longest day she lived. We also told her she knew it was contrary to the Scriptures, and it would be the quickest way the devil could concoct to destroy her life and usefulness in the Kingdom of God.

With heavy hearts we left her, viewing the situation from the natural. But, as we turned our faith to the promise of salvation for our household in Acts 16:31, we encouraged ourselves in the Lord.

After we returned from Spain, the Lord gave me assurance that Carole would come to her senses, and would heed the call of the Lord upon her life that she had had since childhood. The Lord spoke to me through Isaiah 43:5-7: "Fear not; for I *am* with you; I will bring your descendants from the east ... and My daughters from the ends of the earth ... whom I have created for My glory."

About a month later, we received a letter from her, saying she felt she was wasting her time in Spain, and was "ready to go to work for God and for daddy." She returned to Dallas and became deeply involved in the work of Christ For The Nations. The Lord finally called her to Israel where she has been laboring for the Lord since 1967, as well as making Bible films.

God at Work in Dennis' Life

Later our youngest son, Dennis, began having problems as a result of selecting companions at school whose lives were anything but exemplary. Gordon counseled with him, and when that didn't work, he would use his belt. But finally the day came when he said to me, "I have whipped him for the last time. We will have to choose another method." We gave ourselves to more fervent prayer.

Dennis later enrolled in a secular college. He had no respect for some of his teachers, saying that one was an alcoholic, and another would remark, "I can't teach you anything before I light up," as she lit her cigarette before beginning the class.

While Gordon was away, I could not get Dennis to go to school. He would stay out late at night and would want to sleep all day. When his father returned home, there was a real confrontation. Dennis ran from his own bedroom into ours and locked the door. When he didn't open to his father, his dad knelt in front of the locked door and prayed for almost an hour, calling on God to stop him in his tracks at any cost; to save his soul; to rain judgment upon him, if necessary, but to use love, if possible.

Dennis did not have even a radio in the room, so there was no way of escaping hearing his father praying. I am sure that prayer made a lasting impression upon his life, for shortly after this, Dennis decided to go to a Christian college where he found God's purpose for his life and also met his future wife.

A week or so after enrolling in Southern California College, Dennis phoned to tell me excitedly, "Guess what? The coach took me out to a steak dinner!" He had found a friend who would

have a tremendous effect on his life in the days
to come. Several years later in one of the school
publications, it stated, "Dennis is one of the best
all-around athletes in the school."

Dennis arrived home from college in the summer of 1967. He was debating whether or not to
go with his coach and the Youth With A Mission
group to Jamaica and the West Indies. However,
not having a passport it seemed impossible
unless by a miracle, the process of securing one
could be shortened.

By now, our house was teeming with young
people who were congregating there from various parts of the nation, using it as a launching
pad for this particular trip. The day before they
were to leave, Dennis' passport arrived.

He spent the summer going from village to
village in the West Indies, during which time we
had very little correspondence from him. One
day late in the summer, I received a collect call
from him. His plane had landed in New Orleans.
He was just getting ready to leave for Dallas and
needed someone to pick him up. He had borrowed a dime from a stranger to make the collect
call, as he was completely broke.

When he arrived home, he looked like a starv-
ing war refugee. He was absolutely skin and
bones. I could not believe what I was seeing, and
I wondered what was the reason for his

emaciated appearance.

Then he told his father and me the story of how he had drunk some contaminated water and had become desperately ill — so sick that he thought he was going to die. The group leader took him to the doctor who said that he had typhoid fever.

Back he went to the place where they were staying and to his sleeping bag. There he realized that unless he got ahold of God, he would be left behind as the party moved on from village to village, and worse yet, he could die. So the pages of his diary (which he later gave me) show that he grappled for several days with the devil and this dreaded disease.

Pulling himself from his sleeping bag, he continued on with the young people. He claimed the strength of the Lord every step of the way and was able to keep up with the party the rest of the summer — though I must admit, he looked the worse for the wear. Nonetheless, it was his first big test, and by faith, he had conquered! He came back a changed young man.

After Dennis had finished sharing with us, his father reminded him of the time the devil had tried to kill him, too, with ptomaine poisoning when he first started out in the ministry at the age of 19. And had he not gotten the victory then, he would well have been in his grave these many years.

Dennis later worked with Youth With A Mission for four years in Europe, Israel and the communist countries. He is now Chairman of the Board, President and CEO of Christ For The Nations where he has been teaching since the passing of his father in the spring of 1973. And his lovely wife, Ginger, ministers with him as they counsel and pray with young people. Ginger coordinates and hosts CFN's Annual International Women's Conference. Her dedicated parents, Clark and Mildred Krickbaum, are now a part of the ministry here at CFN, helping in vital areas.

It Pays to Pray

Our second son, Gilbert, always seemed to have his feet on solid ground as far as his personal relationship with the Lord was concerned. Only when he began dating while in college, did the devil calculate to destroy him, when he became enamored with a worldly girl.

After much praying and fasting, God broke up the mismatched courtship. And Gilbert some years later on May 28, 1971, married Shirley, the daughter of a local pastor and his wife, Rev. and Mrs. H. S. Cowart. On January 10, 1973, they presented us with our first grandchild, Michael Jason. Shortly thereafter, Gordon and I had the privilege of helping dedicate him to the Lord, along with his maternal grandfather. I told Gilbert, "If you had gone the world over, you couldn't have found a more beautiful, dedicated Christian girl than Shirley — nor a finer set of in-laws." Proof again that it pays to pray!

Sometimes in later years, folk would come to me and say, "Isn't it wonderful how all of your three children *happen* to be Christians?"

I would feel like saying (and sometimes did), "Happen? Absolutely not! It took years of fasting, praying, guiding, teaching and sometimes depriving ourselves, in order to give them exposure to the right companions, speakers, teachers, conventions, music and entertainment to influence their lives for God and eternity." But it was worth it all!

Chapter Eleven

It has been said that the life of a writer must of necessity, be a lonely one, because he must isolate himself in order to be able to formulate his thoughts. He must likewise be extremely disciplined. Otherwise, a thousand demands upon his time would rob him of his purpose. The world is full of hundreds of thousands of would-be-writers — men or women who are forever talking about what they are going to produce but never do. Why? Because there is never enough time.

These qualities of self-discipline and a willingness to be alone were two of Gordon's characteristics. (Carole later in life would sometimes chide her father saying, "Daddy, you'd have made a perfect hermit. All you'd need is a cave with a candle so you could read and write.")

Gordon's father was a school teacher, and in later years, a high school principal. He was well read, and perhaps it was from him that his son developed a love for reading. Gordon was himself an avid reader, and personally collected a vast library from secondhand bookstores all over the world. (I always knew in what cities he had stopped, for from there would usually come the most interesting boxes of old or occasionally new books.) Sometimes in preparation for writing on a given subject, he would read hundreds of titles.

When Gordon was a young man of 19 preparing to go into the ministry, Dr. John G. Lake, in whose church Gordon found Christ, spoke prophetically. He said Gordon would one day write books that would be used as textbooks the world over. Some Christians, if after receiving a word from the Lord and it does not come to pass immediately, utterly reject it. However, Gordon didn't write his first book — *The Wonders of Bible Chronology* — until 1940, which was 15 years after the prophecy was given.

How well I recall that first book which he tediously wrote and rewrote in longhand, and which I typed and retyped, page after page, until it was finally ready for the printer. How excited we were when at last we leafed through the first printed copy! How thrilling to be an author! But little did we realize then that in the next 33 years, Gordon would write some 250 books which would be translated into 76 languages, with some 50 million copies presently in print. Yes, textbooks that would be used the world over as the prophecy said!

Gordon's second book, *Bible Days Are Here Again*, appeared one year after the first. After that, it seemed something within Gordon's soul had been born, and life began to stir in earnest. Soon he was turning out books at a rate of one a month which he came to call the book-of-the-month.

During the last three years of his life, he wrote incessantly. On every plane trip, in every airport, in every hotel lobby — in fact, whenever he had a few minutes interval, whether it was between appointments or when someone was running late for an appointment, his pen never took a rest. Thanksgiving, Christmas, New Year's, all were the same to him — another day in which to put on paper the message that burned in his heart.

I recall in particular one Christmas when our family had gathered together. It had been our custom since our wedding to read the story of the birth of Jesus on Christmas Eve. After that, each member of the family would take a turn thanking God for His supreme gift, and then we would exchange gifts. During that time of prayer, something had been mentioned that prompted some comments and discussion afterward.

Before we knew it, Gordon had left us, gone to our room, and the next we saw of him, he was carrying his briefcase with his hand on the door-knob ready to depart. When I asked where he was going, he had a perplexed look on his face and replied, "Why, to work, of course." (It had usually been his custom to write until midnight at the office.) When I reminded him that it was Christmas Eve, and we had just finished praying and were getting ready to open the gifts, he had the most surprised look on his face as if he had already forgotten what the occasion was!

Gordon was always one to encourage others. I recall my first magazine report assignment. We were just returning from a very successful Voice of Healing convention in the East. I would generally scribble down notes of what impressed me, along with the pertinent excerpts from the various speaker's sermons. Then Gordon would write up the report.

Riding along in the back seat of the car, I was reading these notes out loud to Gordon. Suddenly, he said, "This time, you write the report." I objected, but he overruled my objection. After that, I had a "steady job" of reporting the conventions. Later, I wrote a number of articles used in several magazines, as well as contributing certain chapters in some of Gordon's books.

For years, Gordon carried his ever-present portable typewriter with him everywhere he went. But toward the end, he wrote everything in longhand. Only rarely did he use a recorder, and that was when he was on foreign trips.

The last three years of his life were his most
disciplined and intensive. By then Gordon was
producing not only one book a month, but aver-
aged two or even three. He seemed as a man who
knew his time was running out, and the never-
dying flame in his bosom drove him relentlessly
to share with the world insights into the Scriptures that few of our generation had.

Gordon's final writings were the combined
product of 40 years of active Charismatic ministry with its untold experiences, his life of daily
prayer, an in-depth study of the Word, and a keen
sensitivity to the leading of the Holy Spirit
through the gifts.

"A Merry Heart Does Good" (Prov. 17:22).

Gordon had a unique sense of humor, and
often in a serious situation, he would say something that would break the tension and cause
everyone to burst out laughing.

He loved to tell the story of a friend of his who
in spite of the fact that he had few educational
advantages, was nevertheless a man of great faith
and ability. He was able to reach the common
man for the Lord as few men have.

Gordon would relate the story as follows:
"One night, this minister preached on the ten
leopards. 'You remember there were ten leopards. All ten of the leopards were healed. But you

know that only one leopard came back to give God the glory. Now, which leopard are you like? The nine leopards or the one leopard?'" Everyone, of course, would split their sides laughing, but it was a true and accurate account.

Then Gordon would tell about another preacher who said, "You know, the children of Israel were led by God. He gave them a pillar of cloud by day and a pillar of fire by night. Now, you all know what a pillar is. A pillar is something you lay your head on at night."

Another of Gordon's favorites was the account of the brash young preacher who came to an elderly minister with the startling pronouncement, "I have all the nine gifts."

"No, you have 10," the veteran replied. "You also have the gift of bragging."

Gordon used to chide some who were afraid of "getting out on a limb." He'd say, "Before you can get out on a limb, you've got to get out on the branch; and you haven't even gotten out on the branch yet."

One time I said to him, "Gordon, you know, you have improved 50 percent since I married you."

He answered me, "Well then, I still haven't caught up to you, for you've improved 95 percent."

I didn't know if I exactly liked that remark. I

asked, "Are you inferring that I started out that far back? If so, why did you marry me?"

"I married you for your potential!" was his reply. He almost always had the last word.

Trial in Miami

Our telephone often rang in the middle of the night. Sometimes it was to report the marvelous meetings that were going on with an invitation to come immediately to share in the great things God was doing — the thousands who were being saved, healed and filled with the Holy Spirit. Many times Gordon would drop everything and go to get a firsthand report for the magazine. Most of the time, I stayed behind with the children, though on occasion, I did manage to go with him.

Sometimes the calls at night were distress calls — not only from laymen but from ministers. One such call came about 2:30 a.m. when Jack Coe was to be tried in Miami for "practicing medicine without a license." He had prayed for a boy who had polio, and the child had thrown aside his crutches. When there was apparently no visible sign of improvement in his condition, the mother was encouraged by the leading atheist of the city to file civil charges.

Jack Coe was arrested and put in jail. He was released shortly after, but his trial was soon to come up. Brother Coe said on the phone he needed Gordon badly. So Gordon dropped everything and went to his side. He stayed with him for several days, methodically helping lawyers prepare the case. When the trial came up, Gordon was placed on the witness stand as a "key witness" to testify in Brother Coe's behalf. The result was that the judge threw the case out of court, and Jack was set free.

Branham and the IRS

On another occasion, William Branham called to say that he was being indicted by the IRS for failure to pay income tax, which amounted to $390,000.

Gordon had warned Branham to keep proper records and to be businesslike in all affairs pertaining to his finances. But being the simple man that he was, Branham informed Gordon that "some friend of mine told me I don't have to file income tax, because all this money coming to me is not really mine. I am just having to pay a lot of bills." Hence he had never, at any time, filed his income tax.

Gordon told Branham again and again that he was going to find himself in serious trouble with the IRS, and urged him to file. But all to no avail. So now the phone brought the distress call: "Come and help me." Gordon again laid aside his own affairs and went to Brother Branham's side.

The IRS agents were noticeably aggravated with Brother Branham's explanation of why he had not filed. They regarded him as a crook and a fraud. But Gordon persuaded them that Branham was not a crook, but that he was a simple, uneducated man, who had taken the advice of a friend who didn't know much more than he did about such matters.

After several days of interrogation with Gordon present, the result was that instead of the IRS claiming that Branham owed several hundred thousand dollars in back taxes, they finally arrived at a figure of $40,000.

Of course, Brother Branham had no money to pay them inasmuch as he was supporting numerous relatives. So a plan was worked out for him to pay it out over a period of years. (At the time of his death, much of the amount remained unpaid.)

One day Kenneth Hagin came into our offices. He handed Gordon a piece of paper on which was written a prophecy he said the Lord had given him. The prophecy stated that the leader of the deliverance movement was soon to be taken in death because he was getting into error, and the Lord was having to remove him from the scene for that reason. Gordon took the prophecy and placed it on his desk.

After Brother Hagin left, I asked, "What do you think about this? Is this Branham?"

Gordon answered gravely, "Yes, it is Branham. He is getting into error. He thinks he is Elijah. He thinks he is the messenger of the covenant. The sad thing is that unscrupulous men around him are putting words into his mouth, and due to his limited background he is taking them up."

Two years later, William Branham, who had moved from his home in Jeffersonville, Indiana, was driving to Tuscon, Arizona, his new base. In West Texas he had a head-on collision with a drunken driver and was taken to the hospital. His head became terribly swollen. A tube was placed in his throat to assist his breathing, but on Christmas Eve, 1965, he departed this world, even as the prophecy had stated. A tremendous ministry that had veered from the course!

"Start Fishing!"

I recall a spiritual dream the Lord gave me one night. In it, I had decided to go fishing and was walking along a country road with all the paraphernalia necessary to be a fisherman. There was the pole on my back, the fishhooks and the bucket to put the fish in. I had all the required equipment.

As I walked along this road, suddenly I saw what looked like a deep hole. It was large, more like a huge well. The top was completely covered with a green, oily-looking pollution. I saw this big hole and was walking right by it, when I heard a voice saying, "Start fishing." I stopped in my tracks, surveyed the scene and said to myself, "There can't possibly be any fish in that dirty water," and resumed walking down the road.

The second time, I heard a voice say, "Start fishing." Again I argued that there couldn't possibly be any fish in that dirty place. So for the third time, I started walking and again the third time came a loud, strong voice saying, "Start fishing." I repeated my doubts, "How could that hole ever have any live fish in it?"

But because the voice had been so clear and urgent, I removed the fishing gear from my back and threw in the line. Immediately, there was a tug. I jerked up the line and to my utter amazement, there was a huge, beautiful fish! I instantly awoke.

As I reflected on the meaning of this dream, the Lord spoke to me that there were fish in all waters at Christ For The Nations, not just in those that looked "clean," but wherever the opportunity arose. He had fish in all waters that needed to be caught for Him, and we were to obey the command to "start fishing." Many Christians are always looking for the ideal fishing hole instead of fishing in all waters.

Chapter Twelve

In meetings we held over the country, we noticed how the devil would use one method of attack after another. It would be impossible to enumerate in one book all the methods, means and tricks he pulled out of his bag to disrupt and halt the work of the Lord.

I recall how, as Gordon, his sister Gladys and brother-in-law, Leon, and I would pray, the Spirit of the Lord would speak through prophecy. Once while we were managing the huge Branham campaigns, the Spirit spoke and said that because we were in the foreground of the deliverance ministry, we were special targets for the devil. Being on the pinnacle, we were susceptible to the attack of the enemy, as a small army would be on a mountaintop with the enemy shooting at it from every direction. This was oft an accurate picture of our situation.

On the last night of one of those tent meetings (in Topeka, Kansas), Gordon and I planned to help the pastor for whom we held the meeting to raise the money he had borrowed for his new tent. Gordon felt I should be the one to receive the offering. The preliminaries were over, and

Gordon had made some introductory remarks. Just as I arose from my seat to receive the offering, there came such a downpour of rain it was impossible to be heard above the din.

Some people started to get up to leave for their cars, but I motioned for them to stay and to stand, as I pointed to heaven to get them to start praying.

Gordon and I began to walk back and forth across the platform commanding the rain to stop in the Name of the Lord so we could continue the service. We definitely felt that this was a trick of the devil to end the service. No sooner had we touched God when instantly, as one would turn off a water faucet, the rain stopped.

I continued with the service. All the financial needs for the tent were met without any delay, and the Lord gave us wonderful results at the altar that night. All the people on the front row were filled with the Holy Spirit. Praise His Name!

An hour and a half later after the meeting was over and we had said our last goodbyes, we left the tent and drove two blocks. A deluge came suddenly, and we had to stop our car by the side of the road as we couldn't see to drive. Finally, we crept along in the car to reach the motel. It literally poured all night!

A Constant Warfare

The fact that we believed in divine healing did

not mean that the devil did not periodically attack us. One diary entry on April 1, 1965, says: "Gordon fainted during the night. He prayed all night, and God gave him victory."

What had happened was that Gordon had gone into the bathroom and while there, had fainted and hit his head on the door. He said from then on, he remembered nothing. Later he found himself lying on the floor, picked himself up, and got back into bed. He said he was aware that it was an all-out attack of the devil. After spending the night in prayer, he got complete victory. Twenty-four hours later, he left for an extensive trip to the Mideast and suffered no reaction.

Dennis Healed of Blindness

We had always tried to teach our children faith in God, not only for their salvation, but for their healing as well. In fact, during our 35 years of married life, the Lord was good to us. Not one single time did our family need hospital attention, except when I gave birth to our three children. I don't suppose we spent more than $100 in all those years on doctors' bills, and that was generally for vaccinations required for overseas trips.

One day when Dennis was around 10 years old, he came home from school and said he was nearly blind in his right eye. Later that evening, the phone rang; it was the school nurse. She said that she had been observing Dennis for a couple of months. He appeared to be nearly blind in one eye, but since children sometimes fake blindness because they want to wear a pair of glasses like someone they know, she thought she would wait for a few weeks and test him on several occasions.

During one test, she pretended that his medical chart indicated it was the left eye that was blind, to see if in fact he was attempting to fool her. But he insisted she was wrong: It was his right eye and not his left that was blind. This proved to her that he was indeed nearly blind in that eye.

She urged a medical examination. Had he been hit by a ball or received a hard fall? I was at a loss for the answer. We tested the eye and confirmed what the report showed.

When Gordon came in that evening, I told him what the nurse had said. He answered, "I will pray for him, but I want to take a little time to wait on the Lord first."

Shortly after this, Oak Cliff Assembly of God, the church we attended, held a revival. The evangelist seemed to have faith to pray for the sick. On the last night, Dennis was sitting on the front row. When he turned to look at me, I motioned for him to get in the prayer line but he shook his head. Several times he would look around, and I would nod my head for him to get in line. Each time, he would shake his head, "No."

The line became increasingly long. Finally, after ever so long, Dennis meandered toward the end of it. The service went on and on, and by the time the evangelist had prayed for nearly everyone and was getting toward the end of the line, he finally came to Dennis, who was next to last.

Not realizing that Dennis was the son of his good friend, Gordon Lindsay, and being very tired, the evangelist just slapped Dennis on the top of the head and said, "Go, and be healed."

I thought to myself, "Now he could at least have prayed for him." I was disappointed, to say the least, as he had not even asked Dennis about his need.

When we left the church and got in the car, I decided not to express my disappointment, but asked Dennis if he could see out of his bad eye. Matter-of-factly he said, "Yes."

Nothing further was said until we arrived home. Immediately I pulled the calendar down and asked, "Dennis, can you really see out of that bad eye?"

"Sure," he answered.

I tested him by asking him to close his good eye. He could read everything on the calendar. Then I gave him the Bible, which had smaller print, and he read that without any trouble. Next, I offered him a New Testament with fine print, but he could not see that.

With my faith encouraged, I became bold. "Now tomorrow morning, we will test your eye again, and by that time you will be able to read the fine print," I told him. The next morning, I tested him, and he was indeed able to read the fine print without any difficulty.

Some days later, I called the school nurse and found she had been transferred to another school, so I asked the nurse on duty to examine him. She did and found he could see in both eyes. After checking his medical card, she asked me what had happened, and I told her. But she totally rejected the fact that God could have healed him. She said she knew of instances where a person was blind for a period and then received sight again, and possibly his case was one such example.

I then made it a point to call the nurse who originally checked him. I told her the present results, and that God had healed him. She rejoiced with me over the phone, and said she believed God did heal him.

The Motor Scooter Accident

Dennis was now 16 years old. It was Memorial Day, and the last day of school. His dad had helped him get a motor scooter so I would not have to drive him to classes anymore.

The office was closed, but Gordon was none-theless in the middle of some work at the office. Suddenly he felt a tremendous burden to pray. He did not know what for, so he just began to pray in the Spirit.

About one hour later, I received a telephone call from the hospital. It was Dennis on the line. He said, "Mother, come get me."

"Where are you?" I asked.

"The hospital."

"What are you doing there?" I excitedly questioned.

"I've just had a bad wreck on my scooter."

"Are you hurt?"

"No," he responded, "but the boy with me is."

"How badly?"

"I think real bad."

So I ran across the street to the office and knocked on Gordon's window. He was praying so loudly and earnestly he didn't even hear me. I knocked several times before I finally caught his attention.

When I told him what had happened, we jumped in the car and drove to the hospital where we found Dennis who was uninjured. He gave us the following report: "I was going on a very busy six-lane thoroughfare with my friend sitting on my scooter behind me, and suddenly out of a side street there came a large car that failed to stop, hitting my scooter broadside."

The driver told me personally that the first thing he noticed was arms and legs flying through the air. (The arms and legs he saw were those of Dennis!)

Dennis said when he was hit, he quickly remembered what his coach had told him: Curl up and roll like a ball. This he did, and when he landed on the pavement, he rolled across three traffic lanes. His body finally unwound against the curb. Miraculously, there was not a single car in that busy intersection at the moment!

The boy with Dennis did not fare as well. His leg was pinned under the motor scooter and was broken in several places. He spent the whole summer in and out of the hospital, and the car driver's insurance adjuster finally settled with the boy's family, and reimbursed Dennis for the total amount of the scooter.

No doubt God's protecting angel was with Dennis because his father had obeyed the voice of the Holy Spirit and had prayed.

The Day Kennedy Died

November 22, 1963, was a day which stunned the whole world. It was the day when the president of the United States, John F. Kennedy, met death from an assassin's bullet.

The tremendous impact of this event was felt throughout the world; yet greater still, was its effect on the city of Dallas where it took place. And to those who actually witnessed the scene, it was a day never to be forgotten. Dennis was among those watching the horrible spectacle.

On the morning of November 22, 1963, Dennis with two other boys got into his little red Volkswagen and started to the Dallas Love Field Airport. On the way, they noticed it was a little after 11 a.m. by the big clock on a building just off the expressway. They had to hurry, for they knew the president would soon be landing in his big jet plane.

They arrived at the airport just before the plane came in. Soon it landed, and in a few minutes, the president's car was coming off the field through the gate. One of the boys was on top of the Volkswagen taking pictures. The president glanced at the boy, smiled, and waved at the crowd as the procession passed on.

Dennis and his friends had managed to get tickets to the Mart (one boy's father worked there) where the president was scheduled to speak in just one hour. Later while they were walking around the Mart, they saw a reporter with a walkie-talkie running for the photographer's stand.

At that moment, a car came roaring down the

highway with sirens screaming. It had to slow down to make the corners. What Dennis saw startled him beyond words. The president was slumped down on the seat, and Mrs. Kennedy and a man were leaning over him. One of the photographers exclaimed, "The president has been shot!"

The boys got into the Volkswagen and followed the racing car to the hospital. Secret Service men had not yet been stationed at the doors. And with boyish curiosity, they went in. They followed a reporter to the room where the stricken president had been carried. A nurse came rushing out asking what their blood type was and if they would give blood for a transfusion. Dennis said he would be glad to, but before any decision could be made, an orderly called the nurse back and told her that it was no use. The president was beyond any human aid. The announcement came shortly that the president was dead!

As the boys drove toward home, they were very solemn and deep in thought. No one said anything. They passed the clock that they had looked at only two hours before. They did not yet know that it was under that clock that an assassin's gun had rung out.

They crossed over the Trinity River into Oak Cliff. Then they had another shock. They came upon the scene of a shooting on the street. Blood was on the pavement, and policemen were frantically pursuing the man who had killed a policeman. The officers quickly captured him in the Texas Theater and took him to the police station. There they learned he was Lee Harvey Oswald, alleged assassin of the president.

It was an eventful and sobering day for the boys. We asked Dennis after he had witnessed this tragic but historic event what impression it had made on him. Very soberly he replied, "It showed us boys how short life can be and how suddenly death can come. It caused me to realize that even if you have hundreds of men guarding you, you can be taken away in a split second, and you have to be ready."

The Judge and the Jury

After we had started the printing plant and had been operating it for several years, we turned its management over to one of our fellow ministers.

We decided we should perhaps lease part of the building to a typesetter in order to expedite our printing. Later the manager was contacted by a man who said he knew typesetting and wanted to lease the space. He wanted a few weeks to secure equipment. So an agreement was signed between the printing plant manager and this man. (The document plainly stated that The Voice of

Healing was not involved in the agreement.)

Several months went by, and the man finally told our manager he had decided not to go ahead with the project, as he had not found the proper equipment at a price he could afford to pay. (Unfortunately, the manager did not get this in writing.)

In the matter of a few days, another man who already had typesetting equipment arrived, and the space was leased to him. (This typesetter was with us for many years.)

But the first man later found and purchased some equipment. When he came back to our print shop and learned the space had been leased to someone else, he came to the conclusion that here was a good chance to pick up some extra money.

Soon a letter came from his lawyer notifying us that he had filed a suit against The Voice of Healing for $60,000 plus lawyer's fees, court costs and punitive damages. We tried to talk to the man, but he was completely unreasonable.

The thing dragged on for several years but finally came to trial. To our dismay, the jury awarded him $3,400. In my diary that day it says: "Still believing God."

During the trial, testimony came out to the effect that this man was illegally operating a typesetting office in his own home (which was

zoned for residential use only). We also learned
that he had gone bankrupt a couple of times prior
to his moving to Dallas.

One thing that particularly baffled us was that
our manager, learning that the man had set up his
own typesetting plant in the garage of his home,
asked him to do some of the typesetting, but the
man replied that he was so busy he could not take
on any more work.

According to his own testimony during the
trial, he later turned around and sold the equipment, actually making a profit on it. Neither had
he lost any time off work as he was still working
on the job he had for several years.

Following the jury's decision, we worked
with our attorney and prepared a brief contesting
the verdict. To our joy several weeks later, the
judge laid aside the decision of the jury, inasmuch as he felt it was an unfair verdict. (A few
days after this, I cut a clipping from the newspaper which stated that rarely will a judge overthrow the decision of a jury. But God used this
Jewish judge to render justice.)

Beside Still Waters

After living for eight years in the house the
Lord had built us, we began to make plans to
relocate our office to a more strategic area.
Therefore, we started looking for a home in that

immediate vicinity also.

I had spotted a little lake with about 12 families living on it in that vicinity. One day as a minister's wife (who was my prayer partner) and I were praying, the Lord gave a message by the Spirit. My friend gave the interpretation that the Lord was going to give us a house and "lead us beside the still waters." The moment she said that, my heart leaped within me for joy, for I knew God intended that we have a home on the little lake.

Whenever a house went up for sale on the lake we looked at it, but the prices were always outlandish — nothing we could afford. After several house-hunting excursions, Gordon finally became impatient with my insistence on securing a house on that lake. But I kept holding on.

Some months later, one evening he and I were eating at a cafeteria a block away from the lake. After dinner, I suggested to him again, "Let's drive around the lake and see if there are any more houses for sale."

"You will only be wasting your time," he replied.

"No, not really," I said. So after prevailing upon him, he drove around the lake. Lo and behold, there was a house for sale! But Gordon would not stop long enough for me to inquire.

However, the next day I went back, looked at

the house, negotiated with the owners, and within an hour had made a small down payment on it. The man's business was going into bankruptcy, and he needed cash immediately. For this reason, he sold it far below the market value.

I had looked for a total of 15 months. But God had said He would lead us beside still waters, and He did just that! We lived in that house for nine years, and never did the children and I enjoy a home as much as we did that particular one.

Lost and Found

We were looking for commercial property on which to relocate our office and print shop; the existing facilities were entirely inadequate due to continuous growth. (Actually, the floors of our storage area overhead had begun to sink, due to the heavy weight of our inventory of books.) Finally we found several beautiful, level lots situated one block between two freeways. After prayer, we felt it was the location we needed, so we purchased the property with a small down payment, planning to build after the lots were paid for.

Two months after this, I attended a Full Gospel Business Men's Saturday breakfast at the Adolphus Hotel in downtown Dallas. After a wonderful morning, I picked up our car from the Adolphus parking area, then drove home. As I climbed out of the car, I noticed my lovely wedding anniversary watch (that Gordon had purchased at a big savings from a friend who was in the jewelry business) was missing.

I looked on the floor of the car, on the pavement beside the car, ran into the house and searched the kitchen, bathroom and the entire house. I was sick at heart when I was unable to find my watch. Finally, I calmed myself and began to pray. Suddenly, I remembered that when I went to pick up the car in the Adolphus parking building, I had looked at the time in order to determine how much I owed.

Hurriedly, I drove back the five miles. By now a full hour must have gone by; it was lunchtime and traffic was exceedingly heavy. When I arrived at the Adolphus, I asked the parking attendant if anyone had turned in a beautiful, white gold watch. He said, "Lady, you'll never find that!"

I left him and walked over to the pay window. I told the lady I had just been there about an hour before and lost my watch; that I remembered looking at the time as I stood at her window.

As she answered me, "No watch has been turned in," I looked down at my feet, and there to my total amazement was the watch lying in front of me! I grabbed it up and showed it to the lady at the window. She was dumbfounded and couldn't believe it had been lying there all that time without someone seeing it.

I then told her I had prayed about it and asked God to return it to me, and I felt He did. She agreed it must have been God, or it would never have been lying there all that time.

When I examined the watch, I saw what had happened: the band had broken. On Monday, I took it to the jeweler for repair and discovered that the manager of the jewelry store was the same man who had sold us the lots for our future office building (he sold real estate on the side). He asked if we had begun building, and I answered, "No. It will take a couple of years to pay for the land." Then he informed me that the nightclub facing Kiest Boulevard (a main thoroughfare) which joined our property had gone into bankruptcy and was for sale. He wondered if we were interested.

I made an appointment with him to see it, and Gordon and I with the children who were now grown, went to look at the place. The sheriff had padlocked the building, and we had to get permission to enter.

"Something Worthwhile"

The children and I felt immediately that we should purchase the property. But Gordon could see no practical purpose for it and so rejected the idea. Finally, after praying about it for several weeks, he said he felt we should go ahead and see whether we could indeed purchase the club.

I called the owner who was an oil man in San Bernardino, and told him we were a religious organization and wanted to turn the place into a Christian Center. I told him we had heard the place had gone bankrupt three times before. No doubt he had made a sizable sum on it already, and wouldn't it be a splendid thing if he would make it available to us at a price we could afford? His answer was, "I would like to see it used for something worthwhile."

To make a long story short, we finally agreed to pay $125,000 for that club (the land alone was probably worth that). To duplicate the building and buy the land would undoubtedly have cost a quarter of a million dollars at that time. Plus, it was completely furnished. It had kitchen equipment (including 13 freezers and refrigerators), tables, chairs and dishes, etc.

I remember a breakfast meeting Gordon and I had with a dozen or so Christian businessmen concerning the purchase of this building. We had wanted their opinion and hoped they might help us in financing it. But at the breakfast everyone who spoke discouraged us from getting it. They said, "This place is a white elephant. It has gone bankrupt several times. What would you do with it?" And on and on they went, strongly advising against securing it.

However after the meeting was over, an elderly retired layman, J.B. McMath Sr., came to us and said, "Brother Lindsay, if you feel God wants you to get this place, then go ahead. I will give you the first $1,000 toward the purchase of it." That was just enough to encourage us to go ahead and buy it. So we did. Or we thought we did!

When we met with the real estate agent, we gave him the $1,000, and told him we would need 30 days in order to secure a loan for the balance. He took the $1,000. We tried several places to negotiate the loan without ever getting a firm commitment.

Several days before the deadline, the real estate agent called me and said, "Mrs. Lindsay, I want to inform you that the club has just been bought by another party."

Startled at the news, I asked him, "How could this be possible? We have a contract. Our time hasn't expired, and you have our $1,000 down payment."

He answered, "I'm sorry, but actually the other client has already given me a $5,000 down payment. I have taken it to the title company and put it into escrow. So it is just too late."

I asked him what he had done with the $1,000 we had put down on the club. He replied, "I never did anything with it because I figured you could not get the loan. It is lying here on my desk, so you can come by and get it."

By now I was indignant and told him so. I said, "You had no right to sell it to someone else when our time had not yet expired." He agreed it was a little unethical, but said it was too late to do anything about it now. He added, "I just didn't think you could come up with that kind of a loan."

I called Gordon to tell him what had happened, and we made an appointment to see our lawyer the next day.

The frustrating thing about this was that two hours after talking to the real estate agent, the bank president phoned me and said, "Mrs. Lindsay, you can come up and get the full amount of the loan. The board approved it last night." I had to tell him I was sorry, but apparently the property had slipped through our hands, though we were going to see a lawyer the next day.

We did go see the lawyer and told him our story. His answer was, "No doubt you have a case. But the question is, do you want to go to court over it?"

By now Gordon had thought it over and said, "No, we don't want to go that route. If God wants us to have that building, we will get it."

I questioned him, "What are you saying? How

can we possibly get the building? That was a Jewish investment company that put $5,000 down on that club. Have you ever heard of a Jewish investment company putting that much money down on a building and losing it?"

"I still say if God wants us to have that building, we will get it," was Gordon's reply.

We thanked the lawyer and left his office, stopping on the way home at the real estate office where we picked up our $1,000 check.

Several months later as I opened the telephone book one morning, my eyes suddenly fell on the name of the investment company (a very odd and unusual one) that was buying the night club. The type seemed to stare up at me in bold letters. Thoughtfully I mused, "God, what are you trying to say? Can it be that we are still going to get the club?" I prayed a short prayer and dropped the matter.

Three weeks later, I received a telephone call from the real estate agent. His voice dripped with a hollow-sounding solicitude. He asked, "How are you, Mrs. Lindsay? You know that night club? Well, I *always did feel* you should have that place. And I just wanted to tell you that it doesn't look as if the investment company is going to be able to raise the balance of $125,000. Their time will be up this week. If you want it, come down next week, and I will be so *happy* to sell it to you."

Without showing much emotion, I thanked him and hung up the phone.

When I called Gordon, he teased me with, "Shall I say, 'I told you so'?"

The following week we went to the title company and finalized the purchase. As we were going out the door of the title company, the real estate agent was laying claim to the $5,000 the investment company had placed in escrow.

After securing the club, we had to make repairs and alterations costing $12,000. Within a matter of several days, a man in Georgia deeded to us some 15 acres of land, and within a few more days, that property was sold. This gave us enough to pay for remodeling.

We found again that the waters of the Jordan River never part until we step into them.

A New Career

Our son, Gilbert, attended Baylor University, majoring in business administration. Scarcely was the ink dry on his college diploma, when a notice came through the mail saying he was to appear for his physical for army induction. We had been anticipating this; however, it was a tremendous burden to me personally to see him inducted so soon. For during the years Gilbert was in college, I had assisted him on a part-time basis as he managed our print shop. He had quite a knowledge of printing because he had started working in the print shop as a teenage boy, first sweeping the floor, and then gradually working up to the manager position.

I was eager for him to finish college so he could be in the plant full time and relieve me of my responsibility there. Nevertheless, I knew there was a good possibility he would be drafted.

After we prayed together, Gilbert felt led to check a National Guard unit that was based about two miles from our home. To his surprise, there was an opening, and he was immediately accepted.

Gordon felt strongly that I should take over the print shop while Gil was away for six months of basic training. I strongly resisted Gordon's suggestion at first, telling him I was already 50 years old and that most people do not start a new career at 50 — especially a career in printing, which is so technical and involved. Besides, I felt I already had all I could do in helping Gordon with his books, the magazine, traveling with him and assisting in the public meetings we held.

However, he prevailed upon me, saying it would be impossible to get a manager for a few months, and then let him go when Gil returned. I knew he was right, so I reluctantly accepted.

Realizing my inadequacy and lack of background, I threw myself entirely upon the mercy of the Lord. I knew if I bid the printing jobs too high, we would not get work and our employees would be standing idle, drawing their salaries with nothing to do. If, on the other hand, I bid a job too low, we would get the job and then lose money on it. So the printing business with all its technicalities and its myriad details was not one for a speculator nor a novice.

Before Gilbert left, he and I called a meeting of all the employees and informed them that I would be running the shop. I told them I would need their help daily, as most of them there knew much more about printing than I did. I informed them that many times I would be coming to them with what they would consider foolish questions, but their cooperation was a matter of life and death for the print shop. I was there to keep the shop running, to do the work for God and make secure their own jobs.

The result was beautiful. Everyone was most cooperative. Each day I would go to the Lord in prayer, and I asked our employees to do the same. I told the Lord, I was entirely dependent on His mercy; He would have to give me the "know-how" and the ability which I lacked. God marvelously answered prayer, and in the six months Gil was gone, the shop made more profit than it had in the several preceding years.

After Gil returned and some of the bids that I

had figured came in, he said to me one day, "Mother, I am amazed when I look at some of the jobs you figured, how near right you were. I know you don't know all that much about printing, so the Lord must have helped you." I assured him He had and gave God the glory.

The moral to the story is that you can do anything that is necessary, if you take God as your partner.

While Gil was in the service, an entry in my diary of April 27, 1967, says: "Gil called to say he was the only one who had dry feet after 13 hours in two-inch rain in Fort Leonardwood, Missouri. Praise God!" When your children grow up believing in a God of miracles, they can even on their own believe Him to keep their shoes dry in a downpour!

Chapter Thirteen

Gordon was receiving increasingly more invitations to speak at conventions around the world. Yet he always found time to pray and to write. Here are several of his letters:

Portland, Oregon
February 1963

Dearest Freda and All,

... Was too wide awake to immediately go to sleep the night before, so was compelled to continue my writing until 4 a.m. ...

Tonight I leave at 8 p.m. for the Orient. At 10 p.m. I will be in Anchorage. Three hours later by the clock, I will be in Tokyo. However, due to complications of time on a round world, it will not be tomorrow but the day after tomorrow. Alas, I shall never, never see Tuesday, February 19. For me, the day never exists. Please pray daily for the success of my trip.

Love,
Gordon

✳ ✳ ✳ ✳ ✳ ✳

Lagos, Nigeria
March 1963

Dearest Freda,

... Nigeria has one-fourth of the total population of Africa and represents a tremendous field of opportunity. Below the clouds where the lightning is flickering in Nigeria, are thousands of primitive people, the great unreached, some viciously savage, others pathetically friendly and responsive to the Gospel if they only had a chance. But now as the Gospel is spreading through evangelism, it is important to build churches for the converts. Every important official I have met says the old plan of the compound and the outstation where somebody preaches under the stars on occasion is dead. Moreover, governments are beginning to crack down on open-air meetings in some places as it occasions disturbances, so they claim.

Love,
Gordon

✳ ✳ ✳ ✳ ✳ ✳

Jerusalem, Israel
March 1963

Dearest Freda and All,

... It's always a change after I have been active

to lie down and relax by writing. ...

We drove to Amman where I had met the prime minister and his secretary. Both of them were later blown to bits in the same office we had been in a few days before. ...

In the distance on the way back, I saw Mount Nebo where Moses looked out on the Promised Land. Medieval monks built a monastery on top of it. They were always sure to get far enough away where they would be of no earthly use to anyone. ...

The old mother of my hostess was a study. Her lower jaw is the color of bluing. A ghastly blue it is, like the color of a corpse. To get that color, they painfully inject a dye into the skin. The effect is quite comical. In my ignorance I asked my host what that is for. That, he explained, is to make her look pretty. Rather startled at this explanation, I looked toward her, and she was grinning happily at what she assumed was my look of admiration. My host rather apologetically explained that his mother-in-law put on the blue, just as the American girls put on the red — to make themselves look beautiful. I could see however that the mother-in-law after all had by far, the best and most advanced system. While the Americans have to everlastingly renew theirs, hers is there to stay — the tattoo marks are permanent.

That reminded me that in India some swarthy matrons wore nose jewels. No doubt this gives them extreme gratification, for they imagine this gaudy ornament adds substantially to their pulchritude. And if they think so, is not the cause served? ...

This evening, we had all the missionaries out to dinner and laid plans for the morrow — a 400-mile round trip to North Israel and then to Tiberias for a baptizing. Up at 6 a.m., we chartered a bus to take 46 people to the baptizing. We picked up about 30 in Jerusalem. We had no more than got out of town, than they began to sing. And what singing! What was lacking in quality was made up in quantity. One had a tambourine, which added to the din. Just to make sure they were getting enough volume, they used the bus's loudspeaker. And they never stopped all the way to Tiberias. They made more noise than Alexander's Ragtime Band, but they were singing unto the Lord! I doubt if there was a band of singers in Israel like this since the destruction of Jerusalem in A.D. 70. One Jew got so happy, he danced up and down the aisle on the bus.

One of the amazing things was the fact that the Christian Arabs and Jews got along so well together. As you know, there are 150,000 Arabs in Israel who did not flee at the time of the war. This means we have a work to do among the

Arabs as well as the Jews. We picked up passengers at two or three points. Some had to stand the last lap of the way.

We reached Tiberias in the middle of the afternoon, and soon were ready to baptize several of the boys in the Sea of Galilee. Tiberias, you remember, was built by Herod who beheaded John the Baptist. The reason he selected the site was that there are hot springs there. I had not particularly looked forward with anticipation to getting in the icy waters of the Sea of Galilee which have flowed down from the melted snows of Mount Hermon. But then I found that the water from the hot springs flowed out into a sort of a cove and did not immediately mix with the water of the lake. It was delightfully warm, and the baptizing proceeded without incident — after I preached for about 20 minutes. The boys all gave testimony afterward at our meeting in the village.

Incidentally, I could not resist the temptation to swim a little in the waters of the sea after the service. But the sun was dropping lower in the west and would soon submerge behind the towering hills, so we bid adieu to the city of Tiberias.

As we ascended, we had the most beautiful view of the northern part of the lake. Our minds rapidly reviewed the historic events that took place along the shores of that sea. Straight across was the scene of the feeding of the 5,000. Halfway across the lake the disciples met Jesus walking on the water. To the north and west were the flourishing cities of Capernaum, Bethsaida and Magdala. There the great trade route to the East crossed. And in those cities, Jesus preached and performed many of His miracles. Alas, that very prosperity was their ruination. So engrossed were they in making money that when Jesus returned, He found the revival had completely subsided. And so He pronounced the woes against these cities. Today you can scarcely find a trace of them and strangely enough, the Jews have not built upon these sites. After the services in the village, we started retracing our journey back to Jerusalem, arriving around midnight.

... Today is the Feast of Purim, in honor of Esther's deliverance. The youngsters all paint up and wear masks as American youth do on Halloween. ...

Love,
Gordon

✳ ✳ ✳ ✳ ✳ ✳

Kampala, Uganda
March 1963

Dearest Freda and All,

A man came to me right after the service and had a remarkable story to tell. Quite a few years ago, about 1953, he was a total cripple and had to crawl on his hands and knees and had a severe case of asthma. He found *The Voice of Healing* magazine which told him he could write for a prayer cloth. After some weeks, a letter came to him with instructions to pray twice a day and believe God for deliverance. He prayed once and was *instantly healed*. He began to preach and has built a grass church in Uganda. He has a congregation of about 70 and wants to build a Native Church. ...

Love to all,
Gordon

* * * * * *

Nagpur, India
March 1963

Dearest Freda,

Well, for the first time on my trip, I felt indisposed. Because I was short of sleep, I lay down for a while and suddenly began having chills and fever. I remembered the mosquitoes that bit me in Vietnam and thought of malaria. The feeling of nausea came upon me, and no one feels less like praying than at that time. Most Christians get sick for two reasons: They let their strength run down or secondly, when the signs of some sickness strike, they fold up because it is easier to do that than to fight it out. I knew I could not allow myself to be delayed by anything like that so I had to get the victory.

At first I did not get anywhere, but after a while, the Spirit of God began to pray through me, and in a matter of seconds, it was all gone. Praise the Lord!

People who have been in India describe it by telling about the Taj Mahal or the burning of the bodies on the Ganges. That however is not the real India — they are only its great extremes of wealth and poverty. The real India is the life of the dull, plodding masses — 400 million of them. What a pool of manpower and how it is wasted! Six men get less done than one in America. Let me describe to you this example, which typifies the real India.

Nagpur is a town of two-thirds of a million people in the very heart of India, so it can be said to be a metropolitan city. The great Indian Airlines cross here and exchange traffic. It has a touch of the outside and therefore cannot be said to be truly provincial.

I went to the best hotel, which cost only $4 per day with meals. Now, after my slight indisposition, I asked the porter if it were possible to take a hot bath in the hotel, supposing they had a bathtub — surely they had at least one in the best hotel of such a large city. The porter nodded gravely and set to work. He said he would be back in an hour. At the appointed time, he brought two large buckets of hot water into a side room and told me all was ready. Not being versed in the methods of India, I asked him how I could take a hot bath without either a shower or a tub. His face looked pained in puzzlement. I said, "Do you know what a bathtub is?" And I tried to describe it. A slow look of recognition came on his swarthy face. And again he disappeared.

I heard him setting his crew to work, but could not quite figure out what was being done. After a long time, he appeared again and showed me a rusty tub, the kind they used in the depression days in America, only much larger. He explained that they had been scrubbing it and now it was "much clean." Apparently, it had not been used for a considerable season, and had now become rusty from disuse. The natives see little use for such a superfluous article, but kept this on hand for foreigners who had fancy notions.

Well, I decided this was the best that was available. So I told him to pour in a bucket and a half of water. I would save the half bucket to keep the water warm in the tub. He thought I did not know what I was doing and insisted on pouring it all in. Finally, I thought I got him to do what I wanted him to do. He disappeared and so did the rest of the water.

I noticed now the tub had developed a leak,

and that I had better hurry. Perhaps this was in the plan also. They never came back for the tub while I was in the hotel, so perhaps this was their method of emptying it. They had thoughtfully provided a drain at one corner of the room so the water did not accumulate on the floor. It seemed that they had thought of everything but the soap. I was afraid I would not have time to explain this Western commodity to him, so I appropriated a tube of brushless shaving cream I had handy. Then I looked for the towel. Surely I had seen it somewhere? But now I looked in vain. So I had to use some of my own undergarments for that purpose. After I had dressed, I saw a towel had been placed in another room, in a place naturally calculated to miss the eye.

... The more I see and talk with the missionaries, the more I am convinced that this program (Native Church Crusade) is the one to push. ...

... It is so strange the number of people who know me. I talked at length with a lady and her husband who seemed well educated and knew the Far East quite well. Then we got to discussing missions, and after awhile, she asked if I happened to know Gordon Lindsay. I said, "Yes for some time." When I finally explained that I was he, she and her husband almost exploded.

Love,
Gordon

✳ ✳ ✳ ✳ ✳ ✳

Jerusalem, Israel
February 1964

Dear Mother, Carole, Gilbert and Denny:

... I believe my trip to Israel has been measurably successful. The prayer band has been set up and is functioning excellently. I believe we have better unity now than at any time in history since the days of the apostles.

Translation is beginning on my first book in Hebrew with the first printing at 50,000. Arrangements have been made for all equipment that is needed. Booklets will be sent out by mail. We will give a free Bible to all responding.

We plan to support several full-time workers — some for preparation of literature. Most of them to go out in the settlements to distribute literature. The missionaries will never reach Israel waiting for the people to come in. We must reach out — sending out literature and workers over the cities who can pray for the sick. ...

Lots of love,
Daddy

✳ ✳ ✳ ✳ ✳ ✳

Saigon, Vietnam
January 1966

Dearest Freda and All,

It was 5 p.m., and I had not seen Gordon

Smith (the veteran missionary in Vietnam). I began to fear that my telegram had not gone through, and I had missed him altogether. Actually my telegram had been held over Saturday-Sunday. On Monday noon, his wife received it in Toulane, 500 miles north. He had come to Saigon, but had not received accurate information as to when I would arrive. His wife phoned him then that my telegram said I would be arriving Saturday and would stay over till Monday. He then thought he had missed me, and that I had already flown out.

By the merest "coincidence," he stopped in at the Continental Hotel for some information. At that split second, I finished my lunch and went up to the desk clerk to remind him I was expecting a visitor, Mr. Gordon Smith, and to notify me at once when he arrived! I did not pay particular attention to a tall man who was standing by. But when I said I was looking for Gordon Smith he turned swiftly and asked me if I were Gordon Lindsay. Upon my responding in the affirmative, he said, "I am Gordon Smith." Since he supposed that I had already gone, he was in the hotel for other purposes, and I would have missed him. The chances of meeting him "accidentally" in the way we did were less than one in a hundred. It was evidently providential.

Brother Smith and I spent the evening

together, and the conversations were very
enlightening. ...

                Love,
                Gordon

Chapter Fourteen

It would be impossible to say how many times the Lord protected our family from certain death. Daily we appropriated the verse, "The angel of the LORD encamps all around those who fear Him, and delivers them" (Psa. 34:7).

One such incident was when Gil and a friend, Jack, decided to go sailing on a cold wintry day in February. The craft they had was a small sailboat which the salesman had said was "unsinkable."

Gil and Jack had pulled out about 50 yards from shore when suddenly the boat tipped over. Gil, who had played in the Baylor University band, wore his thick Baylor jacket that day. He also had on his heavy army boots which were laced to the top. When he was thrown into the turbulent cold water, he was not able to extricate himself from either the Baylor jacket or the heavy army boots. Though he was a good swimmer, he knew the chances of his making it to the shore were exceedingly slim — and in fact, were getting slimmer by the second.

He called on the Lord to help him. And

miracle of miracles, he made it to the shore! He realized that, had the hand of the Lord not been upon him, he would have gone to a watery grave. (Jack, his friend, also a good swimmer, was not encumbered with such heavy clothing, so made it to the shore with only minor indisposition.) The boat apparently sank, for it was never found.

The Plane Crash

A month later that same year, God again showed forth His mighty hand. Gordon had left for a round-the-world trip. Before he went, Mrs. Anna Schrader had said by the Spirit that this would be a dangerous trip. The prophecy mentioned that when Gordon got to Hong Kong, as he would look to his right, there would be danger.

After Gordon left, Mrs. Schrader called me and urged that we get several people to pray for Gordon, as Satan was going to try to take his life. We did pray, and I committed the matter to the Lord.

Gordon went to Tokyo, and after he finished his business there, he planned to go to Hiroshima. He had wanted to do that for several years, but each time had been too busy. Now this time he had told me in advance he definitely planned to visit Hiroshima.

But in Tokyo the man who was to take him there, suddenly found it was impossible for him to go. Gordon was greatly disappointed. He then was confronted with the decision whether to take a train by himself to Hiroshima or to go on to his next destination.

He said he struggled all evening in prayer, not knowing what to do — wanting to go to Hiroshima but yet somewhat hesitant about going alone. Finally, after several hours of indecision and vacillating back and forth, he felt a strong urge to go on to his next destination.

He caught the first plane out, and when he stepped off the plane in Hong Kong, remembering what Mrs. Schrader had said, he looked to the right. All he saw was a big Canadian plane sitting there with a long line of people climbing the ramp. His Hong Kong host appeared shortly, and Gordon dismissed the matter from his mind.

The next morning when he awoke, he found a newspaper that had been placed under his door. Pictured there were the ruins of the large Canadian plane which he had seen loading! It crashed and 64 people were dead!

The following day, he picked up another paper and to his amazement read that the BOAC plane he was scheduled to fly on had he gone to Hiroshima had crashed, killing 124 people! It had exploded over Mt. Fuji, killing everyone on board, including 89 Americans. The papers listed that day, March 4, as the "darkest single day in commercial aviation" with both planes going down — yet our great God was able to protect Gordon!

At home, I was seated at the breakfast table when the first report came of the crash. As I listened closely, I realized Gordon could not have been on that particular plane as it was going from Hong Kong to Tokyo — the opposite direction he would be traveling. So I put my mind to rest.

The next day as I was on my way to do my grocery shopping, the car radio was on. Suddenly the newscaster announced that a large plane taking off from Tokyo to Hong Kong had crashed; all were dead. Being human, for a moment my heart was in my mouth. When I collected my wits, I said, "Lord, if he were going to get killed on that plane, why would You have alerted us to pray for him? Surely You must have preserved his life somehow." But I wondered how.

When I returned home, the phone started ringing. Just before Gordon had left on his round-the-world tour, we had held an open house on February 27, 1966, at the newly remodeled Christian Center with Kenneth Hagin as our guest speaker. Gordon had announced that his first stop would be in Tokyo, and he would go from there to Hong Kong. Therefore, a lot of people in the city knew he should have been in

Tokyo at the time, so they called to inquire about his safety.

For two days, I had no information; however, I had a peace about it that only the Lord could give. Finally, a cable arrived from Gordon saying, "Not on ill-fated BOAC."

After the opening service, the Center stood unused for several months. Gordon and I did not seem to know exactly what God wanted us to do with it. It began to seem that the businessmen had been right — that we had purchased a "white elephant." Yet in the back of my mind was the feeling that somehow young people would be associated with this place. At the time, we had no plans for a Bible school.

So we let a young man try to start a youth work in the Christian Center. The first Saturday night found the place fairly well filled. But because he did not keep a promise concerning showing a film the second Saturday night, by the third Saturday, hardly any young people showed up. The work quickly disintegrated, and we were left with several bills to pay.

Then the devil harassed me by saying, "You got your husband to buy this white elephant, and you will be the laughingstock of the community." Secretly I began to pray, "Oh, Lord, let me live long enough to see this fiasco paid for. This $125,000 is a tremendous strain on us, and I don't want Gordon to be left alone with this burden on him."

"This is Just the Beginning"

It was in the first Kenneth Hagin seminar that summer that a little 76-year-old lady from South Africa, Catherine Raper, stood to her feet and began to prophesy. She opened her eyes and seemed to point her finger right at me where I was sitting on the platform and said, "Not only will you live long enough to see this place paid for, but this is just the beginning. This whole hill will be covered with the work of the Lord, and you will live to see it."

I thought to myself, "Dear Lord, that little old woman is just getting carried away." I was sure she knew nothing about my prayer to live long enough to see the Christian Center paid for. Yet I felt she had just stepped beyond her bounds. (In fact, I thought to myself, "That is one reason why women get themselves in trouble. They talk too much, and they talk out of turn." And I reinforced my position of doubt with the thought, "Now, Mrs. Raper doesn't know what is out here on this hill, but I do. There are motels and apartment houses, and how in the wide world could they ever fit into anything we would be associated with for the work of the Lord?" It was beyond my wildest imagination.)

I hoped no one would come to me after the service with questions about it. I was embarrassed over the prophecy, and prayed people would forget it. Then I dismissed it from my mind.

Some eight years later, a lady who was present that day came to me and asked, "Do you remember that little old lady's prophecy? How she said this whole hill would be covered with the work of the Lord?"

Tornado in Topeka

Attending that first seminar were Mr. and Mrs. Bert Line of Topeka, Kansas. They were very interested in receiving the baptism in the Holy Spirit; so after the service, we took them into the office and gave them a few simple instructions. Both of them received without any delay.

Later that day, news came over the radio that a tornado had gone through Topeka, doing $10 million worth of damage. The Lines came to me with this information. Immediately I encouraged them in the Lord. I said, "When you were receiving the Holy Spirit this afternoon and were using your prayer language, you did not know for what you were praying. But our great God Who knows everything, surely must have known that tornado was coming. And I just have a feeling that you prayed for God's protection over your home and all that belongs to you."

They were not able to get a phone call through because the power and telephone lines were down as a result of the storm. However, they decided not to go home but to stay for the remainder of the seminar. When finally Mr. Line was able to make contact, he found that the dividing line of the tornado was the street on which their house stood. The buildings across the street from them were almost all completely destroyed. Their house had not been touched!

A New Name

Through all these years, the work of The Voice of Healing had been taking on greater and greater dimensions. It had evolved from a magazine which initially had reported the ministry of only one evangelist (William Branham) and now was a worldwide missionary organization with an ever-increasing scope of activities. Therefore, we began to see the need for changing to a name which would accurately reflect our enlarged ministry.

Thus it was in May 1967, some 19 years after The Voice of Healing was started, the name Christ For The Nations was adopted.

The Stamp Collection

For years, Gordon had only one hobby, and that was collecting stamps. As a result, there wasn't a country in the world, no matter how small, whose location he did not know. Usually, he had a lot of additional information about it, also.

He used this hobby as one means of keeping contact with his two sons when he was home, as generally he was able to inveigle them into helping him paste the stamps in his albums. This he had done for many years, but by now his work was so demanding that he felt he did not have the time to continue. Besides, the boys were now grown, so there was no longer this incentive.

Thus, he decided to sell the albums, and accordingly ran an ad to that effect in a stamp journal. He had no idea of their actual value. It would have cost perhaps several thousand dollars to have ascertained the exact value because of the huge quantity of stamps he had.

The first person to inquire about the albums was a man who offered him $3,000. Gordon refused to sell. The next person who came offered him $5,000. Again he refused to sell.

One day when I was in prayer suddenly the figure $10,000 kept coming to me in connection with the sale of the albums. When I went into Gordon's room, I asked him, "Do you know what figure keeps coming to me for the albums?"

"What?" he asked.

I replied, "Ten thousand dollars."

With a big smile on his face he said, "That is just the figure that has been coming to me!" In faith, we began to thank God that it would be so.

A few days later, a man called on the phone and made an appointment to see the stamp collection. When he arrived, Gordon showed him the work of Christ For The Nations. And finally, the man got around to asking what he wanted for the stamp collection. Gordon replied "Ten thousand dollars."

The man gave it a quick inspection and said, "I will take it." He gave Gordon $10,000, and the sale was made. Gordon invested that money in the work of the Lord.

God Supplies Missionary's Needs

It was during the August 1967 seminar when I had gone to the platform to make some announcements between the morning teaching sessions, that the Lord moved upon me in an unusual way. As I walked to the podium, my eyes were drawn to a denominational missionary, Ford Wilson, who had just lost his ministerial papers in Mexico because of being filled with the Holy Spirit. He had been asked to vacate the parsonage and leave the automobile which belonged to his organization. Missionary Wayne Myers had encouraged him to come to Christ For The Nations Seminar, and there he sat that particular day.

I had heard of his circumstances, but just did not know how we could possibly help him. We were already struggling to fulfill the obligations we had in building Native Churches, supplying literature, and making payments on the Christian Center.

But that morning, my eyes were attracted to him. For a moment, it seemed the Spirit of God was drawing me in his direction. I could not understand it, for I had no intention of receiving an offering then. I stood there, not knowing exactly what to do, and yet fearful of missing God. So I urged everyone to pray.

After a few moments of prayer, I felt impressed to share the predicament of the Ford Wilson family, and the need for securing a car, furniture and money to rent a house. No sooner had I stated the facts when Helga Zidermanis, who had escaped the clutches of Hitler and had lost her husband, gave the first $100. (My diary one week later states: "Helga needed $27 to go to New Mexico for a week of prayer services where she was to speak. She had no money. She looked in her purse and found an envelope with no name on it with ten $20 bills!!! Praise God!")

Next an elderly, retired Methodist minister said he wanted to give $1,000. Then a young woman with three stair-step boys who had a few months earlier buried her missionary husband in Mexico, said she felt impressed to draw her savings of $1,165.15 and give it to the Ford Wilsons. (A couple of days later, she came into the office bringing her check for that amount.)

The superintendent of schools from a northern city who sat in the rear of the auditorium began to weep. In a moment, he raised his hand and said, "The Lord told me to give $4,500 for the purchase of the car."

Within five minutes, God met the needs of this missionary who had dared to follow the Lord in spite of rebuffs by his organization. Eight years later, his oldest son studied for the ministry at Christ For The Nations Institute.

Today (May 1998), all of Ford Wilson's three children are in full-time ministry as are also the widow's three stair-step boys. One of them, Marcos Witt, is Mexico's leading Christian singer/songwriter. Many thousands attend his crusades in Spanish-speaking nations.

Chapter Fifteen

Through 35 years of my diary notes, ever and anon I see the words, "Fasting and praying today," "day of fasting and prayer," "fasting today," "concluding several days of fasting and prayer." When we came to a difficult decision, we knew we must follow the example and admonition of Christ to fast (Matt. 17:21). Also Paul enjoined us to "give yourselves to fasting and prayer" (I Cor. 7:5).

The Joggers

In our dedication to spiritual matters, we sometimes tended to neglect the physical. Therefore, every so often Gordon and I would take steps to incorporate some type of physical exercise into our already overcrowded schedule.

In 1968, we had decided to start jogging a mile each day. We lived near a shopping center, and on this particular brisk day in March, we were running through that area. Gordon, always somewhat faster than I, was a little ahead of me. As I was tagging along behind, panting and running, I saw a car with two policemen in it.

They were observing me, and after a bit they pulled alongside of me and stared. Finally they inquired, "Anything wrong?"

"No, I'm just jogging," I said.

Both of the policemen began to laugh. They said that one of the employees of the shopping center had put in a call to the police department saying that a man was running through the shopping center with a woman close on his heels! They had assumed there was trouble and no doubt a homicide was about to be committed! I assured them that all was well and thanked them for their concern.

After that, Gordon and I chose other routes for our jogging, rather than the shopping center where employees could observe us.

God's Compensations

Sometimes the children of ministers and missionaries seem to be at a disadvantage because they move around, as the old saying goes, "from pillar to post." Oft times they are transferred from school to school even in a single year. Sometimes as in the case of our children, when we traveled, there were periods when we, the parents, actually taught them by correspondence course.

Nevertheless, through the years I have observed that when a family is dedicated to the

Lord, the children don't actually lose a thing by way of education. In fact, often the "handicaps" have a way of turning into advantages. For these children learn the cultures of different people and learn to adjust quickly to various situations. After all, travel does broaden a person.

As I read my diary, I see every so often where one of our children was honored. For instance, when Dennis started his senior year at Southern California College, he was president of his class. He also received an athletic scholarship during the same year and was honored as best all-round athlete of the year.

So we felt that God amply compensated our children for any sacrifices they had to make for the ministry.

"From Martha to Mary"

After the purchase of the Christian Center, we began to hold seminars in it two or three times a year, with leading Charismatic ministers such as Kenneth Hagin and John Osteen. During one such seminar, John Osteen spoke to me through the Spirit that my ministry had been submerged in Gordon's, but that God was going to give me signs and wonders, and my ministry would one day come forth in its own right.

I did not immediately see myself launching out, as I felt my ministry was being a helpmate to Gordon. However I was to find some nine years later, that God would indeed give me signs and miracles, and there was a need that I launch forward in faith through the open door which the Lord had presented me.

Another time the Lord spoke directly to me at the Christian Center through Clara Grace, a woman with a beautiful spirit of prophecy. She said that my ministry was changing "from Martha to Mary." I pondered that prophecy, and in time saw that my ministry was shifting from an administrative one and one of being exceedingly given to detail, to one of spiritual leadership.

The Warning Dream

After paying for the property we had purchased behind Christian Center, we were now ready to launch into the construction of the headquarters for Christ For The Nations and the printing building. Actually, we were overcrowded in every department — to say the least.

Throughout the Bible, there are instances where God spoke to individuals through dreams. One such experience came to me the night of November 13, 1968. I dreamed that the men who were constructing our new headquarters building were placing it at the wrong end of the property. After a bit I woke up, fell asleep again, and dreamed virtually the same dream. Again I woke up, fell asleep and dreamed the same dream a third time.

When morning came, I couldn't figure out what it was all about, as I was sure the contractor knew exactly which end of the property on which to put the building. And so I dismissed it from my mind.

We were leaving in two days to take a tour group to Israel. The day before leaving, Gordon and I drove over to the building site. As I stood there looking at the pegs outlining the location of the building, I was surprised to see that it was at the opposite end of the property from where we had planned it. I mentioned this to Gordon, and he calmly remarked, "Oh, these are no doubt just preliminary stakes and have nothing to do with the location of the building."

Suddenly, recalling the three dreams I had had the night before, I said to Gordon, "Let's talk to the foreman."

To our amazement he confirmed what I suspected. He had misunderstood, and was actually putting the building at the opposite end of the property from where we wanted it. This would have caused no end of problems as we needed the print shop loading docks next to the street. The warning dream had come just in time!

Miracles Unlimited

God has always been our help as we have

conducted numerous tour groups of varying
sizes to the Holy Land and to other countries.
One such instance was when we were in Egypt.
We were preparing to mount camels in order to
ride to the pyramids. The camel corral was across
the street from where our bus had stopped on an
incline. Traffic came down the hill at a rapid
pace, and we warned the tour members of this as
they left the bus to cross the street.

But a heavyset, 82-year-old gentleman,
apparently failing to hear the instruction, crossed
the street without looking. A taxicab coming
down the hill at top speed struck the old man on
his side, tossing him into the air, and severely
injuring his arm. As he lay by the side of the road,
we quickly gathered around him and prayed for
him. He chose not to go to the hospital, and in a
matter of minutes he was up and about.

But by next morning, his arm had turned quite
blue, and by the third day, it was completely
black. A medical doctor was with us, and I asked
him privately to go to the man's hotel room and
check him over. He came back with the report
that because of the man's age and excess weight,
a blood clot could very easily develop, which
could take his life.

I was greatly concerned. But the marvelous
thing about it was that the physician was a strong
Christian and encouraged me to believe the Lord

for a miracle. This we did. As a result, the old gentleman had no ill effects, but made the trip without further difficulty, as each day we watched more of the black areas fade and recede. Two months after this incident, he came to our Dallas seminar, a thousand miles from his home, none the worse for wear.

Later in this same tour, we met Gordon in Israel as he had preceded us there.

It was while we were in Jerusalem that I felt led to change the schedule for our next day's itinerary. We had first thought to go to the Red Sea for a swim, but as I was praying, I felt we should start the day off in a more serious vein. So I decided to go instead to the Shepherd's Field at Bethlehem where we could have our devotional service. Then in the afternoon, we would go to the Dead Sea and let those who wanted to swim in the salt water do so.

When we arrived at the hotel from the Shepherd's Field at noon, the moment we walked into the lobby, there was so much excitement at the registration desk that we were puzzled. Everyone was speaking at once. They were asking, "Oh, did someone in your group get killed this morning?"

"No, why?" we asked.

"You went to the Dead Sea, didn't you?"

"No," I answered, "we changed it. We decided

to go this afternoon."

The manager of the hotel looked quite relieved as he said, "We thought surely it was your group. For we heard on the news this morning that 17 rounds of ammunition were fired across the Dead Sea from the hills of Moab in Jordan. The shells hit the Lido Restaurant, and a young American missionary woman was killed and others were injured." (Fortunately, there were only a very few people at Lido so early in the morning.)

Then we realized God had miraculously redirected our steps. For had we not first gone to our devotional service at Bethlehem, our whole tour group would without doubt have been at the Lido Restaurant when the shells began falling. God had spared our lives.

That same Israel tour saw no limit to God's miraculous interventions. Another such occasion was when we were leaving Rome. All of our tour members were on board the big jet, and we had fastened our seat belts. Gordon and I sat back and breathed a sigh of relief. This was the final leg of our journey back to the states.

As this plane which was loaded to the hilt sped down the runway, I found myself waiting for the liftoff. But as the seconds ticked off, the plane did not lift. Instead all of a sudden, there was a tremendous grinding noise as though some mechanical part had broken.

The next instant we realized the pilot was desperately attempting to stop the plane as we heard the tires screeching along the concrete runway, and smelled rubber burning. The passengers were all thrown forward and were sitting on the edges of their seats. Finally, after what seemed an eternity, the plane came to a sudden halt.

The moment it did, Dennis (who was seated behind me and on his first trip to Israel, having just graduated from college) said, "Look at the hole in the wing!"

Seconds later, we saw ambulances and fire trucks come screaming alongside the plane, and we were ordered to evacuate the plane as readily as possible for fear of fire. Dennis then pointed to the end of the runway — we had only a few feet to spare!

The pilot later told us that had the equipment breakdown come a second or so later, he would never have been able to stop the plane on the runway. Not only was every seat filled, but the gas tanks were also brimful for the transatlantic flight. He told us that under the circumstances a fire would have been impossible to prevent. But God had again miraculously spared our lives!

After transferring passengers and cargo to another plane, we left for New York some six hours later on what turned out to be from then on an uneventful trip.

"Dry Bones"

It had been in October 1967 that we took our first tour group to Israel. Carole, who was working with us at Christ For The Nations headquarters, had told us on a couple of occasions that she had a real burden for Israel. She made plans to go with us on this trip to Israel. She talked as though she might stay there.

But the night before we were to leave, I noticed she was packing her suitcase with just enough clothes for a two-week trip. When I mentioned this to Gordon, he replied, "Don't say anything to her about it. Unless God lays it on her heart to stay in Israel, it would be useless."

So she accompanied us to Israel. Finally, the tour was over, and we were leaving the hotel in Jerusalem for the airport in Tel Aviv. All the tour members and the baggage were already in the bus. I was paying the bill at the desk, when Carole came hurriedly up to me, saying, "I've decided to stay in Israel." When I reminded her that her suitcase was already on the bus, she wouldn't be dissuaded. So her dad suggested she ride the bus with us the 45 minutes to Tel Aviv, and she could pull off her luggage there. This she did.

She has lived and worked in Israel ever since,

and her love for the people of that land has never waned. Mastering the Hebrew language has been a challenge to her. But by attending the Ulpan, the Hebrew University of Jerusalem, and for a period, living and working on a kibbutz, she was able to do this. Now she is able to teach the Bible to Israelis in their own language, and God seems to have given her a rapport with the officials of that nation from the least to the highest.

In 1969, Gordon asked Carole to produce a film on Israel. (She had helped make one film earlier — of Mexico.) She began shooting the Israel film which she titled "Dry Bones." When it came time to write the script, she was at a total loss. She made several attempts to write, but each time came to an impasse.

After several days of earnestly waiting on the Lord, the Holy Spirit began to lead her. Suddenly, she found herself saying, "What better scriptwriters could there be to show the fulfillment of prophecy in Israel than Isaiah, Jeremiah, Daniel, Ezekiel and Zechariah?"

This then was the answer. So instead of writing her own script, she began to search the Scriptures. Thus the words of the ancient prophets became the complete narration for the film. Not a word was used apart from the Old Testament Scriptures.

One day while Carole was shooting "Dry Bones," I received a telephone call from her. She said it had rained steadily for three months, and this had greatly hindered the completion of the film. She needed eight days of sunshine as the crew was committed to start work on another film in eight days.

I told her we would join our prayers with hers and assured her that she would have sunshine. Gordon and I went immediately to prayer. Later, we received word from her that the sun began to shine and shone unfailingly for the next eight days. She was able to complete the filming on schedule!

After the film was finished, it was shown not only in some of the largest churches in America, but it was also used as Israel's official entry into film festivals in San Francisco, California, and Barcelona, Spain. The Israeli minister of tourism has also shown the film, and often when it is viewed by Jewish audiences, it brings copious tears to their eyes. They are made to realize that their dispersion throughout the world and their regathering back to Israel, is not by accident, but was foretold by God Himself through Isaiah, Jeremiah, and the other Old Testament prophets.

At the time the film was completed, Golda Meir was prime minister of Israel. She asked to have a private showing of "Dry Bones" in her home, and was exceedingly gracious to Carole on that occasion.

Other Films

During the 1972 Olympics, Gordon, Carole, Dennis and Ginger were in Munich, Germany. Carole was able to produce a tremendous sound and color 40-minute film, "My Witnesses," showing the effectiveness of the Christian youth witnessing during the international event which was so tragically marred by the hatred and violence of the Palestinian terrorists.

Carole had also helped produce a number of other shorter films in Israel — including one on the archaeological findings at what is believed to be Solomon's stables in the area of Armageddon.

For a few years, Gordon had talked about filming a documentary on the outreaches of Christ For The Nations, but the price quoted by commercial film companies was always about $1,000 per minute. So because he never had the funds in advance, he would drop the idea.

After Gordon's death, Carole volunteered to do the film for Christ For The Nations and was assigned the task. She produced a 32-minute documentary which I like to call, "Acts in Action." Many believe this is her finest film, as she has grown up with the ministry of Christ For The Nations and has a personal insight that no doubt a less familiar person, even though professional, might have lacked. The intimate touch comes through in her production.

About 125 copies of Carole's film are in circulation and are in constant demand throughout the world. Harry Spykerman, missionary in South Africa, told me that several thousand young people had accepted Christ as Savior as a result of the showing of Carole's Munich film, "My Witnesses," in that country.

Fire!

Shortly after Carole had finished the CFN documentary film, she was spending a few days with our dean of women's daughter, Bobbi Hromas, in Rolling Hills, California.

A forest fire was raging all about them, destroying many homes in the area. By now it was burning across the street from the Hromas' home. A heavy wind was blowing. Bobbi and Carole went outside and commanded the fire to cease, praying in the Spirit as they walked back and forth. And a miracle of miracles happened. The wind changed its course, and the Hromas' home was saved!

A few weeks later, I had the privilege of speaking in the Hromas' home to about 100 of her neighbors — lawyers, doctors and scientists. Twenty received the baptism in the Holy Spirit that day, including her son, who studied at Wheaton College.

Praise the Lord for Petunias!

For years, Gordon had depended upon me to handle most of the business affairs of Christ For The Nations, leaving him free to speak in conventions and seminars, to write his many books, to serve as editor of our monthly magazine, and to oversee the worldwide foreign missions program.

He told me one day that he would like to have the two and a half acres of land that joined our property to the rear. So for three and a half years, I negotiated with the elderly woman and her son, who owned the land — and got exactly nowhere. Finally one morning while in prayer, the Lord spoke to me by a still, small voice and said, "The property is yours already." I rose to my feet and felt led to go immediately to the owner again.

I knocked on the front door several times, but there was no response. The devil said, "Ha, ha, ha! So the Lord told you to come, did He?"

I stood there a moment wondering what to do and what my next step should be. Then a still, small voice said, "Go around to the back. You will find her working among the flowers."

That's what I did ... and there she was! Instead of talking about the property, we started talking about flowers. I told her how my mother had over 100 different kinds of flowers in her garden, and how she always got "starts" from every neighbor in the vicinity.

At last it appeared that I had found a point of common interest, and for the first time seemed to have a rapport with the little old woman. And the next thing I knew, the trunk of my car was filling up with "starts" and "shoots." Before I left, she had called her son, and we had negotiated the purchase of the property! Today it is part of the lovely campus of our institute.

Just in Time!

When we had made the move to Dallas from Shreveport, we bought property just across the street from the city limits. There we built the headquarters office and the print shop. It so happened that soon a beautiful residential district developed all around us. So, when that whole area was later zoned residential, our print shop was considered nonconforming.

On July 30, 1969, when our new, larger headquarters was completed, we moved into it. According to the law in Dallas, the owner of a nonconforming building is given six months to sell it, should he move out. But if it is not sold in that length of time, the zoning of the property becomes the same as the adjacent property, which in our case was residential.

When we attempted to get a commercial appraisal, we were informed that the property on which these two large buildings sat, could be appraised only as residential, since if we failed to sell within the allotted six months, the buildings would have to be torn down, and the land sold for residential property! This would have meant a substantial loss for Christ For The Nations.

So after the move into the new offices, we began to pray more earnestly about the sale of our older buildings. One month passed ... two months ... three months ... four months ... five months. We were now in our sixth month and, by this time, we were not only praying fervently, but desperately. We felt it was not God's will that we should take such a loss of property due to the zoning that had resulted, and which was in no way our fault. So we implored the Lord to intervene in our behalf and to send us a commercial buyer.

Three days before the deadline, my diary reads: "Sold Bonnie View property for cash. Great miracle! Three days short of the six-month city law before land would revert to residential." It truly was a great answer to prayer!

The Grand Piano

One of the unique features of Christ For The Nations' ministry has been a monthly interdenominational ladies' luncheon that began shortly after we bought the Christian Center in January, 1966, and continued once each month for many years. I carried several reports in *Christ For The Nations* magazine, encouraging other Charismatic women to organize similar luncheons in their own communities. And when time permitted, I accepted invitations to help start some of them.

Now through the years, we have been happy to see several large groups do that very thing. In fact, the Women's Aglow fellowship is one example. It now has regular meetings in many cities throughout America and many nations.

Our own ladies' group has been responsible for helping build well over 100 churches in foreign lands. Besides that, we have helped missionaries in securing equipment such as cars, refrigerators, stoves, washing and sewing machines, etc.

I recall one particular time Carole said to me, "Mother, you really need a grand piano in that Christian Center."

I responded with, "Where would we get the money for a grand piano?"

But when we had our next Ladies' Day meeting, I felt impressed to say, "Perhaps there is someone here today who would like to give a grand piano in memory of a loved one." It so happened that a lady was present who had just come to Dallas from California to bury an aged aunt. This aunt had purchased a new grand piano, but had not really even broken it in. The niece came to me after the service and said she would like to give the piano in memory of her aunt.

We secured a piano company's moving truck, and within a few hours, the almost-new instrument was placed in Christian Center and has been a source of blessing ever since!

Pat Boone

Throughout the years, Gordon and I have been privileged to meet some celebrities. One such time, was when we received a call from Gordon's friend, George Otis, saying that Pat and Shirley Boone would like us to spend Sunday afternoon with them.

It so happened that when Red Foley, Shirley Boone's father and well-known country and western singer, died suddenly, she and her family were nearly overcome with grief. Friends revealed that she would "commune" with her father by attending seances. In her grief, she was being drawn in that direction, when the Otis family learned about it. Immediately, George called Gordon and asked him to airmail a set of books on sorcery. Gordon did, and when the Boones read the books, their understanding was enlightened, and they avoided this pitfall.

Since Gordon had been promising a minister friend in Los Angeles that he would speak for him the first opportunity he had, he called his friend. The minister invited him to speak that Sunday night. So we left the next day for Los Angeles, and on Sunday, visited the Boone home.

When we entered the spacious home, I was a little uneasy until the radiant Shirley arrived. She said Pat was at the hospital visiting one of his actor friends who was dying. Immediately, George suggested that we join hands in the foyer and have a special prayer, both for the dying man and for Pat. As we did, Shirley and her two sisters began at once to pray in their prayer language. Upon hearing this, I felt perfectly at home.

Fifteen minutes later, Pat walked in, modestly dressed, wearing his familiar white shoes and California suntan. His friend had taken a turn for the better, so he felt he was able to leave him to keep his appointment with us. He shared with us the blessings that Gordon's books had been to him in his search for truth. Then he told how the Lord had baptized him in the Holy Spirit (he was a Church of Christ minister) after Shirley had received the experience.

Later when Pat went to Israel, he was very well received by the nation, partly because he had written the music for the film "Exodus." Carole renewed her acquaintance with the Boones, and accompanied Pat on the piano in his singing engagements during that visit.

Chapter Sixteen

As I read through my diary, I marvel at the preservation of the Lord. One such time was on February 17, 1970, when Carole was driving her car in Israel. A couple of servicemen suddenly stepped out into the road in the night wanting to hitch a ride. To avoid hitting them, Carole swung the car quickly. She lost control, and the car turned over three times, shattering the windows and practically demolishing it.

As the soldiers saw what had happened, they ran excitedly to the scene of the accident. But to their amazement, Carole and her girlfriend crawled out of the car unscathed. Fortunately, the car was insured.

Several times my youngest son, Dennis, was in similar accidents in which his car rolled over. One such time was after he had married his college sweetheart, Ginger, and they were working with Youth With A Mission at the Munich Olympics. He had borrowed a chaplain's car, and he and Ginger were headed toward Munich, when suddenly a large truck, coming toward them from the opposite direction forced them off the road. They turned over, and the car was demolished. But worse yet, both Dennis and Ginger were thrown from the car.

As Dennis hurried to Ginger's side, she lay with blood pouring out of a wound in her head. Suddenly her eyes rolled back and she began going into convulsions. Dennis felt that unless he got ahold of God, she was gone.

Kneeling beside her at the side of the road, Dennis laid his hands upon her and rebuked death, asking the Lord to preserve her life for the ministry. Immediately, the convulsions stopped. When the ambulance arrived, they rushed her to a hospital where she was examined and told that she had a brain concussion. However, after several days, God had completely healed her, and she was able to leave the hospital.

A notation in my diary of July 18, 1970, says: "Today, God answered four prayers. Some people pray all their lives and cannot really say the Lord answered a single prayer."

A Burden for a Bible School

Four years had gone by since we purchased the Christian Center. One day after Gordon had been in prayer, he came to me and said he felt we should start a Bible school. I reminded him that starting a school was work for a younger man, and he was now past 60. I suggested to him that he was already doing more than most men, that his schedule was too heavy, and why not leave something for someone else to do?

When we talked to our three children about it, each one in turn discouraged him. Carole said, "Daddy, have you ever heard of a single Christian college making it financially? They are always in debt, and some of them are going bankrupt." Then she asked him, "How much money do you have?" When he didn't answer, she answered for him, "You don't have one red cent to start that school, so forget it."

Several weeks later I heard her tell a friend, "My dad acts as if he doesn't hear one word we're saying about that school. He's going right ahead making plans as if to start it."

Another few weeks passed, and one day he brought up the subject once more. I said, "You are not really serious?" And again I reminded him of his age.

He looked at me earnestly and added, "The Lord told me that He would not take me until this school is established."

That sparked faith in my heart, and I said, "If the Lord told you that, then let's go." Immediately, we threw things into motion and made an announcement in the magazine that we were going to start a Bible training school in September 1970.

When we began to pray about teachers, I suggested to Gordon, "In place of having a large faculty, which we really can't afford, why not bring in special speakers for the 11 a.m. class? That way both students and the local people could benefit." He thought the idea was a good one, and we made plans accordingly.

So we started the school with Gordon and one other teacher on the faculty, and brought in a number of excellent faith teachers during that first year for the 11 a.m. classes. Before the year was completed, we added the third full-time teacher. Our enrollment was about 50 students.

The day after the zoning was granted, we were visited by a gentleman who owned five apartment houses joining our property. He informed us that he had been told he was dying of cancer and had only six months to live. He did not want his wife to have to worry about the apartments after he was gone. (His wife told me privately that on two occasions the doctor told her he probably would not live more than a month.) In his early years, he had pitched in major baseball leagues for 12 years, but now the ravages of cancer were plainly visible on his face.

He urged us to take the apartments off his hands, and asked no down payment on four of them. We were able to name our own price, and he graciously accepted.

A Step of Faith

So now we owned five apartment houses and had 50 students. It was a tremendous step of faith. But to top it all off, this gentleman concluded by saying he had a building 75 feet from our campus next to the freeway. Half of it was leased to a restaurant chain. He wanted us to pick up the existing indebtedness against it, and we could have his equity.

It was a difficult decision to make because the payments on it were $500 a month, and the restaurant was bringing in only $300. However after prayer, both Gordon and I felt we should go ahead. We did, and within a week I had leased the other half to a beauty shop for three years for $300. Thus the building was able to pay its own way.

After the beauty shop's lease ran out, they moved to another location. I ran an ad in the paper for a full month without receiving a single inquiry. One day as I was in prayer, my youngest son said to me, "You know that place where the beauty shop was would make an ideal bookstore — right on the freeway."

"I don't want any bookstore," I said. "We are too involved already."

Within a few hours, two other employees came to me, each unknown to the other, and made a similar suggestion. The Bible says that by the mouth of two or three witnesses a matter shall be established (Deut. 19:15). I knew it was God.

So we opened our bookstore, which has been a great blessing to the community and to our students as well. (Gordon had always talked about a bookstore but had never gotten around to opening one. And this lovely bookstore was opened on the date of his first anniversary in heaven.)

Across the street from our headquarters building was a small piece of property (50' x 175') that joined the land we already owned. The owner felt he had us "over a barrel" so was asking an exorbitant price of $15,000. Actually, we owned the land on all four sides of him, so we reminded him that without even a front, he might have to get to his land by helicopter, for we would just build the new institute around him.

We then committed the matter to the Lord. Three days later, the owner called back and offered to sell us the property for $3,000, which was a fair market price, and to which we agreed.

Gordon's New Shoes

As I have indicated, it never took much of this world's goods to make Gordon happy. Usually, he had just one pair of good shoes. He would wear these until a "full moon" would appear on the soles. He always considered it an imposition to take time to shop. Shopping for a suit or shoes was a necessary evil.

But now, he was getting ready to make a trip around the world, and seeing the sad condition of his shoes, I implored him to get a new pair. With the usual reluctance and lack of enthusiasm, he finally responded.

Because I had a speaking appointment, I did not get to take him to the airport to see him off the morning he left. I had, however, packed his suitcase. I didn't include shoes because he never wanted that extra weight, and besides, he always kept just one good pair.

Two years later his host in India, Dr. Rao, minister of tourism for Andhra Pradesh, South India, attended our annual seminar in Dallas, and when he spoke, he brought greetings from India. Then he told how he and a large gathering of people had gone to the airport to meet Gordon. There as they watched, Gordon came walking down the ramp, smiling and waving. But when he reached the bottom step, Dr. Rao noticed he was wearing two different-looking shoes — one *very* old and one brand new! Before taking him to speak to the 1,100 denominational ministers at the conference, Dr. Rao quickly rushed Gordon to a friend's shoe store and bought him a pair of shoes — that matched!

By now, everyone at the seminar was roaring with laughter. As I observed Gordon, he had that little boyish smile on his face and twinkle in his eyes that told me he would have the last word.

When he went to the pulpit, he said, "The thing that troubled me was not finding out in India that I had on a pair of different shoes. What really disturbed me was when I got back to Dallas and looked in my closet. Lo and behold, there was another pair just like the one I had left in India!" The truth of the matter was, he usually bought new shoes only when forced to, because his old ones were beyond repair, and I would dispose of them immediately. For some reason, this time I hadn't. Just how complicated could life get? He was confused, so he just picked up the first two shoes that caught his eye.

One thing that puzzled me about that episode, was that Gordon had already made several stops with missionaries in other countries before arriving in India. Why hadn't they called attention to his shoes? Surely they must have noticed. Perhaps they were being polite or maybe even a little embarrassed. They probably all had a good laugh after he was gone.

And had Dr. Rao not told about it that day in Dallas, I would never have known, for Gordon hadn't said one word to me about it.

What happened to that mismatched pair of

shoes in his closet? I have an idea that on one of
the very first nights home when he was writing,
long after I had fallen asleep, he probably crept
silently to the garbage can — shoes in hand.

Such a man was our daddy!

Indira Gandhi

Through Dr. Rao, we received a personal
invitation to meet Indira Gandhi. He had
arranged the appointment in conjunction with
our annual Israel tour, so we would be able to
continue our journey on from Israel.

On March 29, 1972, in New Delhi, we had an
audience with Indira Gandhi, and I presented her
with a Bible. (Gordon had written several Scriptures the Lord had given him for her in the
flyleaf.) We also gave her a check of $5,000 for
relief for the children who were victims of the
war between East and West Pakistan. India
finally joined forces with East Pakistan in order
to stop the carnage, and in the fighting, a goodly
number of Indian soldiers had lost their lives,
also.

Mrs. Gandhi's response was very warm in
receiving both the Bible and the check, and we
assured her that the Christians of America were
praying for her in the tremendous responsibility
that had been placed upon her shoulders in gov-
erning the land. She told us she had received

many encouraging letters from America and was grateful for them.

Riot in Bangladesh

From India, we flew to Bangladesh, where we met with some of the missionaries who had suffered tremendously at the hands of the invaders. One particular instance concerned a missionary and his wife who were in their home in Dacca when the invading army of West Pakistan overran the city. Several soldiers came into their home and ordered the husband out of the room. They then told the woman to remove her clothes and lie on the bed, intending to rape her. Both of the missionaries began to look to God for strength and direction, whereupon the husband defied the invaders, and told them he would not leave the room, and his wife would not disrobe and subject herself to them. And having said it, he stood defiantly before them!

This boldness seemed to disarm and amaze the soldiers momentarily. Then they hastily withdrew from the house, without harming either of these dedicated missionaries.

Upon our return from Bangladesh, I wrote the following account in *Christ For The Nations* magazine:

"The bright sunshiny day had begun in a leisurely way with early morning Bible-reading

and prayer, then breakfast at 8 a.m. with one of
the missionaries who had labored in Bangladesh
for nearly two decades. Her husband was at the
airport, seeing off their co-worker who had
become ill. So, Gordon and I listened intently
over breakfast at the Intercontinental Hotel to an
eyewitness report of the war conditions in
Bangladesh during the past year, from the lips of
this brave, but tired-looking, little woman. She
told how first the foreign property owners were
liquidated, then one to three million of their own
people killed.

"In the course of conversation, the missionary
called attention to three people sitting not far
from us — a physician and two concerned citizens of Europe, who were there to give help to
the women who had been raped in the war. The
missionary had attended a meeting the day
before in which they were appealing for funds
for a rehabilitation home for these unfortunate
girls.

"After concluding our breakfast, she took us
to their table, introduced us, and from the three,
we heard a heartrending story. Nearly 200,000
women had been raped by the West Pakistani
army upon orders from their superiors, thinking
this was one of the quickest way to subjugate the
nation.

"The missionary and I were invited to

accompany the doctor to the clinic where these young women were being given medical attention. We were to meet in the lobby in 20 minutes.

"Fifteen minutes later I came into the lobby, and seeing no one I knew, walked onto the large front lawn. There I saw and heard what papers later said were 600 demonstrators, loudly yelling and marching on the street in front of the hotel. A press photographer with a camera was filming the procession from atop a large, locked iron gate and tall fence which completely enclosed the grounds, so I took a couple of snaps, thinking those shots would be interesting. Noticing that the men were angrily looking in the direction of the hotel, I became uneasy. Suddenly, I noticed that by now the men had stopped at the main gate of the hotel, and apparently were trying to force entry. Several uniformed guards were remonstrating vociferously with them.

"Suddenly, the pressure of the force gave way, and the marchers broke through the gate as they headed running and screaming for the hotel. By now the missionary had spotted me, and together we rushed into the lobby, hoping to get to our seventh floor room. I suggested the elevator, but she cried, 'No!' Then I started through the door for the narrow stairway right beside it as I saw half a dozen employees run through it. But she grabbed my arm and shouted, 'Don't get caught in there!' A second later, the flood of raging men poured into the stairway. Apparently, they wanted to get to the hotel manager's office on the second floor.

"The riot was inspired by outside forces, we were told later — namely communists. Some of the protesters were from a closed, nearby hotel and were in pursuit of employees who had not backed the protesters in their strike against the Intercontinental Hotel.

"The missionary and I raced for the doors and headed for the garden area where we hid behind tall shrubs. Soon we were joined by a man wearing a Red Cross insignia along with several other men and a woman. From inside, we heard the breaking of glass amid loud shouts.

"After about 25 minutes of hiding, we started again for the lobby which was in shambles with strewn glass from dishes, bottles, broken doors, and plate glass windows. Just then the army trucks and soldiers arrived, whereupon machine guns began to spue forth a volley of rat-a-tat-tat, interspersed with single gunshot sounds. We ran for cover to the high 10-foot garden wall, thinking at first to climb it. The missionary advised against it, saying that if we were caught on the wall, we would be fired upon. So we crouched low against the building among some thorny bushes. In another 20 minutes or so, we tried unsuccessfully to mount the stairs. But by now the wounded were being carried out (about 20 in all, the papers stated, six of whom were shot), as fighting once more erupted with staves, iron bars, wooden clubs and guns.

"We ran into the ladies' lounge, but after staying there for a short time, the missionary was reminded that in the adjoining men's room, a bomb had been planted a few months earlier, which caused $100,000 damage to that very hotel. We left for the dining room, which was completely deserted of all personnel. Furniture was overturned. Glass was everywhere. Food was on the floor, the drapes and the walls. We tried several doors of shops, but each by now had been tightly locked. We later found one open, but after entering it, decided the glass windows were a hazard. Finally, we started for the elevators again, but by now they were out of commission. We asked some men if the stairs were safe and were told that possibly they were, and that we must go to our rooms and stay there for safety. We ran up seven flights of steps as rapidly as possible, and breathed a sigh of relief as Gordon opened the door for us. Our room was high up away from the street side with the noisy air conditioning window unit droning away. Gordon was busily writing, and had not even heard the firing of the machine guns or the riot.

"By now soldiers were everywhere. We watched from our window as they flushed the rioters (who papers later said also robbed the hotel cashier of all the monies) out of the block-long garden, and patrolled the roofs and halls.

"Later that night, we learned that the European lady had talked to the leader of the mob and told him she was personally responsible for the safety of two American women, and that they were not to be touched. She had helped escort us on the steps to safety. How we thanked God that He had spared our lives. Two hours later, we watched from our windows as hundreds of additional strikers again assembled a block away. Carrying their banners, they crossed the street as if to march on the hotel a second time. After about 10 minutes, we saw them disband. (As we opened our door the next morning to check out, there were two soldiers standing with long guns outside our room, apparently to protect us.)

"After the riot had subsided, the doctor came and informed us that he had a plane to catch later that afternoon, and if we wanted to see the clinic, we must go at once. He had ordered a Red Cross ambulance, and felt we would be safe. Once more, following closely on the heels of the doctor, we made it through the glass-strewn, blood-spattered lobby, still filled with soldiers and fiercely shouting rioters. Inside the ambulance, we felt a measure of safety as soldiers motioned us through the hotel gates.

"The scene we saw inside the clinic is one we shall never forget. The elderly doctor put his arm around a young 12-year-old girl as he told us her story. Raped and pregnant, both parents killed in the war, she had been brought to the clinic. Here we saw girls in all stages of pregnancy. The European lady said that when they came into the waiting room, they often crumpled to the floor in a small heap, facing the wall, with their saris covering their faces to hide their shame. She then would go over to them, crouch on the floor beside them and put her arm around them. Suddenly, two big, brown eyes would peer out from under the sari, eyes oh, so sad, and not a little bewildered that someone would love them. No questions were asked, no names were given, no forms filled out, no money required, as generally they brought nothing in their hands. After the baby was delivered, there was no place for the girls in the clinic to go. The doctor told us that most of the girls in the clinic were between 12 and 16 years of age. As we passed from room to room, we witnessed the truthfulness of his statement — they were just little girls.

"The culture of the Muslim people prohibits marriage for any girl not a virgin. In many instances, she is rejected and cast out by her own family. For a higher-class family, the injustice seems even harder to bear. Some hide their daughters to cover their shame. In the case of a married woman, she would be rejected by her husband. Their Mohammedan religion offered them no comfort. Some sources say that nearly 50,000 women committed suicide.

"That night over the dinner table we talked to the husband and wife, faithful missionaries in this land. They had prayed for an open door to minister to these girls. That day it came to Calvin and Marian Olson.

"Though we had difficulty getting in and out of the country because America had not recognized Bangladesh, we finally secured the necessary police papers for our exit.

"As we listened to one government official tell how he was imprisoned for six months without paper, pencil, book or a watch, simply staring at blank walls, he concluded, 'It's been a long year!'"

How can we ever forget this trip, the millions of eternal souls, and God's hand of protection upon us?

Chapter Seventeen

It was while we were in Philadelphia holding a seminar, that the Lord spoke to me one afternoon, telling me He was going to provide an organ and a piano for the new Christ For The Nations Institute (CFNI) which was then under construction.

That evening when I started to receive the offering, I was a little nonplussed at exactly how to proceed. So I stood there momentarily, and then told the audience that the Lord said He was going to supply an organ and piano, but that I didn't know exactly how He was going to do it.

As I waited on the Lord, suddenly a kindly-looking little woman with graying hair came forward. With a whisper, she handed me a beautiful diamond ring which she said her late husband had given her as a wedding ring. He had paid $2,500 for it, and she wanted us to have it to buy the piano.

I was overwhelmed and deeply moved. Nothing like this had ever happened to me in a public service. I left the ring on the pulpit and said, "If you change your mind at the close of the service,

please come and claim it." However, at the conclusion of the meeting when everyone had left,
the ring was still lying there.

I took the ring to Dallas. There I talked to a
long-time friend, V.E. Morgan, who is a
co-owner of the Arnold-Morgan Piano Company, and he gave us a beautiful grand piano in
exchange for the ring.

Attending that same seminar in Philadelphia
was a hippie-looking, young man who had
recently surrendered his heart to the Lord after
having tried everything, including drugs. His
desire was to attend CFNI, and we prayed about
it at the time.

When fall came, this young man, Jimmy,
arrived in Dallas with his beard, long hair and
unkempt appearance. But within a few days,
Gordon had completely cleaned him up. Shortly
after this, he became a part of a campus singing
group. Before the school year was out, he was
the pianist for a newly-formed singing group
called the Luminaires (composed of CFNI students). They have since traveled to Africa,
Europe, Asia and around the world several times.

The lady who gave me the ring also appeared
at the institute. She took a personal interest in
Jimmy and helped him make some of the necessary adjustments to school life. While attending
school, she met a bachelor who was also

enrolled. After graduation along with other delegates, the two went to Korea to attend the Pentecostal World Conference. There they decided to get married. Guess who sang and played at the wedding? Jimmy, the young man she had helped so much, and the Luminaires!

CFNI Harvest

Many of the students who have come to CFNI have tried everything, including narcotics of every kind. While the government spends thousands of dollars trying to rehabilitate a single dying addict, often losing the battle, we have seen young people (former narcotic users, and a few still secretly using drugs even when they arrive) completely delivered, and in the two years of their stay with us, become sound, solid citizens, with a burden for lost souls.

Many former CFNI students are now scattered throughout the world preaching the Gospel. Here are just a few of their stories:

Joseph Skinner (India)

"I have been very busy since returning from CFNI. In the beginning, I did a great deal of evangelism, but in February 1974 the Lord led me to take the pastorate of the city church here in Shillong (India). The Lord told me He has many souls in the city, and He has done wonderful things by bringing many souls to the cross. We have become almost like the Early Church where the Lord added daily those who believe.

"At the same time, I traveled every month on evangelistic outreaches, preaching the Gospel to many villages in India. The main bulk of the population in India is in villages. Only 20 percent of 650 million population live in the cities and towns; the 80 percent are scattered in the villages. Last year, the Lord used us to raise up seven churches for His glory in different villages, and many more are interested.

"I do a great deal of preaching on the streets and in open-air marketplaces where the sinners are. We have seen wonderful conversions of many Hindus, animists and the untouchables, such as drunkards, gamblers and prostitutes.

"There is a definite and wonderful move of the Spirit of God in our land at the present, evident from the interest shown in the Gospel. We have seen people by the hundreds coming, and in some places, thousands of them come. This is unusual for India, but we expect to see greater multitudes in the following days. Of the total population of India, 500 million have never heard the Gospel even once. Vast areas have never been reached.

"We have to do a good deal of teaching and training for the Lord's work, as the Lord is raising up new churches. I am glad for the training I had at CFNI. It has given me a new understanding, vision and a fresh anointing from the Lord. It has really helped me a great deal in my work at present. Please continue to pray for me and the work on this side."

(Christ For The Nations later cabled Joseph Skinner $20,000 to purchase a building for a Bible training center in Shillong.)

Jeries Rihany (Jordan)

Jeries, the eldest son of Ayoub Rihany, and his two brothers attended Christ For The Nations Institute. Christ For The Nations had built Christ For Jordan Bible School in Zerka, Jordan. Some 50 students enrolled when the school opened in September 1975. Jeries is teaching in that school along with his father. Here is Jeries' story:

"As a child it was not hard to understand Jesus because He loved me, and I loved Him. As I grew up, this did not satisfy me any more. I was very curious and wanted to know more about Christ, and logically understand God and His creation. I reasoned that God created the mind for a useful purpose; therefore, it was necessary for me to develop my mind in order to understand God.

"To fulfill this desire, God provided me with an excellent opportunity. I completed high school and enrolled in the American University of Beirut, Lebanon. At the age of 24, I graduated with a B.A. degree in education.

"Immediately after graduation, I taught for a year in Al-Riyad, Saudi Arabia. Then I transferred to Jordan and taught high school physics and mathematics for three years.

"Still desiring to study more, I came to the United States and received my B.S. degree in chemistry from Eastern Mennonite College, Harrisburg, Virginia.

"All this education brought me to the conclusion that God is a master scientist with an infinite mind beyond our imagination and understanding. Christ, in Whom I believed as a child, and Whom I accepted in my heart, changed into simply God the Creator with an infinite mind. It was as if I lost my Christian faith of love and mercy. I was unsatisfied, and I condemned the world. Finally God's providence intervened.

"After graduation from Eastern Mennonite College, I gained admission to East Texas State University to work on my master's degree in organic chemistry. But being physically exhausted, I felt the need for rest. I landed in Dallas, and decided not to go to school immediately. It was as if I had reached a stalemate. God had to have a purpose for my life, but what was it?

"I remembered that Christ For The Nations had worked for many years with my father,

Ayoub Rihany, and I planned a visit to the headquarters. Mrs. Gordon Lindsay received me at
the office and invited me to enroll at Christ For
The Nations Institute. At that point, I was unde-
cided, but agreed with much hesitation to enroll.
I had been determined not to go to school immediately, but suddenly here I was back in school
again.

"I was overwhelmed by a feeling of indecision and depression. I wanted to find a purpose
to live, but where was it? I was not sure that Bible
school was the answer, so I ran away. I could not
face the reality of making a decision, so for three
days I wandered around Dallas, spending each
night in the bus station. As I wandered about, I
met by chance another student from Christ For
The Nations Institute who had been introduced
to me a few days earlier. She encouraged me to
return to the school and talk with Gordon
Lindsay.

"Brother Lindsay heard my story and told me
to go and read the book of Jonah in the Bible. A
sudden explanation flashed inside me! Could my
flight be like that of Jonah, whom God called to
preach to the inhabitants of Nineveh, and who,
because of his disobedience, spent three days and
three nights inside a great fish? It could be! But
it was certainly more convenient to spend three
days and three nights in a bus station than inside

a great fish.

"Finally I decided to stay at the institute. A few months after the semester began, Allen Beck, then institute director, suggested that I seek the baptism in the Holy Spirit. Although I had believed in the message of the Full Gospel, my immediate answer was that this baptism was not necessary. I faced no difficulty in believing in the baptism in the Holy Spirit. I had even defended it with scriptural evidences, but I never wanted it to become a part of my personal Christian experience.

"However one night with an urgent desire to pray, I had fellowship with two of my classmates, Scott Hinkle and John Lieberman. It was on that night and through these believing friends — who were Jewish — that I, an Arab, received the baptism in the Holy Spirit.

"What a marvelous experience to become like a child again and to accept Jesus by love and faith only! It is a valuable thing to have the education that life offers, but it is more valuable to have Jesus and His love. All the knowledge in the world can never save you; but Jesus surely can, for love conquers all.

"As a Christian in a Muslim country like Jordan, I felt great frustration as a student because I did not receive any Bible teaching in school. Since Jordan is a country which is 90 percent Muslim and 10 percent nominal Christian, the Muslim religion is presented as part of the public school system. There is no form of Christianity presented in the public schools to balance the spiritual education. There are a few private schools founded by various traditional religious denominations, but none presenting an evangelical view of the Full Gospel. Hence, there is an urgent need for a Bible school.

"However, since the natural resources of Jordan are very limited, and students find it hard to make a living while enrolled in a Bible school, it becomes necessary to take this fact into serious consideration, and to make arrangements to meet the vocational needs of the students. Jesus was a carpenter, and Paul a tentmaker. Now Christ For The Nations is first to establish a Christ-centered school to meet both the spiritual and vocational needs of the nation of Jordan."

Bob Humburg (U.S.A.)

Can Jesus change a man's life — even if he lives in the innermost recesses of the Bronx and is a compulsive gambler and an alcoholic? "Yes!" says Bob Humburg, a man with a vibrant and convincing personality.

To see him is to see a miracle of Jesus. His life is a living epistle that fairly advertises, "Made by Jesus." The life Bob Humburg had made for himself was a total loss. Since a teenager, he had been a drinker and a gambler. When he entered the family business in New York, he began to embezzle corporate funds to support his selfish living. "I was very self-centered," Bob confesses. "My whole life was a lie. I would lie endlessly to cover another lie, which was told to cover yet another lie."

Bob married his childhood girlfriend, Emma, who was a nominal Christian. He managed to get the huge A&P grocery account in New York City. But success never lasted long. "One of the big problems," explains Bob, "was that I always had my hand in the till. I knew I was wrong. But I couldn't quit my gambling, bookmaking and drinking. In my mind I thought I could pay everyone back. But really, I was destroying myself and everyone around me."

At 32, Bob finally called it quits and left home. Everyone was after him. Loan sharks, underworld figures to whom he owed bad debts, and people to whom he had given hot checks. In Cleveland, Ohio, he gambled until he made a big score, but he lost it as quickly as it had come. Lonely and in despair, he got a job and tried to straighten out. He even quit drinking.

Proud of himself, Bob went back to his home in New York. Again his life deteriorated — only it became worse. He lost his friends, even his old drinking pals. No longer the sharp high roller, he was looking more like a shabby tramp.

His family (he then had three children) somehow never lost all hope for him. Day and night his wife, Emma, tuned in to a Christian FM radio station. This annoyed Bob. Also, everywhere he looked there were open Bibles, tracts and books. Emma, in the desperation of her lonely situation was drawing nearer to God. Unknown to Bob, she had committed him to the Lord.

"I came home one night all bombed out," Bob recalls. "I flipped on the radio and the first thing I heard was this man asking, 'Do you want a new life?'"

"Do I want a new life?" Bob thought out loud. He had even contemplated suicide. He really did want a new life — more than anything in the world. This led him to begin listening to the radio more. Because he didn't want Emma to know, he would sneak in at night and listen. He even started reading the Bible, though he didn't understand it.

Finally at the invitation of a radio minister at 3 a.m., Bob prayed a sinner's prayer. This was the first time he had ever prayed. God dealt with him, and he wept like a baby. He was so happy, so surprised at himself, that he ran and woke up Emma with shouts of, "I've done it! I've done it!"

Emma, at first, was suspicious. It seemed Bob

had told her a million lies before. But at work the next day, the change became obvious. When Bob routinely started driving to the bar after his morning deliveries, the Lord directed him to take a left turn instead of a right. He ended up in the park reading his Bible, and this time he was enjoying it. But most of all, it was a great victory — for it represented Bob's first sober day. "If anyone *is* in Christ, *he is* a new creation; old things have passed away; behold, all things have become new" (II Cor. 5:17). Things were going to be different.

Jesus also helped deliver Bob of his gambling. The hardest thing to do was to make restitution for his past. He owed everybody in the world it seemed. But he was free in Christ Jesus. Hope had come to his life.

The Lord immediately moved him to New Jersey. There Bob found a good Bible church and began to grow. It took Bob eight years to pay old debts. His marriage was healed, and soon he came into a home prayer group which led him into the baptism in the Holy Spirit. At this juncture, Bob realized the Lord was calling him into full-time service. "I prayed mightily for direction," Bob recalls. "When I saw the great change in my daughter after her first year at Christ For The Nations Institute, I knew the Lord would have me study there."

At CFNI, Bob was soon marked for

leadership. His role among the students had been outstanding. He always bubbled over with Jesus' love. It was at the institute that Bob was impressed with a burden for Germany. His two oldest daughters, Kay and Lynn, were called to Germany, also.

"It is surprising," Bob explains, "how many people God is calling to Germany. It is as if some great spiritual battle is going to be fought and won on German soil. If Jesus can change me, He can change Germany!"

Bob and his family resided for a couple of years in Wolfenbüttel (suburb of Braunschweig) where Christ For The Nations purchased and renovated a 45,000-square-foot former factory building. Under Bob's direction, it was used as a Bible school for Germany, a seminar center, an American servicemen's retreat, a base for CFNI students laboring in Europe and a literature distribution center for Europe and the Iron Curtain countries.

In 1988, God opened the door for a new location for the school in Bad Gandersheim — a Hilter-built training camp. The school is growing, as are their month-end conferences. The Humburg's son-in-law and daughter, Mike and Kay Chance today direct the whole operation.

Anthia Hendrix (U.S.A.)

"I was raised in a Baptist church, and then

became involved in the Catholic church as I searched for a personal contact with God. I wasn't able to find this experience in the churches I had attended, and as I began to get discouraged with the Church, I began to turn away from the Christian principles I had been taught as a child.

"At 15, I had my first drug experience; by the time I was 16, I was smoking marijuana and experimenting with various kinds of drugs. My disappointment in the Church grew into a hatred and rebellion against God. Finally, I became convinced that Christianity was nothing more than a false religion centered around a dead prophet. Jesus was a vague figure Who had said and done some great things in His life, but I saw Him on the same level as Buddha, Krishna and Mohammed.

"I was on my own at 17, and had become deeply involved in drugs and in various Eastern philosophies. For two years, I traveled all over the country living in communes, working for short periods of time, and singing occasionally for enough money to make ends meet.

"While I was in Berkeley, California, God began to deal with me through the ministry of 'Holy Hubert' Lindsey. God used that man and many other people to get me to the end of myself.

"At 19, I had become very discouraged with

life, feeling I had done everything, seen everything, and been everywhere I had ever wanted. At this point of total surrender, the Lord Jesus met me, and I was gloriously saved and later baptized in the Holy Spirit.

"Almost immediately after I committed my life to the Lord, I felt a definite call to the ministry. I began seeking the Lord about a Bible school, and God gave me many confirmations about coming to Christ For The Nations."

(After completing the two-year course at CFNI, Anthia began working for the Lord in Germany.)

Ezekiel Guti (Rhodesia — Now Zimbabwe)

Ezekiel Guti was raised in a pagan home in Chipinga District near Umtali in Rhodesia. His father died when he was a very young child, and he was reared by his mother who believed in the ancestor worship of the Mashona tribe. One day, Ezekiel's mother visited a neighboring village where a white missionary was holding a revival meeting. Mother Guti rushed home telling her children about an eternal place called "hell" and that it actually burned forever.

As young Ezekiel heard the story, he imagined himself in this burning flame. He would neither sleep nor eat — all he could see were the eternal flames. The next morning, he rushed to the village and found the missionary and begged him to tell him about this place and how he could keep from going there. Mother Guti did not accept the Gospel message at that time for herself, but her young son invited the Lord Jesus into his heart. Several years later after Ezekiel received the baptism in the Holy Spirit, his whole family including his mother was brought to the knowledge of the Lord.

Following his call as an evangelist, Reverend Guti went throughout the country of Rhodesia preaching. People began to change their ways, becoming new creatures in Christ. They gave up their ancestor and idol worship, bringing their idols and fetishes to be burned as a sign of true repentance. Miracles were witnessed as demons were cast out, people were raised from the dead, and many unusual healings took place.

Everywhere great crowds of people came to see the young man who would kneel down and start praying in the street or main thoroughfare of the village. As the crowds gathered, anointed by the Holy Ghost, he would make known why he was there — to teach them of Jesus and His redemptive work on the cross.

Of the 80 Christian fellowships in Rhodesia, Malawi and Mozambique, only a few have churches or stationary meetings in place. The rest meet in home prayer meetings, in the open fields, near streams, or in tents.

(Ezekiel felt his need for further training, so applied for a work scholarship at Christ For The Nations Institute. He was accepted as a student, and after graduation returned to Zimbabwe where his minstry, Forward in Faith Ministries, expanded to more than 3,000 churches and into 19 countries.)

Priorities

By now our ministry had become so expanded that it seemed the normal things of life took on less and less importance. For example, on November 14, 1972, which was our 35th wedding anniversary, I later made a notation in my diary under that date saying, "Both of us forgot about it."

Carole's Apartment in Israel Bombed

Six weeks later, I received a call from Gordon's sister, Ruth, living in California. She had just read in the morning paper that Carole's apartment in Israel had been bombed the day before. The details were scarce. Had we heard?

I told her we had not heard a word, and after the conversation was over, I immediately went to prayer, wondering how I could get further information. Scarcely was I on my knees after calling Gordon when the phone rang. It was Carole!

She said that the Orthodox Jews, who were perturbed over her witness, were the instigators of the incident. Though the bomb outside her fourth floor apartment had exploded and caused damage in the hallway, evidently burning itself out, she and members of a young singing group staying with her were inside, unharmed.

Newspaper clippings of the bombing were sent to us from all over the world, and Carole had a fantastic opportunity to witness on Israel's only TV station, as well as to correspondents from around the globe. The leading Israeli magazine carried a two-and-a-half-page story about her telling of her faith in God.

In speaking to people who are candidates to receive the baptism in the Holy Spirit, I often point out the necessity of praying in the Spirit every day. For it is when we let the Holy Spirit pray through us that we can become instruments to pray for situations about which we know absolutely nothing, as in the case of the bombing of Carole's apartment. I am sure that the effectual prayers of God's children have covered her and kept her safe to this date. This is true of many of God's workers.

Too, praying in the Spirit is not only effectual but it is also the most unselfish way to pray. It is impossible to pray a selfish prayer when praying in the Spirit.

Chapter Eighteen

In March 1973, we were taking what was to be Gordon's last tour. Our large group of 116 had all climbed safely aboard the 747 jet for the flight to Israel. As we settled down and taxied for the takeoff, we suddenly noticed our plane coming to a dead stop. Moments later fire trucks and ambulances came racing onto the field. The steward came through the plane, excitedly telling us to leave everything and deplane immediately. Once off the plane, we were told someone had called the airlines and reported there was a bomb on board the plane.

We were taken back to the terminal while every inch of our luggage was searched. Later, we were informed that no bomb was found. However, a source close to the airlines told us that actually there were explosives found on board the plane.

During the six-hour delay at John F. Kennedy Airport in New York, we encouraged ourselves in the Lord. We began to sing, "He's got the 747 in His hands!" In fact, it ended up with a Jericho march, and everyone began to dance before the

Lord, including other passengers from other flights. Before we knew it, there were photographers and news reporters looking on. They had probably never seen the likes of it at Kennedy!

The rest of the trip was uneventful. From Israel, Gordon and I went to Spain to be with Ginger and Dennis, whom I had not seen in two and a half years. We spent several days with them. Gordon was busy writing while I visited and did a little sightseeing.

From Spain we returned to Dallas, arriving on Saturday night. The next day, Gordon spoke from the platform of the new Institute Building for the first time. He announced he was preaching his Easter sermon on "The Hope of the Resurrection." At the time, I wondered why he wasn't saving it for Easter, which was still several weeks away. At the close of the service, three men came forward to accept Christ as Savior.

The following Monday, we received a telephone call from Carole in Jerusalem. She said she felt led to come back to Dallas to finish the film she was producing on the Munich Olympics called "My Witnesses." I told her I was not in favor of her doing so because of the expense involved, and advised her to remain in Jerusalem. I told her I would talk to her father and send her a nightletter.

When Gordon returned from teaching his

class at the institute that morning, I mentioned Carole's desire to come back, and he said, "I will let you know later in the day. I want to pray about it." Two hours later, he phoned me from our apartment saying, "Cable Carole to come immediately. This is the time." I was a little surprised but was busy at something else and didn't question him further. I followed his request, and four days later, Carole arrived in Dallas.

That week was a busy one for him, as was usually the case when he had been away for a couple of weeks.

The next day was Saturday. We decided to take a rare day off and go to the lake with our family. In our family devotions that morning, Gordon asked Gil to read I Corinthians 15. The whole chapter deals with the resurrection of the dead. It was the first time I recall Gordon had ever asked for that specific chapter to be read.

During the day, Gordon went outside three different times, and we could hear him walking around, praying to the Lord in the Spirit. As we heard Gordon through the walls, I remarked, "I wonder what the banker thinks about it?" For he and his son were across the street visiting a friend who was working on his boat. Gordon was walking about the premises praying loudly with the banker's little white poodle nipping at his heels. At the end of the day we drove back to Dallas.

The next day was Sunday, April 1, 1973 — a day I'll never forget. Looking at the day-by-day calendar on my desk, I thought to myself, "I know what is going to happen today. Charles Duncombe will speak at the 2:30 p.m. service at the institute. After the service and prayer time, Gordon and I will take Reverend Duncombe to dinner for a time of fellowship. Then I'll come home, read and pray, while Gordon will go back to his office to write until about midnight." So I made these notations in my daily diary, changed the desk calendar to April 2 and left for the service. Little did I realize what the next hour would bring!

I was on the platform with Charles Duncombe who was to be our guest speaker until the end of school — the middle of May. Just as it was time to start the service, Gordon came walking through the prayer room and sat beside me.

A beautiful spirit of worship and praise was evident in the song service. We concluded by singing, "Jesus, Jesus, Jesus! There's Just Something About That Name." After this, everyone began to sing in the Spirit.

As I stepped to the lectern to make some announcements, I noticed a former CFNI student, a young Jewish man who was working in New York City among the Jewish people. I said, "John, come up here and take over. Tell us what

God is doing in New York City."

At that moment, I was aware of walking going on behind me, and I wondered why the faculty was moving about on the platform. But before I even turned my head, I sensed in my spirit that it was Gordon. As I looked, there he sat in his chair with his head on his shoulder. He appeared to be asleep.

I could not accept death for the moment. I motioned for Carole to come up to the platform. We walked about the platform raising our hands and praising the Lord. Two doctors were in the audience, one of whom came immediately to the platform. He administered mouth-to-mouth resuscitation, but told me afterward he did this for my benefit, as there was no sign of life. After some minutes, Gordon was carried to the prayer room and later to the hospital where he was pronounced dead on arrival.

That afternoon at the institute, Charles Duncombe rose to his feet and ministered to the students and all who were gathered there. A beautiful prophetic message came forth, saying that this work had been founded on the Rock, Christ Jesus, that it had a solid foundation, and that it would continue more gloriously than in the past.

Four hours later as Carole and I stood in his closet selecting his burial clothes, I said to her,

"Carole, is this for real?" It seemed as though it were all a bad dream.

The shock of losing one so active so suddenly can only be realized by one who has gone through a similar experience.

"Good-bye, Gordon"

Three days later, we buried Gordon; and the Holy Spirit, the great Comforter, sustained us all. During the funeral service there was singing and worship and prayer in the Spirit. The gifts began to operate, and through interpretation and prophecy, the Lord assured us all that He would be with us and that we need not fear.

As we stood by the graveside, a bird began to sing, and it brought to mind a prophecy that had been given by Charles Duncombe in a recent seminar which said:

"Your affliction is but for a moment. It worketh for thee a far more exceeding and eternal weight of glory. It will not be long before the shadows will be gone forever, and the time of the singing bird will come. Yea, the voice of the turtledove will be heard in the land. Then shall it be true that God will wipe all tears away from thine eyes, and lead thee beside fountains of living water. Yea, then shalt thou be in the land of broad distances and running streams. Then shalt thou see a loveliness beyond the concept of

thine ears, thine heart, or thy mind. Then shalt
thou understand more fully what thy God hath
prepared for them that love Him. For hath He not
said, 'I go to prepare a place for you?' Loveliness
that is beyond compare. Vistas and grandeurs of
beauty and loveliness that thy mind would reel
and rock, indeed, if thou could see it now.

"But yet a little while and the darkness will be
over and gone, and the true light will shine.
Rejoice, O weary pilgrim, for thou hast almost
reached the end of the way, and soon, though
thou who hast done so valiantly for thy Lord,
yea, thou hast dealt many a valiant blow; yes, and
sometimes the sword in thy hand hath almost
clave to the flesh thereof, and thou hast perse-
vered and struggled, weary and tired. Thou hast
known many a season of loneliness and many a
secret tear. But fear not, for soon thou shall
sheathe the sword in the scabbard. Soon thou wilt
lay down thy shield, dented and dented with
many a blow. Then shall thou remove the helmet
from thy head, lay aside thine armor and step
proudly into the presence of thy King.

"Look forward then to that glorious day when
thou shalt see with thine eyes and not another,
even as one said of old, when, after my skin
worms destroy this body, yet in my flesh shall I
see God, Whom I shall see for myself ... and not
another. Yea, thou shalt behold thy Kinsman

Redeemer. What glory and what joy that day will bring thee! So rejoice, for yet a little while and thou shalt see Him even as He is."

Ministers from all over the nation flew in for the funeral. It was impossible, as much as we would have liked, to have all of Gordon's many friends speak. Some close friends came who, had we known they were present, would also have spoken. The following did participate:

Rev. H. S. Cowart gave the eulogy and shared how the Lord had arranged the last few weeks of Gordon's life in preparation for his departure to his heavenly home.

Allen Beck, who was on the faculty of CFNI, said: "Brother Lindsay had a vision for the world. He always saw the whitened harvest and the need for laborers. CFNI is the result of Brother Lindsay's vision and faith in the Lord Jesus. His favorite poem was, "The Call of the Harvest," which he wrote concerning a young man with the call of God on his life, who due to procrastination, waited until it was too late.

But there is a call; 'tis the Master's voice —
This is our hour; let us not stay;
A call to the harvest is waiting and fields are white;
Will you join the reapers in the morning bright?

Awake, O youth, to the heavenly vision;
Multitudes, multitudes in the valley of
decision.

And what of us who live today?
This is the hour; let us not stay;
A call to the harvest till it shall end;
Work now, work fast, reap my friend.
New dawn and sunrise —
To the faithful, the Master will give the
prize.

Wayne Myers, a missionary to Mexico, who
has assisted us in the construction of thousands
of Native Churches in his field, as well as hundreds in other countries, read Gordon's favorite
Scripture: Psalm 91.

Demos Shakarian, president of the Full
Gospel Business Men's Fellowship International, had been a friend of Gordon's for over 25
years. Gordon had used his influence and efforts
to help start several FGBMFI chapters, including
the one in Philadelphia. Demos shared these
recollections:

"Gordon Lindsay was a very humble man.
When he was in a meeting, you didn't even know
he was there. ... He was a pioneer, one of the most
dedicated men I have ever met ... one of the most
lovable men you could ever meet, one of the
most godly men that you'll ever know. I have

never heard him say an unkind word toward anybody. That's the kind of man he was.

"He literally burned his life to encourage others. Many times in my difficult days of struggling, we would counsel together. Our lives were in certain ways parallel. While my lot was to encourage laymen, Gordon Lindsay's lot was to encourage ministers. I believe I can truthfully say the deliverance ministry largely depended upon this brother. His life brought in the era of healing ministry in a way, and it spread through America and around the world.

"Millions of lives have been touched by this man's life, yet you would not know it just to talk to him. He never boasted. But he had a burden that few men knew about. He carried a load that few men understood. He had a dedication that very few of us could understand. The hand of the Lord was upon him. He was anointed of God. He was directed by God. He had the love of Jesus in his heart. He had the compassion of Jesus in his life. And he had the same love for humanity that Jesus had, because Jesus was in his life.

"Through his efforts, thousands of ministries were launched one after another. I have seen him at some of the greatest trials that he went through, but he kept going. I saw him when he enjoyed mountain peak experiences, but he was still humble before God. I think his life should be an inspiration to every student, to every minister, to every layman and to every person all over the world."

Gordon's longtime friend, the late Jack Moore, came from Shreveport. "How can you explain a life like this? I can almost hear him say, 'Give all the glory to Jesus.' And now he has laid his pen aside and fallen asleep, but his influence will still live on. I don't think today that we should sorrow as others who have no hope, because this man had great hope. He not only had great hope, but he also gave hope to others."

Ralph Hart, who succeeded Gordon as president of the Full Gospel Fellowship of Churches and Ministers International, said: "When I was a little boy he came down to Farmersville, Texas, and held a revival for my father. He held me on his knee. I shall never forget it as long as I live.

"I was only a little lad, but I remember that young man with a fervor and the desire and the compassion for lost souls. It never died. It never changed. That desire, that compassion carried him throughout this world, winning multitudes, establishing missions throughout the nations and building a work for God that will live throughout eternity.

"I'll never forget one night when he spent the night with me. I wake up pretty early in the morning, and I was praying, and got up and walked down to his room. I heard somebody saying, 'Lord, I thank You. Lord, I thank You. Lord, I love You this morning.' And I cracked the door, and Gordon was sitting there with his Bible in his hand. I said, 'Man what are you doing up this early in the morning?' He said, 'I'm communicating before the devil gets up!'"

Pastor H.C. Noah of Oak Cliff Assembly said, "I have observed a lot of preachers, but I have never seen anyone of my acquaintance, who worked harder for Jesus Christ, and tried to do more with his total life than Gordon Lindsay.

"And I have seen him in those moments of testing that will either make or break a man. I have seen him as he faced life's disappointments, but I have never seen Gordon Lindsay once anywhere near giving up or going back on what he believed and what God called him to do.

"And his disappointments, his heartaches, his problems, only brought forth the true strength of God, and all the devils in hell and all the disappointments in life could not deter him. But his goal was to bring glory to God in his life and to carry out a vision that God had put in his soul.

"And when we come down to the facts of life, it isn't the great things we have done — it is the great Christian we are. And we can only be that by doing what Gordon Lindsay did: total commitment, total surrender to be all that Christ wants us to be.

"When my son was tragically killed in an automobile accident, Gordon wrote me a letter in his own hand and said, 'All our life has been a preparation for the inevitable moment!'

"And that's why Gordon Lindsay lived as he did. He believed that this place is just a dressing room. Our great consolation is that we have observed the life of a great Christian. And when it's all over, it's what we are in Christ."

Lester Sumrall flew in from South Bend, Indiana. At the service he said, "To many of us, he was a brother. A brother is one who is strong in time of need. A brother is one you can rely on when you need help. And he was a brother to so many people. ..."

Charles Duncombe presented the final tribute: "This is a time to look back on the footprints in the sands of time. ... This Gordon Lindsay was a colossus; he made giant footprints in the sands of time. He straddled continents and oceans.

"He had one foot in Dallas and the other in Germany. He had one foot in Israel and the other in the Mediterranean Sea. One foot in Texas and the other in Africa. One foot in the Atlantic and the other in Europe. One foot in the Pacific and the other in Indonesia. One foot in the North Sea and the other in the Philippines.

"He served his generation like David. He walked with God like Enoch. He finished his course like Paul.

"We do not have to deplore the fact that he was snatched away by some tragic accident, neither did he linger under the onslaught of disease. We were not harassed and brokenhearted by watching a man slowly become emaciated and die. Had that happened, we might have said it was of the devil. But this was not the devil. It was of God. God said, 'Gordon, it's over. You're through. It's time to come on home.'"

Hundreds of friends filled the large auditorium, and all of the students were requested to go to the balcony, where they sat on the bare cement floor, because no pews nor floor covering had yet been installed.

As my older sister, Esther, and I walked away from the grave with her arms through mine, she said softly, "That is just the way Gordon would have wanted it."

Later, the funeral director told me that when his assistants returned to the funeral home, one of them said, "What was that? We have never had a funeral like that! I wish every one were that happy."

A Methodist lady said to me, "I am going back and tell my pastor how a funeral service ought to be conducted."

God Will Finish the Work

I want to share just one letter of the thousands

that came to me during the next few months from all over the world. It was from a former CFNI student:

Dear Mrs. Lindsay,

Ever since Brother Lindsay's funeral service, I have had many thoughts to send you something the Lord gave me the year I attended CFNI. It may give you some comfort, but it seems the Holy Spirit has done a beautiful job of comforting you and encouraging you already. Of all the people at the funeral service, I admired you the most. There was a joy and victory in your voice at the graveside that others could not touch. My daughter and I came away laughing and singing from the service. For the first time, I got a glimpse of the wonderful future we have in Christ, and I was ready to go, too. That's quite a change for a person who was always fearful of funerals and would never go to any. If all funerals were conducted like Gordon Lindsay's was, and all had the Holy Spirit there pouring out His love like He did in honor of your husband, we would all be like Paul and be torn between going and staying.

You are very fortunate to know the Lord, to have been happily married, to have such dedicated and lovely children, and share with a husband a work that has done and will continue to

do so much good. There are far too many who
have never even tasted one of these privileges.
You have been most blessed, and God will continue to bless you, for the good work He has
begun, He *will* finish. May God bless you richly
and be your husband (Isa. 54:5, Job 29:12,13, Jer.
49:11) until you see Jesus.

Sincerely in Christ Jesus,
K.M.M.

Two meaningful choruses gave great help
and strength to the board, the faculty, staff,
students, family and me. One was, "Because He
Lives," and the other was, "Let Thy Mantle Fall
on Me."

My youngest son, Dennis, and his wife
returned from Spain in time for the funeral.
Dennis and Ginger were to become a part of the
faculty the following September as had been
approved by the board in Gordon's last meeting
with them.

Gordon had been president of Christ For The
Nations for exactly 25 years. For it was on April
1, 1948, that *The Voice of Healing* was started
with Gordon as the editor.

The day after Gordon died, my secretary
checked in at the hospital for a physical examination. Doctors found she had 15 cancerous
lobes. She never recovered her health, and her

death was a great personal loss to me.

Had it not been for the well-trained and dedicated staff which God had supplied to Christ For The Nations, it would have been impossible for me to step into the role that suddenly fell my lot. Almost without exception, the employees rallied around me and gave me their loyal support. With their daily prayers and words of encouragement, joined with those of our splendid, devoted board of fine Christian businessmen, the work couldn't have done anything else but go forward.

Since then with the work growing in every area and the institute quadrupling, God has added some fantastic people to our staff and faculty. It has been amazing to watch God work.

Sometimes, it almost overwhelms me to look back and see what God has done. I now know how it feels to have a thousand decisions to make, and suddenly have the one who has always made them gone — where you cannot even ask his advice. It's then that I fall at the feet of Jesus, and He sends the Holy Spirit to guide me.

Chapter Nineteen

The day after Gordon died, I received a phone call from Kenneth Hagin, a longtime friend of the family. He was in a meeting in Florida and expressed his regret at not being able to attend the memorial service. Then he gave me words of encouragement and ended by saying, "Great new doors of service are going to open to you. Don't be afraid. Don't be afraid. Don't be afraid."

The morning of the funeral I was in my apartment, and Demos Shakarian came to see me. The living room was full of family, friends and several board members. Demos said he was getting ready to go to a regional convention when the Lord told him instead, "Go to Dallas; Sister Lindsay needs you."

In the course of our conversation, Demos said to me, "Gordon's mantle has fallen on you."

That same morning, Evangelist Chuck Flynn came to see me. He asked to pray with me and as he knelt by my side, he began to prophesy. Among other things he said, "The reins are in your hand."

The Scripture says, that *"By the mouth of two*

or three witnesses every word may be estab-lished" (Matt. 18:16). So I told my children that if each of these messengers were sent of the Lord, and I believed they were, then God would verify it in the board meeting.

The day after the funeral, our 10-man board met and unanimously voted that I was to succeed Gordon. I appreciated their confidence in me, and I shared with them the last verse that our family had read with Gordon. I Corinthians 15:58: "Therefore, my beloved brethren, be steadfast, immovable, always abounding in the work of the Lord, knowing that your labor is not in vain in the Lord."

On the following Saturday after Gordon's death while I was in the kitchen fixing breakfast for Gordon's only brother, the phone rang, and it was my sister, Edith, calling from Portland. She told me that my 62-year-old brother, Dave, had just dropped dead in the bathroom.

Fortunately, he had served the Lord for many years and so was ready to go. I did not attempt to attend the funeral because of the many respon-sibilities that had suddenly fallen upon me. But the members of my family who were still with me, left immediately to return to Portland to bury my brother.

One Day at a Time

After friends and family had returned to their

own homes, I was left alone with Carole. I started
to get out of bed the next morning, and found I
had no strength even to stand. I lay back down
and called Carole into my room. I told her the
task was too great ... the responsibility of our
missionary work that was reaching into over 100
nations was too much ... the finishing of the
Institute Building ... the 300 Native Churches we
were at that time helping to build ... the Bible
school in Zerka, Jordan, that we had just started
to build ... they were more than I could carry.

(While making funeral arrangements, my
great additional concern was how we could finish the construction of the Institute Building. The
downstairs auditorium was the only part of the
building completed. There were no seats in the
balcony, and the cement floors were unfinished.
The library walls stood bare and incomplete, the
fellowship area and prayer room, the tape room,
the language laboratories, the offices — everything was only partially done.)

Carole said to me, "Mother, let's just pray.
And let's just take it one day at a time. The Lord
will give you strength for just today." So I
crawled out of bed and prostrated myself on the
floor. For some time I lay there sobbing out my
inadequacy at the immensity of the task, when
suddenly the Holy Ghost took over, and I began
to pray in the Spirit. Then like a rush of a mighty

wind, faith and strength seemed to pour into me. After some time, I rose to my feet and dried my tears. Then Carole said, "You do have enough strength for today, don't you, Mother?" (She had been taught for years that we have what we confess.)

"Yes," I answered, "I do have enough strength for today."

Then I bathed myself, dressed and went to work. And the Lord has each day provided strength sufficient for all the needs that have arisen.

One day, shortly after we began construction on the Institute Building, Gordon had said, "You know, I really believe we ought to build this building larger. We are building it too small." So we talked to both the banker and our contractor and they advised, "If you are going to do it, do it now while we're working on the foundation."

$17,000 Overdrawn!

We had originally asked the bank for a $350,000 loan, and because we extended the size of the building, we had now used up $450,000.

The day after Gordon died, I checked with our accountant, and found we were $17,000 overdrawn — and still a long way from finishing the building. I wondered whether the bank would give us an additional loan. A few days later, the banker came to see me, and said, "Mrs. Lindsay, let's finish this building exactly as Brother Lindsay would have wanted it. I'll extend the loan to whatever you need, the same as if your husband were here!"

So with that assurance, we completed the building, and dedicated it at the August seminar that summer. (The banker had more faith in the future of Christ For The Nations than some preachers did who predicted that in six months Christ For The Nations would fold up. Praise God, they were wrong!)

One of the very first things I did was to write a letter to all the missionaries and national workers with whom we had worked. I assured them we would keep every commitment and complete every project Christ For The Nations had started. And in fact we believed God that the work would expand greatly and not recede.

"I Had to Make You Go"

Before his death, Gordon had arranged for us to hold a series of seven banquets in seven major cities in the interest of Israel. As it happened, these were scheduled to begin exactly three weeks after we buried Gordon.

I felt I was not up to taking these banquets alone, and was greatly concerned. After several days of prayer, I talked the matter over with Carole. I said, "The notices have already gone out advertising the banquets. A lot of people will be attending. There really isn't time to inform them of Daddy's death. So what shall we do?"

She answered, "Mother, I believe we can do it."

"Carole, I was praying that you would offer to go with me, because I believe the two of us can see them through."

We did keep all seven appointments, and God met us in a very spectacular way. In fact, the results of those seven banquets were greater than any Gordon and I had ever done previously.

The day after we returned from the meetings, I was in my kitchen washing dishes. Immediately after Gordon died, I had asked the Lord, "God, why did you not let Gordon live until the banquets were over and the seminar was finished next month in Minneapolis?"

If God ever spoke to my heart, He did then. He said, "I let him live as long as I could. I gave you three weeks to bury him and get things in shape here at home so you could fulfill these commitments. *I had to make you go.* I had to show you that you could do it."

The Work Goes On

Shortly before Gordon's death while seated in his office one day, I said to him, "Daddy, I really hope the Lord will let you reach your threescore and 10 years, because we still have three years to pay on the Headquarters building." He was nearly 67 then, and I was recalling the threescore and ten (70) years the Lord had promised to His own in Psalm 90:10.

I continued, "With the Institute Building coming to completion, we will be under tremendous financial obligation. That additional $6,000 or more a month payment will really add to our burden. If either of us dropped out of the race, it would work an immense hardship on the other."

He replied, "Honey, don't worry about it. Longevity is on my side. Both my mother and my father lived to be in their 80s."

Then he stopped for a moment and looking very serious, he pointed to a whole row of notebooks on the shelf. He said, "But you know, I am really three years ahead on my work." I knew he had been writing nearly day and night for the past several years, as a man racing against time, but I didn't know he was that far ahead. "All those books up there are books-of-the-month. If you ever need them, that's where you'll find them."

His statement puzzled me, for I thought, "Why would I need them? You'll be here to publish them, month after month."

After the Lord took him, within 11 weeks friends of Christ For The Nations had, by small donations, paid off the $83,000 indebtedness against the Headquarters building. An additional

$71,000 was needed to pay off the parking lot property of the institute. This was also paid within several months.

We went ahead with the scheduled seminar in Minneapolis; and through a series of miracles, God met us in those meetings. Kenneth Hagin kindly assisted me.

Gordon had scheduled the first summer school session at CFNI. Now I was faced with the decision of whether to go ahead or to cancel it. A change of some of the personnel at the time, threw an additional burden on me, but I felt led to go ahead. God honored our step of faith, and in that first summer school session, about 130 completed the six-week course and received their certificates. Since then, the summer school has nearly doubled each year.

Six weeks after Gordon went to heaven, Jimmy Swaggart — evangelist, TV and recording artist and personal friend for many years — held a memorial benefit in the new CFNI auditorium. The 1,400-seat auditorium was packed and jammed as every seat was filled, and people were seated on the balcony steps or in the aisles. Some $60,000 in cash and pledges was raised for the new Christ For The Nations Institute Building. This was a tremendous blessing to us, and helped lift some of the financial load. (Jimmy Swaggart graciously refused any compensation.)

Living on Campus

During the 35 years Gordon and I were married, he was extremely conservative. He always felt we should live no better than the average American. And even after the work had grown until it was worldwide, unlike some of his contemporaries, he would accept only a modest income. So with both of us working, it took us 33 years to finally pay off a home. This was now the first time we had ever had a home completely paid.

But no sooner was our house mortgage liquidated than one day as I was praying, I felt the Lord directing us to dispose of our home and move onto the campus.

I had been talking with the man who had sold us the five apartment houses as he still owned a couple more, and we now were needing to buy the one closest to our campus to accommodate the expanding student enrollment. (He was the man who had been told by the doctor he had only from 1 to 6 months to live; but he lived another 15 years in better health than he had been for years. I told him, "God sent you to us and us to you.")

When I suggested to Gordon that we sell our home and live on the campus, he was a little reluctant and said, "Why don't we wait a year?"

After prayer, I again suggested to him, "What do you think if the owner of this apartment would accept our house for his equity in that apartment (for I knew our house was perhaps a little less than his equity in it)?"

Gordon replied, "Well, if he takes our house as the complete equity, I will feel it is the Lord."

When I presented this proposal to the owner, he agreed; and in a matter of a few days, we were moved on campus.

We lived there the last year of Gordon's life, and to us it was like a honeymoon apartment. We were happier there than in any quarters in which we had ever lived for we were now totally unencumbered.

After his homegoing, I could see the hand of the Lord in the whole matter. For now I did not have the added burden of disposing of that large house, and I had the security and fellowship of those who lived in the apartments about me.

"What God Hath Prepared"

One day as we were getting ready to pray while we were residing in that apartment, Gordon looked out the bedroom window, and said, "You see this piece of land across the street? I really believe the Lord is going to give it to us some time, but we are not ready for it now." (I don't know that he actually meant "give it to us" as a gift.)

However one day that first summer after

Gordon had passed away, a lawyer walked into
our office. After introducing himself, he said, "I
represent the two clients who own that large tract
of land south of your apartments that runs on
down into the new shopping center. We would
like to sell it to you."

I told him we were in no condition to buy any
land. But in the course of our conversation, he
told me how God had so richly prospered his
clients. So I said to him, "Wouldn't it be a
fabulous thing for these men to do something for
God and for this school and give us the property?
Why don't you challenge them with this idea?"

The lawyer thought it might be a good idea,
and said he would talk to them. But he added that
one was a Presbyterian and the other a Seventh-
day Adventist. The latter, he said, was very gen-
erous with his philanthropies, but never gave to
anyone outside his own organization.

I told him we would pray. He replied, "It will
certainly take that."

Some days later, the Presbyterian gentleman
arrived. I spent considerable time with him,
showing him over the entire campus. He said he
was very impressed, but he reaffirmed what the
lawyer had previously said — that the Seventh-
day Adventist co-partner never contributed to
any other than his organization. We prayed
together in my husband's office that God's will

would be done.

To make a long story short, at Christmas time (my first one without Gordon) the Lord so beautifully arranged it that Christ For The Nations was given that piece of land, worth $300,000, as a gift.

This shows as I have told the students on a number of occasions, that our prayers do not end when we leave this world. They keep being answered again and again after we depart. This applies to the salvation of loved ones, the extension of God's Kingdom, and physical and natural blessings which we claim for those we love.

One day the Lord impressed the following verse on my soul: *"Eye has not seen, nor ear heard, nor have entered into the heart of man the things which God has prepared for those who love Him"* (I Cor. 2:9). For years I had quoted it. Now suddenly it took on an unusual significance. For too long, Christians have believed this referred entirely to the next world, but there is no evidence to make us believe that that was the intent.

Suddenly I found myself asking: "What is the Lord preparing for me today?" Then I saw what He had been preparing for Christ For The Nations, lo, these many years:

(1) He prepared a 10-story Sheraton Hotel to be built across the street from our first piece of

property, Christian Center, after we purchased it.
(2) He prepared a bank to be built next to the
Sheraton for our convenience. (3) He prepared a
shopping center at the southern edge of our property. (5) He prepared numerous apartment
houses, each property touching the other, to afford us the campus we needed. (6) He first prepared an 80-room motel a block away, and later
the 10-story hotel for our men's dormitory. (And
there are still many other things in the area He
has prepared that will eventually be ours!)

In fact, serving Christ is so exciting that each
morning when I get up I wonder, "What is God
preparing for Christ For The Nations today?"
Not only in Dallas, but in our many projects
around the world — such as the Nigerian Bible
school, or the one we financed in Zerka, Jordan;
the one we purchased in Bad Gandersheim, Germany; the one we helped provide in Shillong,
India, and on and on. Today we have 40 associate
Bible schools. Yes, God has prepared and is
preparing daily "for those who love him," not
only natural and temporal blessings, but spiritual
adventures as well, for those whom we love and
pray for daily.

A Giant Task — A Great God

During the first few weeks after Gordon left
us, the devil would come to me in the night

seasons. As I have sometimes told an audience, the devil can paint a dark picture, but he can paint it the darkest at 3 and 4 a.m.

He would harass me again and again by suggesting, "What are you going to do with all those dormitories now that Gordon is dead? The school, with its enrollment of 250 this year, will probably drop back to half or less next fall, and you will never be able to fill the dormitories. You won't be able to meet the payments, and then you will go bankrupt."

So I struggled night after night until finally I cried out to the Lord, "God, I can't stay awake all night and go to work the next morning. You will just have to take care of this matter, and I am committing the whole thing to You."

When fall came, instead of having only 250 students, we had 450. So now, I was laying awake at night, not worrying how we would fill the apartments, but wondering where we would house the overflow.

Immediately, we looked around for an additional apartment complex. The logical one was a 40-unit complex that joined the girl's dormitory. It was the newest in the area — only two years old. When I learned who the owner was, I was surprised to find out that he had lived right next to us for a year before we had moved onto the campus.

I called him, and we talked at some length about Gordon's passing. When I came to the point of asking about the purchase of the apartment, he said, "Mrs. Lindsay, this is an amazing thing. I have just put that apartment on the market, but I did reserve the right to sell it myself." After negotiations, we were able to purchase it for $40,000 less than it had cost him to build it. We occupied it immediately after Christmas.

Several months later, a Methodist man talked to me on the phone. He said, "I understand you have a shortage of student housing. I have $126,000 equity in an apartment that is half paid. It is four miles from your place. And if you want the equity, you can have it.

I answered, "Certainly, we'll take it."

He then deeded the property to us, and we sent some of our married couples who had cars to live there. But one day in prayer, I asked, "Lord, what do we want with an apartment four miles from here? We don't want to get into commercial renting. And it is a little too far removed from campus."

As I continued in prayer, I suddenly remembered another huge apartment building joining our campus. The owner was having some financial problems and had not been able to make necessary repairs to keep it up. So it was drawing a very poor element of people, and was actually becoming a ghetto. Gordon and I had prayed about it a number of times, and felt we could not allow this to happen, since it was close to our own dormitories.

While praying the thought came to me, "Why not offer this owner the equity in the apartment we have four miles away, in exchange for the equity he has in this one?" We could then pick up the first mortgage, which a large company was carrying at a very low interest rate with low monthly payments.

We contacted the owner, made the recommendation to him, and within a few weeks, were able to work out the entire transaction. We took over his equity and ended up owing a balance of about $200,000 with an interest rate of only $6\frac{1}{2}$ percent. This 40-unit complex with its 15 three-bedroom, two-and-a-half bath apartments, lovely courtyard, swimming pool, etc., had a market value of close to a million dollars. We were immediately able to completely fill it with students and put it to good use for the Lord!

One block away from our campus was the Oak Cliff Inn, a large 80-room hotel which touches the freeway. On one occasion it was up for sale, and Gordon and I walked around the landscaped courtyard several nights. He said he felt in time we would have the place, but now was not the time. Nevertheless, he said, "Let's just claim it for the Lord." So we prayed together about it, and left it in the Lord's hands.

Shortly thereafter it sold, but two years later, it was up for sale again. In my spirit, I felt strongly it was time to move ahead. I prayed for several months along with the board, the staff and the faculty. We all felt to move forward. The board's decision was unanimous, so we closed the transaction.

We were able to purchase the motel for $242,000 less than it had sold for two years previously. God helped us pay off the second mortgage on it. Soon 225 first-year students were using it as a dormitory. In addition, there were beautiful large classrooms, one seating 300, and another seating 150 which was also used as a prayer chapel. Also, there was a lovely, large restaurant which was converted into a cafeteria for the entire school. The kitchen equipment by itself was worth $150,000.

For many years, this building housed the offices for much of the faculty and staff; and the spacious lobby served as a registration center. It contained a swimming pool and the finest land-scaped courtyard of all of our 11 apartment dormitories. The price we paid of $660,000 would have been approximately equivalent to the value of the land.

A local newspaper carried an article about our

acquisition of the Oak Cliff Inn with this tongue-in-cheek heading: "OAK CLIFF INN: FACING BIGGEST CHANGE YET, BAR NONE."

"The growing Christ For The Nations organization in southwest Oak Cliff has acquired ownership of Oak Cliff Inn and will convert the motel into another dormitory. Opened about 15 years ago, the motel has had a string of owners and many different restaurant operators.

"Hailed as Oak Cliff's finest during the grand opening, it booked several name entertainers. However, after a sensational start, both the hostelry, the restaurant and the club had tough sledding. Several major operators attempted to make a success, but failed.

"On several occasions, the motel remained vacant for a time. The biggest notoriety came when a group of independent operators provided closed-circuit X-rated movies in each room.

"The motel's blatant and overt objective became the center of a court battle and some sensational newspaper stories. The subject even became a political issue in 1971 before the courts shut down the pornography and forced the management to retire.

"Christ For The Nations also owns several apartments, dormitories and has erected two major administration and educational buildings on campus. In addition, the school has opened a picnic and recreational area on fallow land acquired by the school, and a large athletic field."

Some have asked me, "Why do you work so feverishly?" Actually, the souls won as a result of nearly 10,000 Native Churches we have helped build in foreign lands, the tens of millions of CFN books in circulation, the *Christ For The Nations* magazine beginning its 51st year of publication, the hundreds of thousands of tapes we have distributed, the 26,000 Christ For The Nations Institute graduates makes me wish I had a thousand lives to live for the work of the Lord.

Chapter Twenty

I had never made a missionary trip without Gordon, and it took a year and a half before I was ready. But after prayer, I felt God wanted me to visit Africa. Our first stop was to be in Nigeria, where a former student, Benson Idahosa, was laboring. He told me later that before he left Dallas, he measured the length of our Headquarters building and found it to be 210 feet long. He said, "If God can do this in Dallas, Texas, He can do it in Benin City, Nigeria." With this kind of faith, he set out to reach his country for God.

His faith did reach out and before long, he was preaching to crowds of 40,000 and 50,000, with many giving their hearts to Christ and others being healed. Several were raised from the dead under his ministry. Feeling the need for training nationals to help him, he began building a Bible school, and invited us to visit Nigeria.

Our plane circled over Benin City for a solid hour. Pockets of fog seemed to be floating over the airport. Again and again, we made a pass to land. But just as the pilot was ready to set the wheels down on the runway, fog would envelop the strip, and the pilot would have to pull back up into the clouds. Finally, he spoke on the intercom saying that he would make one more attempt to land, and if he couldn't make it this time, he would have to take us back to Lagos, the capital.

We were scheduled to speak both that Saturday night and Sunday. We felt this was nothing more nor less than the work of the devil to hinder us. So our party joined together in earnest prayer that God would lift the fog (which seemed to be only over the airport) and let us descend.

By now the pilot had again circled the airport and was coming in for that final try. Breathlessly we watched, and as we came down out of the clouds, beneath us was the clear airstrip! Within seconds, the wheels touched the ground, and there was a host of people applauding when we stepped off the plane. Such a royal welcome we had never before received!

The next morning, it was my privilege to preach the first sermon in the Christ For Nigeria Bible School, which, incidentally was over 200 feet long. There were about 2,000 people present, and such singing and praising I have never heard in my life! In fact, it took Benson's ringing an old-fashioned school bell loud and long to finally silence the people.

Since there was no roof on the building, they had spread huge palm branches across the rafters to shield our heads from the hot sun. At the close of the service, I promised the people that we would return to the states and ask the friends of Christ For The Nations to help them put on the roof. They rejoiced at this, and we later kept our promise. I was privileged to dedicate that school to the Lord in November 1975. When I returned home from that second visit, I gave the following report to the CFNI students:

Nigeria Report

This little story about Nigeria started five years ago when my late husband went there and met a young man by the name of Benson Idahosa. At that time, Benson was an accountant for a large shoe chain with stores all over Africa. Benson said to my husband, "I feel the call of God on my life, and I would like very much to become a minister. But I am a businessman and lack the vital Bible training. I would love to come to this new Bible school you have just started."

My husband responded, "Well, Benson, we will give you a work scholarship, and you can come for a year." And so Benson came.

At that time, the school was in its second year. Benson really applied himself. Of all the foreign students we had, I don't know anybody who circulated more than Benson. By circulating, I mean he preached all over the area. When there was a vacation like Christmas, he would be out speaking at distant points. I don't know how he made all his contacts, because this was his first trip to America. But right from the start, you could tell Benson was a go-getter.

Another thing I noticed was his appearance. Benson was one of the sharpest-looking foreign students we ever had. He was very, very careful about his appearance.

Thirdly (and this was most important of all), he was a man of prayer. Sometimes Gordon and I would talk about it. He would have such a burden of prayer that he was completely oblivious to what was going on around him. Gordon said to me one day, "You know, the hand of God is really on Benson. I feel his country is going to hear from him when he returns."

Well, Benson finished and went back to his country. He pastored a church which was not all that big, but he conducted campaigns on the side. God started to wondrously work through this young man.

He began to have fantastic healings and miracles. And (as I have said before, students) if you want to reach your land, your own country, it is not going to be through coffeehouses — though I am not opposed to coffeehouses. And you are not going to reach your nation by passing out tracts on the street — though I am not against that. Some of you will be called to do that; some of you will be called to go to coffeehouses. But the way you can really get the ear of a nation and a people quickly (the way Jesus did it), is to minister to the physical needs of the people through miracles and healings. That is how Jesus was able to gain the attention of the people. Then He showed them their need of a Savior. And that is exactly the method Benson used in his own land.

Pretty soon the dead began to be raised in his meetings. He really got the ear of the nation. Then he decided he was going to build a Bible school like ours. Who ever heard of Benin City, Nigeria? I hadn't. But he began to pray about the school, and supernaturally God started to work.

Benson was sharp — he looked sharp, and he attracted the top people in his nation. He didn't start with the slums; he started with the top and then worked down. He impacted his entire nation greatly before he went to be with the Lord in 1998 at age 59, due to a heart attack.

A Little Child Shall Lead

He told the people in his audience on a Sunday morning, "I need a piece of land to build a Bible school."

There was present a wealthy lawyer and his wife and their two little boys. The 4-year-old was sitting on the daddy's lap, and he was smart enough to know his father owned some land in the city. So he turned to his father and asked, "Daddy, did you hear the preacher say he needs some land?"

The father answered, "Son, be quiet. I'm listening to the preacher preach." With this, the little boy began to cry.

When the father went home, he couldn't forget what his little boy had said, "Daddy, don't you hear the preacher? He needs some land." So what happened? This wealthy lawyer gave a huge piece of land about three blocks from the airport. (As the Scripture says "A little child shall lead them" [Isa. 11:6].)

Benson started to build in faith, and suddenly we began to get pictures of the Bible school. When I saw the size of it, I shook my head in disbelief. I said, "Benson, what are you going to do in Benin City?" But he was building himself a school.

I preached the first sermon in that place. Then Benson asked that I come for the dedication. It occurred to me that since we were going to the World Conference on the Holy Spirit in Israel in November, it would be very little expense to go on to Nigeria to dedicate that school.

I wrote to Benson, "I will fly down and dedicate the school on November 9." Evangelist Chuck Flynn had preceded me there for the graduation of 43 students on Saturday night. Norman Young (who was our business administrator and is my nephew by marriage) and I had been traveling and had gotten only three hours of sleep the night before our arrival.

There were a couple of thousand people present at the Saturday night graduation. Benson even had caps and gowns, for the graduates. He had borrowed a cap and gown from the University of Nigeria and had one of the dressmakers in his church use that pattern. So all of the students were in these brilliant blue caps and gowns and guess what color I got to wear — bright red! It was so red! You should have seen it. Chuck Flynn, Benson and all of the faculty were in red.

Besides the 43 graduates, there were about 47 others who were dedicated to the ministry. Some had already graduated earlier from one of his smaller Bible schools. Some were ordained to the ministry, others as deaconesses and deacons or elders.

Dedication of Christ For Nigeria Institute

But the next day was to be the day of all days! We arrived about 45 minutes early for this was the dedication day. Already about 4,000 or so were inside, and probably about a thousand who couldn't get in were milling around on the outside. Benson knew it was going to be packed, and so had engaged the police band, all in uniform, to play a concert outside on the steps of this big, beautiful new edifice. And when I say it is beautiful — for Nigeria — believe me, it is beautiful.

What a time we had! The choir was all robed, and what singing! Those people just get carried away praising the Lord. Benson had this old-fashioned school bell. After they have praised long enough, and he wants to continue the service, he starts ringing that bell, loud and long. Finally the sound filters to the back until the people hear and become quiet. Then he continues with the service.

So with the people packed in like sardines, with the police band now down in front of the platform, I had the privilege of bringing the message. I really felt a rich anointing. But I felt such a responsibility. I said, "O God, this is such a tremendous responsibility." Then I said, "Brother Flynn, come over here, you and Benson lay your hands on me and pray for me that I will say the very words God would want said at this time." So they prayed. Then I preached about Solomon's temple and how it was dedicated and about the glory of the Lord that came down.

Benson had told me before the service, "You

are going to take the offering today."

And I replied, "Oh, am I?" He told me there was $26,000 still owing on the building and everything else was paid. So that day, the offering was over $10,000 in cash and pledges. And that was a Nigerian congregation!

At the close of the service, hundreds of people, even some of the police band, gave their hearts to the Lord. Oh, I tell you we had a shouting good time! That service lasted four hours. We could have gone on till the next morning.

Norman had told Benson that I could speak only one time, because I was just coming back from the World Conference where we had our own tour, and I had already spoken four times in Israel. Norman didn't want me to overdo it as we were going on next to Germany. So he told Benson, one time — just for the dedication service. Well, I squeezed in an extra session when I spoke for half an hour on Saturday night at the graduation.

The Children's Bread

When I woke up on Sunday morning, I was waiting on the Lord for the dedication message, when all of a sudden, I saw a little black girl in a vision. She was the skinniest little thing, and I said to myself, "How old is that little girl?" I don't know why I asked her age. I said, "8, 10?"

The word "child" just came, and I said, "Lord, what is this all about?" Then the phrase came to me: "Healing is the children's bread" (taken from the story of the Syro-Phoenician woman in Mark 7:25-31).

The only way I had heard that principle preached about was to say that we, who are children of God, born again sons and daughters, can rightfully claim divine healing for ourselves. But now it was being applied to this skinny, little girl. So I said, "Lord, what are You saying? I'm sure there is not going to be any prayer for the sick in that dedication service. What are you saying?"

As I waited on the Lord, I felt He wanted us to have a healing service. So I told Benson, "You know, I just feel we need a healing service tonight, and I will be glad to speak somewhere."

He replied, "Fine. I will announce you to speak at the largest branch church." Benson had started nine other churches in Benin City. Nine brand new churches. Fantastic! One young man with a vision! So he announced the service.

We had just about an hour to get ready for that service after we got back to the hotel. The Lord impressed me to make it very simple. Really simple. Just use Scripture. So at the meeting, I started quoting several Scriptures, and I had all the people repeat them. Then I would give another healing Scripture and say, "Now I want you to repeat this. This is what God's Word says." I would give another healing Scripture, make a few comments on it, and say, "Now repeat this. Say this out loud."

I could see faith rise, even though it was dark there, for the lights had gone out. (We had a kerosene lamp and some candles.) But I could see those black faces. Their faith kept mounting up. Finally when I came to Psalm 103:3, I said to them, "Now this says, 'Who forgives all your iniquities, who heals all your diseases.'" Then I gave those who wanted to be healed and who had not accepted the Lord an opportunity to find Christ as Savior. We stood and prayed together. Then I continued, "This says, 'Who forgives all your iniquities, who heals all your diseases.' What disease is the Lord going to heal tonight?"

Somebody raised his hand and said, "Heart trouble."

"Cancer."

Another one said, "Arthritis."

"Asthma."

"Heat."

And I asked, "Heat?"

The national worker replied, "Fever, fever."

They used some words I didn't understand.

"Do you mean this is what God is going to do tonight? He is going to heal all your diseases?"

I asked it several times.

"Yes," they shouted, "He is going to do all that tonight."

So I instructed, "Every one of you who has some such disease, I want you to stand to your feet right now, and put your hands on your affliction." Then we began to pray. I asked them to repeat again what God's Word says about their healing. And so we repeated and repeated; and pretty soon, Charismatic pandemonium broke out (if you know what that is). Then I said, "Let's just go ahead and see what God has done in this place. Check yourself carefully, carefully, carefully. Then those of you who have received your healing, come up to the platform and tell what God has done."

A line began to form. All of a sudden, a man came up and said, "I was in an automobile accident five years ago. My hip was injured, and I have had continuous pain in that hip for five years. My knee was stiff. I couldn't bend it too well. But all of a sudden, when we began to say those verses, I heard this snap in my hip, and the pain instantly left and my knee began to bend. I wanted to be sure, because you said to check yourself carefully. So I went outside and ran up and down the street. I hadn't been able to walk well dragging that foot, let alone run. But I just ran all around this place. And I am healed! And not only that, I couldn't bend my knee, but when I was just outside, I touched my knee to my nose."

So I suggested, "All right, do it now." He stood before the people and jerked his knee up so that it touched his nose as everybody shouted and praised God. I asked, "Is there any pain now in that hip?"

And he replied, "No, none whatsoever." He ran all over the place. He was completely and instantly healed.

Suddenly, standing in the line before me was the skinny girl I had seen in the vision. I said to the mother, "What is the matter with this little girl?"

She answered, "She has been paralyzed. My husband left home a number of years ago because of her as she had become such a burden. So I have been raising her myself these past few years." I asked how old she was, and her mother answered, "12."

Then I said, "What couldn't she do?"

She replied, "She was paralyzed. She could hardly move her limbs." Skinny little legs. Skinny little arms. So thin.

I asked, "Can she move them now?"

"O yes, she walked all the way up here."

And she began to move her legs and stomp her feet. "What about your arms? Can you move your arms? Let's do this," as together we swung our left arms in a circle. "Let's do the other one." She began to move it in a small circle. "Oh, no, honey. Both arms. The same way. Do as I'm doing." And I swung both arms in a full circle. All of a sudden, she made a full circle. God had completely healed her of her paralysis. Praise God! She and I jumped all over the platform.

The lawyer who gave the piece of land was there that day and gave about $1,500. His sister-in-law had been examined a month before and discovered she had cancer. She had two lumps on her right breast. One was the size of a half dollar. The other was smaller. That Sunday night she was at the service and said those lumps instantly disappeared. The lawyer's wife came up and testified with her the next morning that she personally had examined the lumps a month ago and then had examined them after the service and again that morning. They both testified that the lumps were completely and wonderfully healed.

That evening I said, "You know, Norm, I just feel like we ought to have a service on the baptism in the Holy Spirit."

He replied, "You are a glutton for punishment."

I answered, "Yes, but we just have to have it. If even one person gets the baptism in the Holy

Spirit, I feel it is worthwhile."

We announced the service for 11 a.m. because we were leaving that afternoon. Norm said he counted 60 people who came to receive. As far as I know, there was only one who wasn't filled.

So we had a fantastic time; I almost didn't want to come back! I just felt I was called to be a missionary to Nigeria. I could have stayed very easily, but there is a job to be done here.

But you foreign students should learn by what I have said here. You can turn your country upside down for God, if you follow the ministry of the Lord Jesus. Pattern your ministry after His, and God will do great things through you.

While in Nigeria on our first trip, Benson drove me a couple of hundred miles to speak at a convention. En route while going through one of the towns, suddenly our car came to a screeching halt. There beside the highway was the chief of that large village. He knew we would be coming through on our way to the convention, so he waited patiently to tell us what God had done for him.

He quickly led us to his home where we met his wife and children. He then gave his testimony of how for 40 years he had vainly sought God, but could not find Him in the empty religions of his land. But one day, one of the workers associated with Benson, came up to his village and told him about Christ. He accepted the Lord as his Savior two months before we arrived, and was also filled with the Spirit. He and his family jubilantly sang and dedicated to us the little chorus, "I Love That Man of Galilee."

For days and nights this chorus rang in my soul, and I could see that ebony face beaming with the joy of the Lord.

On that trip to Mombasa, I had the privilege of speaking on a Sunday night. About 75 were baptized in the Holy Spirit, and the last person I was to pray for was a deaf mute woman whom God instantly healed.

Is the work of the Lord worthwhile? A trillion times, YES!

My Letter to the *Jersualem Post*

The following letter appeared in the local edition of *The Jerusalem Post* on December 9, 1975, and in the international edition on December 16, 1975:

Christian Belief in Israel

To the Editor of *The Jerusalem Post*:

Sir: After conducting my 12th tour of Israel, I am more than convinced that every Christian in America would do well to visit the land of Israel. For many Christians have no knowledge of the Bible, and if they have never visited Israel, they have no understanding of the strategic nature of the Golan Heights, the border problems of the West Bank, Gaza and the Sinai, and the significance of Jerusalem as the heart of the Jewish people.

My late husband, Gordon Lindsay, who made some 25 visits to Israel, founded Christ For The Nations, a worldwide organization, in the belief that the whole world should know the God of Israel. We have helped some 3,700 congregations in 110 countries build their meeting places. All of them are committed to a literal understanding of the Bible, which includes God's promises to Israel.

When Gordon was accused of being pro-Israel, he would simply reply, "Just because I'm pro-Bible." As editor of our organization's magazine, he wrote continually in defense of Israel's God-given right to be a nation in the land which she now occupies. One entire issue was titled, "The Case for Israel."

In our interdenominational Bible school in Dallas, Texas, we have 830 students. They are taught to pray daily for the peace of Jerusalem. We have a young Israeli student to teach them Hebrew.

Last summer, some 25 of our students came to Israel to work on a kibbutz. A few weeks ago, I received a letter from the secretary of the kibbutz, conveying his feelings of gratitude and thanks, not only for the great help the students gave the kibbutz, but mainly for the unique opportunity of getting to know such a wonderful bunch of people.

Last year when some of our congressmen were under great pressure from the oil czars, we sponsored a large ad in the daily *Dallas Times Herald*, probably the largest paper in Texas, giving Scriptures from the Bible in support of Israel. We received letters and phone calls from all over the South, most of which were favorable.

From Israel, I leave for Benin City, Nigeria, to dedicate a Bible school which one of our former students has built. Strong emphasis will be placed in this school on the God-given right of the Jews to the land of Israel.

From Nigeria, I go to Germany, where we shall open a Bible school in January. The director is one of our former students, a committed believer in Israel's right to exist.

This has been the greatest year of growth in our 27-year history. Why? Two reasons: First, we are a people who pray to the God of Abraham, Isaac and Jacob. Secondly, we love Israel — as every true follower of Jesus should. And we believe that is also the reason God has so blessed America. We teach that as long as America is a friend of Israel, God will bless her. And woe to

372 MY DIARY SECRETS

America or any nation that stands against Israel's right to exist.

Shalom.

Mrs. Freda Lindsay
Dallas, Texas

Chapter Twenty-One

Early in 1976, I made a five-week trip to seven Asian countries. Here is a part of my report carried in *Christ For The Nations* magazine:

Korea

When we arrived in Seoul, Korea, we had just been preceded by a snowstorm that had left ice everywhere. Yet our hearts were greatly warmed by what we saw and heard.

We had the pleasure of attending the Full Gospel Central Church (affiliated with the Assemblies of God) at 10 a.m. on Sunday. (Four services are held each Sunday morning to accommodate the crowds.) There were about 10,000 present at the service we attended, and what a meeting! As Jim Hodges, our missions director, later stated, "When that fantastic choir started singing 'The Hallelujah Chorus,' I nearly went into orbit!" And the large symphony-level orchestra added much, too. But best of all, the free flow of the Spirit was so refreshing.

Rev. Yonggi Cho, D.D. is the pastor and his

mother-in-law, Mrs. Ja-Shil Choi, D.D. is the associate pastor. Mrs. Choi is a powerful speaker and a great prayer warrior. Prayer services are held each morning at 5:30 a.m. All-night prayer is held on Tuesdays and Fridays. The congregation is served by 43 licensed and ordained ministers. The women fill an important role in the church. And the ushers, half of them women, attired in their lovely Korean dresses, are a credit to the work.

After services, when I commented to Dr. Cho in his office on the way in which he allowed the gifts of the word of knowledge, discerning of spirits, gifts of healing, and miracles to flow through him that morning, he answered, "I have learned much from Brother Lindsay's books. I have studied them for years."

Then he reminded me that in 1960, Christ For The Nations had given $20,000 toward building Revival Center which was the "mother church" or forerunner of this present church. When the coliseum-type Full Gospel Central Church was completed, all 1,000 members of Revival Center moved with their pastor. However a new pastor, whom we met, took the "mother church," and in a year's time, the church, seating 1,000, was again full.

Here once more was clear-cut evidence of the power of literature and the results of CFN's

Native Church assistance program.

It was our privilege to speak to the congregation of one of these churches that Christ For the Nations had helped build, pastored by Dr. Dong Bin Kim. In fact, we discovered that the Full Gospel had even reached into President Park Chung Hee's family. His daughter, the eldest of his three children, often acted as First Lady at official functions, since the death of her mother by an assassin's bullet. She had been saved and filled with the Holy Spirit.

Taiwan

From Seoul, we flew to the island of Taiwan, with its population of 16 million. Taipei, the capital, has over two million people. As we drove into the city, a large sign greeted us saying, "Welcome to Taipei — the spiritual fortress of anti-communism and prosperity."

I spoke at the Chemghun Full Gospel Assembly where about a dozen Chinese were filled with the Holy Spirit. Several miracles took place as we prayed for the sick.

We met three wonderful Scandinavian missionaries there: Helvi Taponen, Leone Kauppmen and Miss Anderson. Helvi has spent most of her life in the Orient. She has also supervised the construction of several fine-looking churches which CFN helped sponsor. Jim

Hodges and Norman Young visited some of these churches and met the pastors and their people. When I asked the three women where all the men missionaries were in Taiwan, one answered, "It's too comfortable for them in their own countries." It's sad but true that more women by far, answer the call to the mission field than do men. And even the organizations who are against women preachers seem to have no reservations about enlisting them as missionaries.

We were impressed with how clean Taipei looked, and we felt the influence of the strong Christian leadership of the late Chiang Kai-shek, now continued by his son, Premier Chiang Ching-kuo.

Hong Kong

Our next stop was the island on which Hong Kong, then a city of one million, is located. At that time, Hong Kong still belonged to England. Kowloon across the bay with its three million people, was leased to England until the end of the century. It is actually located on the China mainland.

We were driven to the Chinese border and stood pondering what would be the lot of anyone trying to escape from there. Our host, a Four-square missionary, answered our question by saying, "All that land is heavily mined. No one can escape. Occasionally some will try to swim out (pointing to a body of water separating the two nations), but they usually get shot.

Then the thought arose in my mind, "If communism is so wonderful, then why is it necessary to have all the mines, the high walls and the guards to keep the people locked in to enjoy their version of a good life?"

Some of the folk in Hong Kong told us of a revival in Fook Chow on the mainland. It started in a prayer meeting in 1969 when a man was healed of a cancer on his nose. Then a demoniac girl was delivered. By 1972, there were 1,500 saved who were attending underground meetings. When the communists found out about it, they marched the Christians through the streets making them wear dunce caps. They arrested the leaders and put them in jail, dispersing the group. Yet, the Lord's work goes on in China. We met one man who regularly goes into China with Chinese literature; by which means we are not free to share. He meets with and encourages the underground believers.

In talking with Paul Kauffman and David Wang who for years have translated, printed and distributed CFN literature, they virtually begged for more books. They now have 30,000 children, ages 8 to 12, enrolled in a children's Bible course, and are asking us to supply them with our

children's books. Also, they have already translated several of our books into Korean and are
waiting for funds from CFN to print them. Literature seems to be one door open to the Gospel.

Philippines

In Manila, we were met by our friends of long
standing, Dan and Esther Marocco, pastoring
Bethel Temple, the large church started by Lester
Sumrall. We ministered there in the Sunday services with at least 1,000 present. Again, many
were saved, healed or filled with the Holy Spirit.
On Friday night, I spoke on the baptism in the
Holy Spirit and about 45 received. That many or
more received when Brother Hodges spoke.

In the beautiful, mountainous resort city of
Baguio, we met Pastor Soriano. As a young man,
he was playing in a five-piece Filipino dance
band in a city in northern California. An evangelist came into the dance hall and asked if he
could sing and play. The owner granted permission which greatly angered the five men in the
band. After that, the evangelist spoke a few
words and invited everyone to his revival. He
asked the five young men to bring their instruments, and they did. All five gave their hearts to
the Lord! Soriano returned to the Philippines to
preach to his own people and to start a church
and an orphanage.

Ministers came from far and near to attend the seminar we held in high school facilities. The results were the same as in our previous meetings. The Holy Spirit did His work. While in Baguio, we learned that President Marcos had attended a Full Gospel Sunday school for several years as a child.

Thailand

Returning to Bangkok, Thailand, for my third visit was an interesting experience. The millions of U.S. dollars poured into that country (when much of our Air Force was stationed there during the Vietnam War) had brought about marked changes in the Thai living standards.

We talked to one brilliant young missionary who stayed in nearby Cambodia until several days before it fell. He said that the corruption in high places there was unbelievable. Money that was allocated for rice for the soldiers was misappropriated, and instead stashed away in Swiss banks by the military. As a result, the soldiers and the people had no strength nor will to resist the communist takeover.

On the day we landed in Bangkok, six men had just arrived in the refugee camp, having escaped through the swamps from Cambodia. Another 25 who started with them didn't make it; they were hunted down by the Khmer Rouge.

The six men reported that the slaughter going on in Cambodia was beyond comprehension.

It was heart-moving to hear the churches there praying, "Lord, save Thailand." We are happy to say we found some really healthy Charismatic churches in Bangkok. Yet, there are thousands of orange-robed priests and 300 heathen temples which are overlaid with gold, many of them covering blocks of strategic ground and costing multiplied millions of dollars. But one of the curses in the Orient for spreading the Gospel is lack of funds. Men have failed in centuries past to meet their responsibilities. Thus, not only was their generation denied the Gospel, but countless generations since, know nothing of God. The opposite could have been the case.

Twenty years ago, CFN helped send the late Rev. Don Price and Rev. Leon Hall to Bangkok to build a center. We visited that center and met some of the 1,500 students who are attending school there. They receive daily Bible training all the way from kindergarten through high school. What joy it brought to our hearts to see the result of our investment.

On Sunday, we spoke in three different churches — Jim Hodges in one, his wife, Jean, in another, and I at the Full Gospel Church where Nirut Chandhorn is pastor. Some 50 bright, young men and women were filled with the Holy

Spirit that morning in the latter's thriving church, many of them college students or graduates.

The question now is: What will the Church of Jesus Christ do in Thailand while the door is still open?

India

Next was India! How can anyone ever describe India? With its hundreds of thousands sleeping on the streets where they live and die in their filthy rags, never having eaten one square meal, taken one bath, or slept one night in a clean bed. It was a shocking sight as we came from the airport that morning in Calcutta with the temperature at 50 degrees F to see bodies of all sizes lying side by side, their heads completely covered with their rags to keep out the cold. Each morning, the death wagon goes up and down the streets and picks up the ones no longer moving. Yet several hundred thousand sacred cows have the run of the place and are fat and healthy.

We stopped for a few hours to see the famed Taj Mahal, built by the Emperor Shah Jakan in memory of his wife who died in childbirth. We were told that the emperor later lost his mind. Going into the white marble monument that took 20,000 men 20 years to build, he would at night wail away in grief in the tomb. The eerie echoes would resound throughout the entire edifice. But as we stood there, we thought of the empty tomb in Jerusalem, and our party began to sing, "Hallelujah." Its joyful echoes filled that shrine. Shortly other tourists arrived, and a man asked, "Where are those Hallelujah people?" When we identified ourselves, he replied, "Praise the Lord!" We responded with a hearty, "Amen!"

Several hours later, a few blocks from this marble wonder of the world, we stood on the banks of the Yamuna River, tributary of the sacred Ganges. Here we watched as men prepared the funeral bier for a 36-year-old mother of three who had died that morning. Once the wood was piled over the corpse, the father and the oldest son (a lad of about 8 or 10), lit the match that ignited the dry wood covered with butter to make it burn faster. Customs have changed, so now the women in mourning must stay at home and wail. The men had chanted a wail as we watched them carry the body on their shoulders for a mile to the river's edge. Now, as they gazed at the flames, they all stood silently. Once the fire had consumed the body, they bathed in the water and returned to their homes.

But on the riverbank, we noticed a half dozen large, well-fed, vicious-looking dogs. Our guide explained to us that they fish out of the river the bodies of babies, for whom "funerals" are not always held. Hence they always have plenty to eat.

India now has a population of over 600 million, and that number is increasing at the rapid rate of one million per month. What can the government do? In talking to Christians and non-Christians alike, we were told that Prime Minister Indira Gandhi did what had to be done. She cracked down and jailed only those who were taking the law into their own hands, and assassinating anyone who opposed them. As a result, we were told things were more stable in India.

But we know the only real answer for India is Jesus. As long as the heathen gods reign, there will be little help, little change. One would think that the leaders of the nation would look to see what has happened in countries where Jesus is followed. How they have been blessed, enlightened and prospered. Then compare them with their own lands.

In Hawaii, our cab driver asked us what we thought of the teaching of the gurus. I asked him, "What has it done for the people of their own land? Nothing. That's the proof. Why bring a teaching to America when it can't do anything for their own people?"

Yet over and over again, we were thrilled at how God has a way of reaching the top leaders. An American lady, filled with the Spirit, had a

vision about Mrs. Gandhi. She was later granted
a private audience with the prime minister and
told her what she had seen in her vision. She
shared her conviction that God had raised up
Mrs. Gandhi to lead her nation, and that He
desired to lead her in her decisions. (Mrs. Gandhi
comes from a Hindu family, but claims she is an
agnostic.) This Spirit-filled lady told her that she
was praying daily for her in her tremendous task.
Let us join in prayer for Mrs. Gandhi, for "Happy
are the people whose God *is* the LORD" (Psa.
144:15).

In Kumbanad, South India, we spoke for several
days at the conference of the Indian Pentecostal
Church of God. The night crowds ran as many as
6,000, and it was a joy to minister. Many testified
to instant miracles, such as a goiter disappearing, a
growth in the mouth dissolving, etc.

On Saturday morning as I was about to minister on the baptism in the Holy Spirit, suddenly
to my right there was a disturbance. A woman
appeared to be in trouble. The pastor at the
microphone asked me to go and pray for her. As
I observed her, her eyes closed, her head
dropped, and her mouth opened as if she were
dying. For several minutes, I rebuked death
while the women around her stood with me. All
of a sudden, her body gave a jerk, and her eyes
opened in a startled manner, as if to say, "Where

am I?" Later she told Mrs. T.S. Abraham, the pastor's wife, that while sitting there, she felt herself leaving her body as she listened to the death rattle in her throat. Then she heard praying, and she felt her spirit come back into her body. God had spared her life! Then after my message on "How to Receive the Baptism in the Holy Spirit," a mighty visitation of God took place, and about 250 were filled that morning.

Our last seminar in India was to be in the resort city of Shillong. Here one of our Indian CFNI graduates, Joseph Skinner, had started a work, and we helped him purchase a building to use for a center and a Bible school. We dedicated that building, which will be renovated and enlarged. But in the meantime, we held four services a day in a large makeshift tent. A thousand hungry, attentive people were present each night, with several hundred attending day meetings.

It was so interesting to see the Nagaland men and women representatives wrapped in their colorful red and black shawls. Other ministers came from Sikkim, West Bengal, Assam, Manipur and Meghalaya. Some of them were among the hundred or more who were filled with the Spirit. CFN helped many of these people with the building of their churches and supplying them with literature. So God is doing a work in India.

We were delighted to have the Luminaires

assisting us in the meetings at Shillong. There were 10 in that singing group, nine of whom were former CFNI students. This was their third round-the-world tour made by faith. God marvelously used them in many places.

The Return Home

We left Shillong in two old taxicabs, and we all wondered whether the antiquated crates would make the three-hour trip down the outer ridges of the Himalayan Mountains. Our anxieties were increased as we noticed the front taxi developing a large bulge on one of its tires as it went round and round the hairpin curves. However, we encouraged ourselves in the Lord and reminded Him that we were His cargo; we felt assured He would give us "special handling." At long last, we were out of the mountains, only 16 miles from the airport. Suddenly there was a loud grinding noise. Our taxi had broken down — beyond immediate repair! The front taxi heard our driver's honking and stopped. Seven of us climbed into that one small cab with luggage in the small trunk, on the roof and on our laps. With all that weight, we didn't dare dwell on that large bulge in the tire. We rode in silence — everyone was in prayer. We made it to the airport barely in time to catch our plane.

In our visiting of the seven countries, I was

appalled at the nations' attitude toward the United States. As one high government official told me, "All of this exposure of the CIA activities before the world has been most unfortunate. Now every country is asking, 'Is the CIA getting ready to overthrow our government, to assassinate our leader?'" Missionaries are suspect, too, since the disclosure by the CIA that one Catholic priest in South America had received $15 million from the CIA for his covert activities.

So it seems to me that those U.S. officials who are demanding and disclosing every kind of information are either very naive or subversive, making it easier for communism to take over the world. At any rate, they are certainly destroying confidence in the United States, while at the same time aiding the enemy. What a tragedy!

On our flight home, my heart overflowed with gratitude for the tremendous trip God had given us. Beside me sat a fine-looking Australian youth of 18. He and his brother had each paid $2,000 to join a party climbing Mt. Everest in Nepal. He told me that during the 35-day trek, it was bitter cold, the food was poor, and he had been sick with diarrhea. Why did he do it? To reach those 19,000 feet was a great challenge to him!

Then I shared with him how I, too, was looking for a challenge at 18; how I accepted Christ at that age, and found that the greatest challenge any man or woman can ever want or find on this earth is told about in Mark 16:15: "Go into all the world and preach the gospel to every creature." This challenge not only satisfies in life, but will give eternal life in the world to come. I encouraged him to accept that challenge.

Chapter Twenty-Two

The Christ For The Nations Institute Building, plus the land, including the parking, cost over $750,000. It seemed like a giant undertaking. And I must admit, it seemed even bigger when I was left alone with the task of completing the construction on the building after Gordon was gone. But though we had 10 years in which to pay the mortgage, God helped us to pay for it within two years, thus saving $165,000 in interest.

Exactly two years after the Institute Building was dedicated to the Lord, the indebtedness was completely liquidated, and we had a mortgage burning during the seminar in August 1975. (The 1,400-seat auditorium was none too large, for often it was filled to capacity for just our regular Sunday afternoon service, and many times for our weeknight services. (We later enlarged the auditorium to 2,200 seats.)

On occasion I had heard Gordon say, "You know, a lot of people write a lot of books. They can always tell you how to do it, but they can never make anything work themselves." However, as I've sometimes told our students, "As

you study here on this 75-acre campus, and then
hear about the 10,000 Native Churches we've
helped build, and you see Brother Lindsay's
books — of which 60 million have been printed
(in some 79 languages), as you see the Bible
schools that have been built around the world,
plus the audio and video ministry, then you see
what has been done by a man who could not only
tell you in his books how to do it, but also showed
you by his example."

And when special guest speakers sometimes
have differing opinions on Bible matters, I tell
our students, "No two Bible teachers agree on all
the fine points of the Bible. As the various speakers come and go, giving their opinions, this
should drive you to study your Bibles and search
the Scriptures."

Then I remind them that for more than 35 years,
I have read and answered stacks of letters that came
to Christ For The Nations. During those years,
several thousand letters came from pastors, evangelists, teachers and missionaries. Almost without
exception, they would conclude that they felt Gordon was the most balanced author of his generation.
So when in doubt, I admonish them to read what
Brother Lindsay had to say about it, and they
probably won't be far wrong.

The thing that made Gordon unique was that
he never seemed to be aware of the host of lives

he touched, and the worldwide influence he carried. For some ministers, a playback of their words and deeds could be embarrassing. Not so with Gordon. He weighed his words carefully, sometimes almost to the point of delay. But when he spoke, his words carried weight. And as for his deeds, as I told the children, "Daddy accomplished on earth what he wanted to have done when he got to heaven" — not only of that which had been entrusted to him in the work of the Lord, but also of his personal possessions.

There's an old cliché that says, "You can't take it with you." But that's not true. Gordon did take it with him!

To God be the Glory

Dear Freda:

I just happened to be looking over your recent magazine, and I am most grateful for all the splendid ministry that God has given you to do. Please accept this check for wherever you may have a need. God bless you.

Yours in Christ,

[signature]

Pat Robertson
President

Enclosure: Check for $150,000.

(This check, in full, was paid on the Gordon Lindsay Tower, former Sheraton Hotel, mortgage.)

Another visitor was Marjorie Holmes, author of the bestseller *Two From Galilee,* with over two million copies in circulation. After speaking at Christ For The Nations Writer's Conference and touring the Headquarters, she wrote back:

Dear Freda:

You were, of course, outstanding. Elsa, (Elsa Russell, contributing editor to *Reader's Digest*) and I both agreed that we had never met anyone quite like you. So simple, honest, direct, unassuming ... so filled with tenderness and love ... and yet so strong! What power to bring about seeming miracles. What a power — the right kind of power — over lives. You touched us both very deeply.

Marjorie Holmes

A copy of the new *Who's Who of the American Women* 1975-1976 edition arrived, listing me in it as "a religious executive" — whatever that means. Then the new *Who's Who in Religion* included my name, and the *World Who's Who of Women* informed me that I am listed. I said to my sons later, "It really isn't fair. Daddy did all the work, and I get all the credit."

But I am sure heaven will have an accurate record of all accounts, and the righteous Judge will Himself pass out the rewards.

To what do I attribute growth in every

department of Christ For The Nations, especially in the several years since Gordon's homegoing? It's to faith and prayer. Gordon was the greatest man of prayer I have ever met. The answers to his prayers did not stop with his passing. Rather, they seemed to gain momentum.

So we give God all the glory, at the same time realizing that the Lord has to work through an individual. One such individual was Gordon, through whom God could and did work. On his small gravemarker, the children and I put what we felt were appropriate words:

**DADDY
GORDON J. LINDSAY
June 18, 1906 — April 1, 1973
A MAN OF PRAYER**

SPECIAL NOTE: A free gift subscription to CHRIST FOR THE NATIONS magazine is available to those who write to Christ For The Nations, P.O. Box 769000, Dallas, TX 75376-9000. This magazine contains special feature stories of men of faith and includes prophetic articles on the latest world developments. Why not include the names of your friends? (Due to high mailing rates, this applies only to Canada and the U.S.)

The Sequel to
My Diary Secrets:

Freda

This sequel to *My Diary Secrets* shares seven years of miracles in the life of Freda Lindsay, who, as a widow, took up her late husband's mantle to direct the ministry of an international organization.

You will laugh and cry with her as she relates the humorous, the difficult, the tragic, the awesome and sometimes, overwhelming tasks that have confronted her. You will be amazed by this incredible woman of faith who keeps on going because she hears the voice of the heavenly Father, saying, "Keep praying, You're going to make it."